ScottForesman

WORLD ATLAS

 ScottForesman

A Division of HarperCollinsPublishers

Editorial Office: Glenview, Illinois
Regional Offices: Sunnyvale, California • Atlanta, Georgia
Glenview, Illinois • Oakland, New Jersey • Dallas, Texas

Maps prepared by
Bartholomew, a division of HarperCollins/*Publishers*

Picture credits
Cover
Imtek Imagineering/MASTERFILE

Title Page
NASA

Photographs
J. Allan Cash Photolibrary
The Hutchison Library
London Docklands Development Corporation
Meteorological Department, National Centre for Atmospheric
  Research/National Science Foundation, US
Panos Pictures
Science Photo Library
Sefton Photo Library
Tropix Photographic Library
United States Environment Programme

Scott Foresman Staff
Scott Foresman gratefully acknowledges the contributions
of the following individuals:

Editorial
Barbara Flynn, Mary Chase

Design
Barbara Schneider, Virginia Pierce, Ron Stachowiak

Production
Fran Simon, Derrick Everett

ISBN: 0-673-35171-8

11 12 13 14---PT---   00 01 02

Contents

How to Use This Atlas

An atlas is a book of maps. It may also contain photographs, charts, diagrams, graphs, and tables. You can use an atlas as a reference tool to find the location of countries, cities, towns, roads, rivers, mountains and to compare land and water areas.

The *Scott, Foresman World Atlas* is divided into six parts. The first part is introductory. It includes tips on how to use this atlas.

Parts 2, 3, and 4 cover three content areas. The three content areas are Space and Place, Environment and Society, and Spatial Dynamics and Connections. These content areas were established by the National Assessment of Educational Progress in Geography. They draw from the five basic geographic themes. These themes are location, place (physical and human characteristics), human/environment interaction (relationships within places), movement, and regions. Having the atlas organized in this manner will help you gain a better understanding of the world.

Part 2 (Space and Place) will help you develop an understanding of distributions on the Earth's surface and the processes that shape them. This part of the atlas begins with a glossary of geographical terms that provides you with a basic geography vocabulary. The part also contains basic information about the patterns on the earth's surface.

World thematic maps focus on special subjects or themes—such as physical features, climate regions, and natural vegetation. For example, look at the map of natural vegetation on pages 16-17. Suppose you want to know where Africa's deserts are located. Using the color-coded map key, you can see that a huge desert stretches across northern Africa and a much smaller desert runs along the coast of southwestern Africa. Use the map scale to estimate the size of these deserts. You will find that the desert in northern Africa—the Sahara—is more than 3,500 miles from west to east and 1,500 miles from north to south. This desert is larger than the entire United States.

Many of the thematic maps in this atlas use colors to represent a certain quantity. See, for example, the world population distribution map on pages 24-25.

Here each color is used to represent a certain number of people. You can see at a glance which parts of the world are most densely populated (northwest Europe, south Asia, and east Asia).

Also in this part of the atlas, some pages focus on natural forces—such as earthquakes, volcanoes, floods, and tropical storms. By studying the maps and the related visuals and text, you can discover how these natural forces continually change the earth's surface.

Part 3 (Environment and Society) examines the Earth as a human habitat . This part will help you understand how people depend on, adapt to, are affected by, and modify the physical or natural environment. The maps, diagrams, and photographs focus on topics such as deforestation, desertification, pollution, and resources. You will see that many modifications that people make, such as planting trees to reduce erosion from winds, may have positive consequences. However, other modifications people make, such as locating a landfill over a ground water source, may have negative consequences.

Part 4 (Spatial Dynamics and Connections) will help you understand the dynamics of the connections among people and places. These connections include trade relationships, economic diversity, and migration and travel.

The fifth and largest part of this atlas (Regions) contains detailed physical and political maps. Look at the table of contents on pages 3-4. You will see that this part is divided into six regions—North America, South America, Europe, Asia, Africa, and Oceania and Polar Regions.

You will use the maps in this part most often to find states, cities, mountains, lakes, and rivers, and so forth. The easiest way to locate a place is to use the index on pages 123-135 inclusive. The index lists hundreds of place names in alphabetical order. The page on which a place name can be found is listed in bold (dark) type before the name. The numbers following the place name show its particular latitude and longitude.

Let's assume that you want to locate the city of Baghdad which is the capital of Iraq. What steps should you take? First, turn to the index and look up Baghdad. The number in bold type, 95, is the atlas page that you should turn to. Use the geographical coordinates provided (latitude 33°20′N and longitude 44°26′E), to help you find Baghdad on page 95. If you want to see where Iraq is located in relation to other countries, refer to the world political map on pages 48-49.

Note that smaller towns generally appear only on large scale maps, such as the United States regional maps (pages 58-63). In densely populated areas, many smaller towns are omitted in order to make the map easier to read.

Many maps in this part have small black and white locator maps in the upper right-hand margin. For example, look at the map of Central America and the West Indies on pages 66-67. The locator map shows you where this area is located in relation to the rest of the Americas.

Some pages in this part have small maps called inset maps. For example, the map of southern South America on pages 72-73 has an inset map of the Buenos Aires. The inset map shows details of this important urbanized area.

The sixth part of this atlas includes a handy reference table as well as the index described above. Here you will find the flags, capital cities, area and population statistics, major or official languages, and lists of important products for all the world's independent countries.

The Basic Skills of Map Reading

Basically, every map needs to have a title, a scale, a latitude-longitude grid, symbols, and a map projection.

Title. No good map is complete without a map title. It allows you to identify the map's subject matter at first glance. In this atlas, the map titles are in the top margins. Each title identifies the part of the atlas, the area of the world it covers, and the purpose of the map. For example, the title of the map on pages 14-15 is: "Space and Place/The World: Climatic Regions and Graphs."

Scale. Scale refers to the relationship between a map and the part of the earth it represents. It allows you to compare distances on the map to distances on the earth's surface. Scale may be shown in one of three ways. First, it may be shown as a ratio, such as 1:40,000,000. Such a ratio appears on the North America map on page 50. The ratio means that one inch on the map equals 40,000,000 inches on the ground. Second, a map's scale may also be stated in words, such as "One inch equals 631 miles." This statement means that one inch on the map equals 631 miles on the earth's surface. To arrive at this figure, divide 40,000,000 inches by 63,360 inches (the number of inches in a mile). The answer is 631 miles. Third, scale may be shown with a bar scale. This scale is a straight line with distances marked out on it, with each mark representing a set number of miles or kilometers on the earth's surface. Using the bar scale on the map of the Netherlands, Belgium and Luxembourg on page 80, estimate the distance between Amsterdam and Rotterdam. You will see that the distance is about 38 miles.

On most maps in this atlas, scale is shown both as a ratio and by means of a bar scale. These guides will help you estimate distances between places on the map.

The scale on the atlas maps varies from map to map. One inch might equal 100 miles on one map and 500 miles on another. For example, compare the scale of the British Isles (1:4,000,000) on page 79 to that of North America (1:40,000,000) on page 50. The map of the British Isles has the larger scale: one inch on the map represents 63 miles on the ground. The scale of the North American map is smaller: one inch equals 631 miles. Keep in mind that a larger scale map shows a smaller area in greater detail.

Latitude and Longitude. Cartographers use a grid system to locate places on Earth. The system, as shown in the latitude and longitude diagram on page 7, makes use of imaginary criss-crossing lines called parallels and meridians. The parallels run east and west around the earth. They measure latitude—the distance measured in degrees (°) north and south of the Equator. The distance between each degree of latitude is about 70 miles. The Equator is 0° latitude and divides the Earth into two hemispheres: the

Latitude and Longitude Diagram

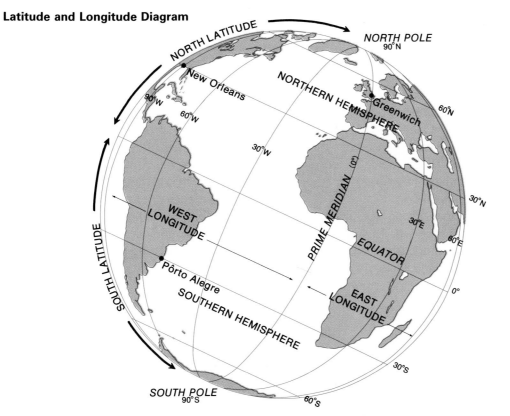

Northern Hemisphere and the Southern Hemisphere. All degrees of latitude are either north of the Equator or south of it. The North Pole is 90°N, and the South Pole is 90°S.

Look at the line representing 30°N latitude on the diagram. You can see that the city of New Orleans is located on this parallel. Because it is north of the Equator, New Orleans has a north latitude position. Pôrto Alegre, located at 30°S latitude, is in the southern latitudes. Now turn to the United States map on pages 54-55 and locate New Orleans. Find 30°N latitude along the margin of either page and move your finger across the parallel until you come to New Orleans. Use the same method to locate the Brazilian city of Pôrto Alegre on pages 72-73.

Meridians are the lines that run north and south from pole to pole. They are not parallel; rather, they meet at the poles. The Prime Meridian, which is shown on the diagram, passes through Greenwich, England. It is located at 0° longitude. The Prime Meridian divides the earth into Eastern and Western hemispheres. Every location to the east, up to 180°, is east longitude. Every place to the west, up to 180°, is west longitude. As you can see on the map on pages 112-113, the 180° meridian passes through the country of Fiji in the South Pacific.

Turn again to the map on pages 54-55. You will see that longitude 90°W intersects New Orleans. Now turn to the map on pages 72-73 and estimate the longitude of Pôrto Alegre. It is about 50°W. Thus, the latitude and longitude of this city is approximately 30°S and 50°W.

Degrees of latitude and longitude are further divided into small units called minutes. There are 60 minutes in each degree, and they are marked by the symbol ('). New Orleans is actually located at 30°0'N and 90°5'W. Pôrto Alegre is actually located at 30°7'S and 50°55'W.

Symbols. Like the other essential elements of a map, the map key serves a special function. The one on page 8 shows various symbols used throughout this atlas. Symbols can stand for many different things. Dots, circles, squares, and larger symbols are used for settlements. These will vary with the size of the community. Larger communities tend to have larger symbols and larger and bolder printed names.

Bold magenta lines show international boundaries—the border lines that separate one country from another. Dot-dash-dot lines are used for internal boundaries, such as states in the United States and provinces in Canada.

Blue represents water, and blue lines indicate rivers. Swamps, marshes, and canals each have their own unique symbols. Notice, for example, the many swamp symbols found in the low-lying areas of southern Florida. (See pages 54-55.)

Color is also used to show varying elevations of land areas and depth of water bodies. As land increases in elevation, the colors change from green to yellow, to orange, to purple and white. As water increases in depth, the color changes from white to light blue to dark blue.

Map Projection. Most maps are not entirely accurate because of a basic property of the earth's surface—it is curved. Map projections are scientific attempts to solve or reduce the problem of distortion, which changes the shape and size of the continents. Many different types have been developed. Each one has some distinct advantages and disadvantages. You can read about the main kinds of projections on page 136.

In this atlas, many projections are used. You will find the name of the map projection below the bar scale on most maps.

Key to Symbols

Relief

		Feet	Relief	Metres
⬭	Land contour	16404		5000
▲ 8848	Spot height (metres)	9843		3000
		6562		2000
⋈	Pass	3281		1000
▭	Permanent ice cap	1640		500
		656		200
		0		Sea Level
		Land Dep. 656		200

Hydrography

⬭	Submarine contour	13123		4000
▼11034	Ocean depth (metres)	22966		7000
∿	River			
⋯	Intermittent river			
∿	Falls			
∿	Dam			
⋏	Gorge			
⊢⊢⊢	Canal			
▭	Lake/Reservoir			
⬭	Intermittent lake			
⋮⋮	Marsh/Swamp			

Road representation varies with the scale category.

═══	Principal road	⎫ 1:1M-1:2½M
───	Other main road	⎭
───	Principal road	⎫ 1:2½M-1:7½M
───	Other main road	⎭
───	Principal road	1:7½M or smaller

Administration

▬▬▬	International boundary
▬ ▬ ▬	Undefined/Disputed international boundary
·········	Cease-fire line
─·─·─	Internal division : First order
─··─··─	Internal division : Second order
◪◉◉ ◎◻▪	National capitals

Settlement

Each settlement is given a town stamp according to its relative importance and scale category.

		1:1M-1:2½M	1:2½M-1:7½M	1:7½M or smaller
◪		Major City	Major City	Major City
◉		City	City	City
◎		Large Town	Large Town	Large Town
⊙		Town	Town	Town
○		Small Town	Small Town	–
•		Village	–	–
⬠		Urban area (1:1M-1:2½M only)		

The size of type used for each settlement is graded to correspond with the appropriate town stamp.

Lettering

Various styles of lettering are used-each one representing a different type of feature.

ALPS	Physical feature	KENYA	Country name
Red Sea	Hydrographic feature	IOWA	Internal division
Paris	Settlement name	*(Fr.)*	Territorial administration

Glossary of Geographical Terms

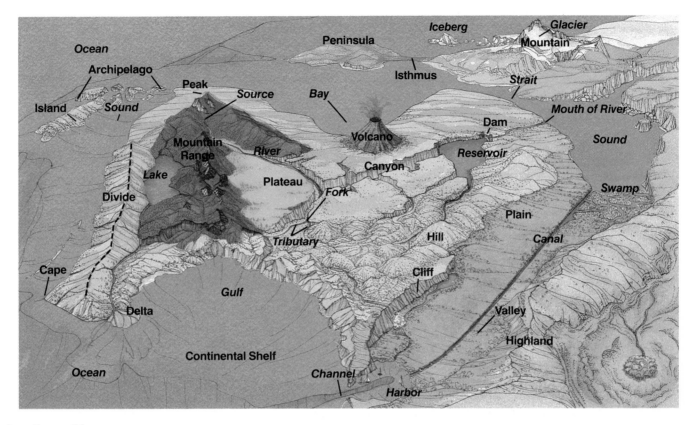

Landforms Diagram

agriculture   science, art, or occupation of cultivating the soil to produce crops, and also of raising livestock.

altitude   height above the earth's surface. The altitude of a place is usually expressed in feet or meters above or below sea level.

archipelago (är′kə pel′ə gō)   a group of many islands *See diagram.* The Aleutian Islands form an archipelago.

atmosphere   the mass of gases that surrounds the earth and is held to it by the force of gravity.

atoll (at′ol)   a flat, circular-shaped coral island or group of islands enclosing or partly enclosing a body of water called a lagoon.

barrier   a wall built by people to break the impact of waves, often near the entrance to a harbor.

basin   **1** all the land drained by a river and the streams that flow into it. **2** land enclosed by higher land.

bauxite (bôk′sīt)   a claylike mineral from which aluminum is obtained; aluminum ore.

bay   part of an ocean or a lake extending into the land, having a wide opening. A bay is usually smaller than a gulf and larger than a cove. *See diagram.*

butte (byüt)   a steep, flat-topped hill that stands alone on a plain; found in the dry regions of the western United States. A large butte is called a mesa.

canal   a waterway dug across land for transportation, irrigation, or water supply. *See diagram.* The Panama Canal connects the Atlantic and Pacific oceans.

canyon   a long, narrow valley with high, steep sides, often with a river flowing through it. *See diagram.* The Grand Canyon in North America is one mile deep, and it contains the Colorado River.

cape   a point of land which projects out into a body of water. *See diagram.* Cape Horn is at the southern tip of South America.

channel   **1** the bed of a river or a stream. **2** a small body of water that joins two larger bodies of water, like the English Channel. *See diagram.*

cliff   a steep slope of rock or soil. *See diagram.*

climate   **1** the pattern of weather a place has over a long period of time. Climate includes conditions of heat and cold, moisture and dryness, clearness and cloudiness, wind and calm. **2** region with certain conditions of heat and cold, rainfall, wind, sunlight, etc.

consumer goods   products made to satisfy human wants directly, such as clothing and food.

continent   any one of the seven largest masses of land on the earth. The continents, in order of size, are Asia, Africa, North America, South America, Antarctica, Europe, and Australia. Sometimes Asia and Europe are considered to be a single continent called Eurasia.

continental drift according to the theory of plate tectonics, the movement of continents on huge plates that slide across the surface of the earth's mantle.

continental shelf the margin of the continent that extends underwater beyond the shoreline. *See diagram.*

copra (kō′prə) the dried meat of coconuts pressed for coconut oil—used for cooking, soap, shampoo, and margarine.

coral a limestone formation built on underwater rocks by colonies of polyps, small marine animals. Coral may form islands or reefs, sometimes developing on the tops of volcanoes to build atolls.

cordillera (kor′də lyer′ə) a system of mountain ranges, usually set in parallel ridges.

cove 1 a small, sheltered bay; inlet on the shore; mouth of a creek. 2 a sheltered place among hills or woods.

crater a bowl-shaped depression in the earth or around the opening of a volcano. The Greater Meteor Crater near Flagstaff, Arizona, probably resulted from the impact of a large meteorite. Crater Lake in Oregon occupies the crater of an extinct volcano.

dam a wall built across a stream or river to hold back water. *See diagram.*

delta a more or less triangular deposit of sand and soil that collects at the mouth of some rivers. *See diagram.* The Nile River has a large delta.

desert a region with sparse vegetation due to little or no rainfall. A desert may be hot or cold. Local words for desert are often used as place names, like Sahara and Gobi.

divide a ridge of land between two regions drained by different rivers. *See diagram.* The Continental Divide in western North America separates streams flowing toward the Pacific Ocean from those flowing toward the Atlantic Ocean.

downstream the direction toward which a river flows.

Equator imaginary circle around the middle of the earth, halfway between the Poles.

erosion the wearing away of the surface of the earth by all processes, including weathering.

estuary (es′chü er′ē) a broad river mouth into which the tide flows.

export article sent to another country for sale.

fiord or **fjord** a long, narrow inlet of the sea bordered by steep cliffs. Formed by glaciers, fiords can be found along the coasts of Norway, Alaska, and New Zealand.

fork the place where a stream or tributary joins a river. *See diagram.*

glacier a large mass of ice formed over many years from snow on high ground wherever winter snowfall exceeds summer melting. It moves very slowly down a mountain, through a valley, or over a wide stretch of land. *See diagram.*

gulf an arm of an ocean or sea extending into the land. It is usually larger than a bay. *See diagram.*

harbor a sheltered area of water where ships can anchor safely. *See diagram.*

highland an area of mountains, hills, or plateaus. *See diagram.*

hill a raised part of the earth's surface with sloping sides—smaller than a mountian. *See diagram.*

iceberg a large mass of ice floating in the ocean. *See diagram.*

import an article for sale brought in from another country.

island a body of land smaller than a continent and completely surrounded by water. *See diagram.* Greenland is the world's largest island. New Guinea is the second largest.

isthmus (is′məs) a narrow strip of land with water on both sides, connecting two larger bodies of land. *See diagram.* The Isthmus of Panama connects North America and South America.

jute (jüt) a strong fiber obtained from two tropical plants related to the linden, used for making rope and coarse fabrics such as burlap.

lake a large body of water completely surrounded by land. *See diagram.*

lowland a region that is lower and flatter than surrounding land. Broad regions of flat lowlands are called plains.

meridians imaginary lines running from Pole to Pole around the earth. They indicate degrees of longitude. The meridian at 0° longitude is called the Prime Meridian.

mesa (mā′sə) a large butte; a steep, flat-topped hill that stands alone on a plain.

metal any of a class of elements which usually have a shiny surface, conduct heat and electricity, and can be hammered into thin sheets.

mineral any natural substance obtained by mining or quarrying; a mineral may be a metal, such as gold, a liquid, such as petroleum, or a combination of various minerals, such as bauxite.

monsoon a seasonal wind of the Indian Ocean and southern Asia, blowing from the southwest from April to October and from the northeast during the rest of the year.

mountain a raised part of the earth's surface with a pointed or rounded top—higher than a hill. *See diagram.*

mountain range a row of connected mountains. *See diagram.*

mouth (of a river) the part of a river where its waters flow into another body of water. *See diagram.*

oasis (ō ā′sis) a fertile place in the desert where there is water and vegetation.

ocean 1 the great body of salt water that covers almost three-quarters of the earth's surface. *See diagram.* 2 any of its four main divisions: the Pacific, Atlantic, Indian, and Arctic oceans.

parallels   imaginary circles running parallel to the Equator around the earth. They indicate degrees of latitude. The parallels at the Poles, 90°N and 90°S, are points not circles.

peak   the pointed top of a mountain or hill. *See diagram.*

peninsula (pə nin′sə lə)   a piece of land jutting out from the mainland and almost surrounded by water. *See diagram.* Florida and Italy are peninsulas.

plain   a broad and flat or gently rolling area. *See diagram.*

plateau (pla tō′)   a plain at a height considerably above sea level. *See diagram.* The Plateau of Tibet is the highest in the world.

polder   a tract of lowland reclaimed from the sea or other body of water and protected by dikes. The Netherlands has extensive polder areas along the North Sea.

population density   number of people living per unit of the earth's surface.

prairie (prer′ē)   a large area of flat or rolling land covered with grass and very few trees.

precipitation   moisture in the form of rain, dew, snow, and so on.

Prime Meridian   imaginary line from which longitude east and west is measured; it runs through Greenwich, England, and its longitude is 0°.

rainforest   a dense forest in a region where rain is heavy throughout the year. Rainforests are usually in tropical areas, though some may also be found in marine west coast climate areas like the Pacific Northwest coast of North American.

range   a row of mountains.

reef   a narrow ridge of rocks, sand, or coral lying at or near the surface of the water. The Great Barrier Reef off the northeast coast of Australia is over 1,200 miles long.

relief   the differences in elevation between high and low spots in a particular area.

reservoir   a place where water is collected and stored. *See diagram.*

resources   the actual and potential wealth of a country; supplies that will meet a need, such as farmland or minerals.

rift valley   a long, narrow depression with steep walls caused by the shifting of the earth's crust. The Great Rift Valley extends from Israel and Jordan all the way to Mozambique. The Dead Sea, Red Sea, and Lake Nyasa are part of this valley.

river   a natural stream of water that flows into a lake or an ocean. *See diagram.* Small rivers are called brooks, creeks, rills, or runs.

river valley   depression cut by the action of flowing water in a river.

savanna (sə van′ə)   tall grassland with scattered trees between equatorial rainforests and steppes. The length of grass depends on the total rainfall.

savanna climate   a tropical climate in which rain falls during the high sun season; also known as the "tropical wet-and-dry climate."

sea   any large body of salt water. The word may refer to the oceans as a whole, to a part of an ocean, or to a smaller body of salt water like the Caspian Sea.

sound   **1** a narrow body of water separating a large island from the mainland. **2** an inlet of the ocean. *See diagram.*

source (of a river)   the place where a river or stream begins. *See diagram.*

staple crops   the most important or principal farm products grown in a place.

steppe   like the savanna, a treeless grassland, but drier and with short grass. Gradually, as the area of dryness increases, it merges into the desert.

strait   a narrow waterway connecting two larger bodies of water. *See diagram.* The Strait of Gibraltar connects the Mediterranean Sea with the Atlantic Ocean.

subsistence farming   small-scale farming in which the final products are consumed by the grower's family.

swamp   a piece of low-lying land in which water collects. *See diagram.*

taiga (tī′gə)   the needleleaf forest that lies south of the tundra in North America, Scandinavia, and northern Eurasia.

topography   the shape and elevation of an area's terrain.

tributary   stream that flows into a larger stream or body of water; part of a river system. *See diagram.*

tropical rainforest   a dense forest of trees, vines, ferns, and flowers near the Equator that receives abundant rainfall the year round.

tundra (tun′drə)   area of land between timberline and polar regions on which only mosses, lichens, and a few shrubs grow. The ground just beneath the thin topsoil may remain frozen the year round, as permafrost. Tundra exists in high latitudes and high altitudes.

uplands   a hilly region; contrasted with highlands, a mountainous region.

upstream   the direction from which a river flows.

urbanization   the growth of cities.

valley   low land between hills or mountains. *See diagram.*

volcano   an opening in the earth's crust through which steam, ashes, and molten rock are forced out. *See diagram.* A volcano may be active (capable of erupting at any time), dormant (not currently active), or extinct (no longer active and unlikely to be so again). The state of Hawaii is located on the tops of some of the world's highest volcanoes, which lie mainly beneath the Pacific Ocean.

weathering   process which wears away the earth's surface by changes of temperature, by wind, rain, frost, and so on; the breakup of rocks into fragments.

Space and Place

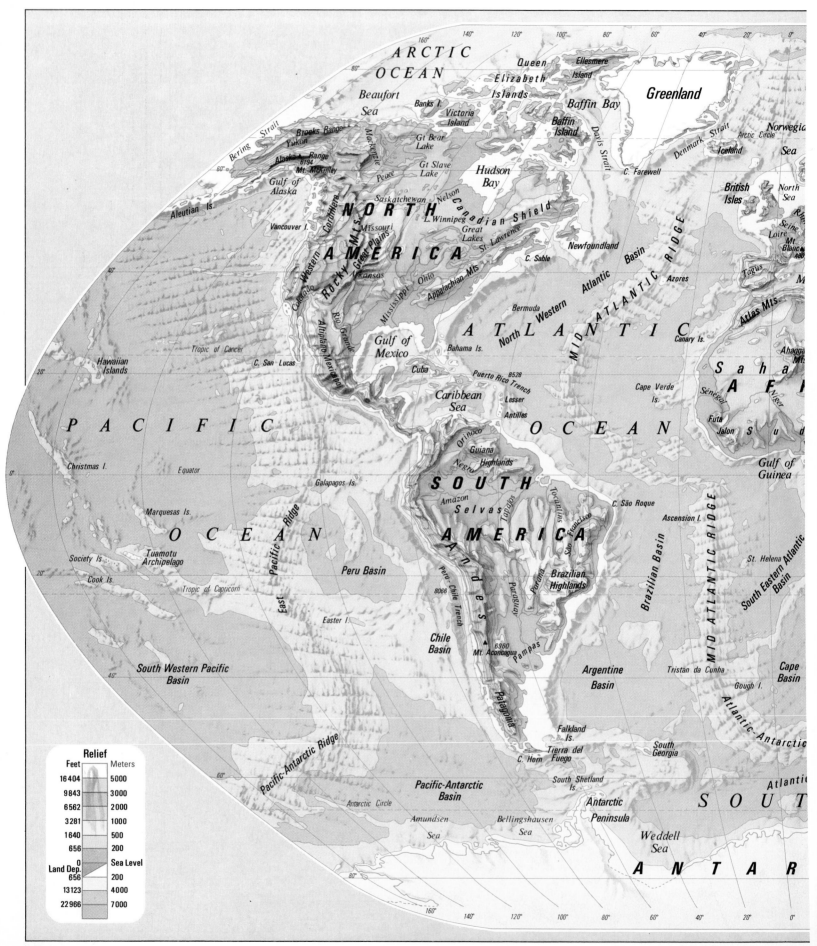

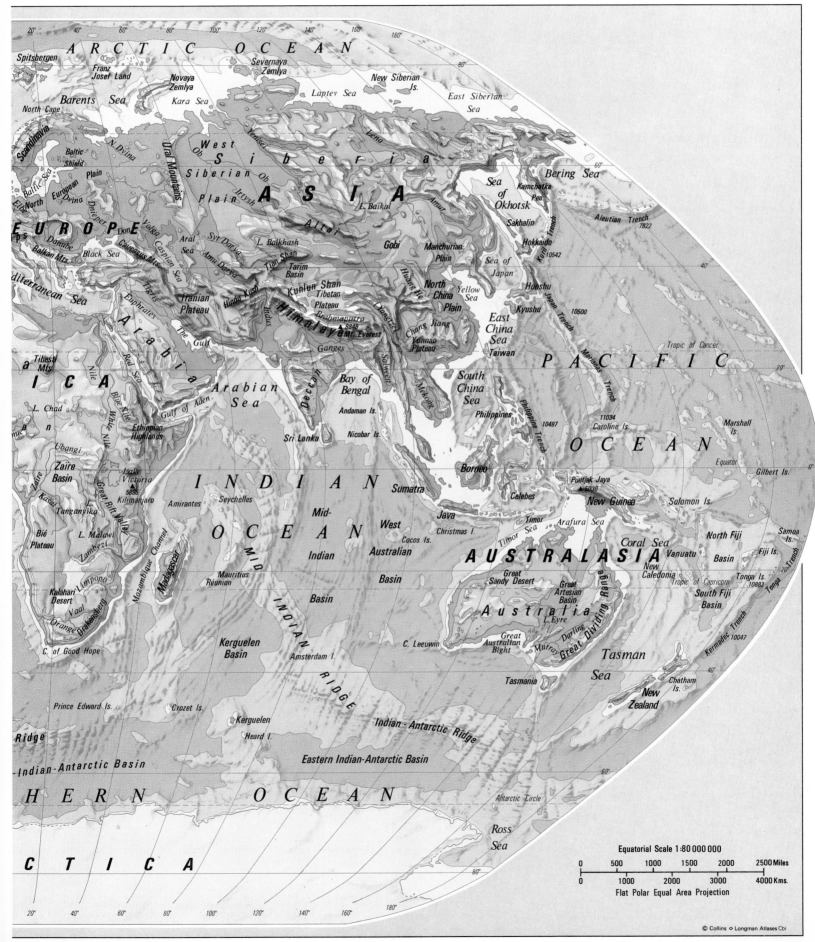

ARCTIC OCEAN

Spitsbergen
Franz Josef Land
Novaya Zemlya
Severnaya Zemlya
New Siberian Is.
Barents Sea
Kara Sea
Laptev Sea
East Siberian Sea
North Cape
Scandinavia
N. Dvina
Baltic Shield
West Siberian Plain
Ob
Yenisey
Lena
Bering Sea
Sea of Okhotsk
Kamchatka Pen.
EUROPE
Baltic Sea
North European Plain
Dvina
Ural Mountains
Siberian Plain
Ob
Irtysh
ASIA
Altai
Amur
Sakhalin
Hokkaido
Aleutian Trench 7822
Alps
Danube
Don
Volga
Caspian Sea
Aral Sea
Syr Darya
L. Balkhash
L. Baikal
Gobi
Manchurian Plain
Sea of Japan
Kuril Trench 10542
Balkan Mts.
Black Sea
Caucasus Mts.
Amu Darya
Tian Shan
Tarim Basin
Kunlun Shan
Huang He
North China Plain
Yellow Sea
Honshu
Japan Trench 10500
Mediterranean Sea
Euphrates
Tigris
Iranian Plateau
Hindu Kush
Indus
Tibetan Plateau
Himalaya △8848 Mt. Everest
Brahmaputra
Chang Jiang
Yangtze
Yunnan Plateau
East China Sea
Taiwan
Kyushu
Arabia
The Gulf
Red Sea
Ganges
Deccan
Bay of Bengal
Salween
Mekong
South China Sea
PACIFIC
Tropic of Cancer
Marianas Trench
AFRICA
Tibesti Mts.
Nile
Blue Nile
Gulf of Aden
Arabian Sea
Andaman Is.
Nicobar Is.
Philippines
Philippine Trench 10497
Caroline Is. 11034
Marshall Is.
OCEAN
L. Chad
White Nile
Ethiopian Highlands
Sri Lanka
Borneo
Equator
Gilbert Is.
Ubangi
Zaire Basin
Kasai
Lake Victoria
Kilimanjaro 5895
Amirantes
Seychelles
INDIAN
Sumatra
Celebes
Puntjak Jaya △5030
New Guinea
Solomon Is.
Zaire
L. Tanganyika
OCEAN
Mid-Indian Basin
West Australian Basin
Java
Christmas I.
Timor
Timor Sea
Arafura Sea
North Fiji Basin
Samoa Is.
Bié Plateau
L. Malawi
Zambezi
Mid
Indian
Mauritius
Réunion
Cocos Is.
AUSTRALASIA
Coral Sea
Vanuatu
New Caledonia
Fiji Is.
Kalahari Desert
Limpopo
Madagascar
Mozambique Channel
Amsterdam I.
Great Sandy Desert
Great Artesian Basin
Great Dividing Range
Tropic of Capricorn
Tonga Is. 10882
South Fiji Basin
Orange
Vaal
Drakensberg
Kerguelen Basin
Indian
Basin
Australia
L. Eyre
Darling
Murray
Tonga Trench
C. of Good Hope
C. Leeuwin
Great Australian Bight
Tasman Sea
Kermadec Trench 10047
Prince Edward Is.
Crozet Is.
Kerguelen
RIDGE
Tasmania
Chatham Is.
Ridge
Heard I.
Indian – Antarctic Ridge
New Zealand
Indian-Antarctic Basin
Eastern Indian-Antarctic Basin
SOUTHERN OCEAN
Antarctic Circle
Ross Sea
ANTARCTICA

Equatorial Scale 1:80 000 000

| 0 | 500 | 1000 | 1500 | 2000 | 2500 Miles |

| 0 | 1000 | 2000 | 3000 | 4000 Kms. |

Flat Polar Equal Area Projection

Space and Place

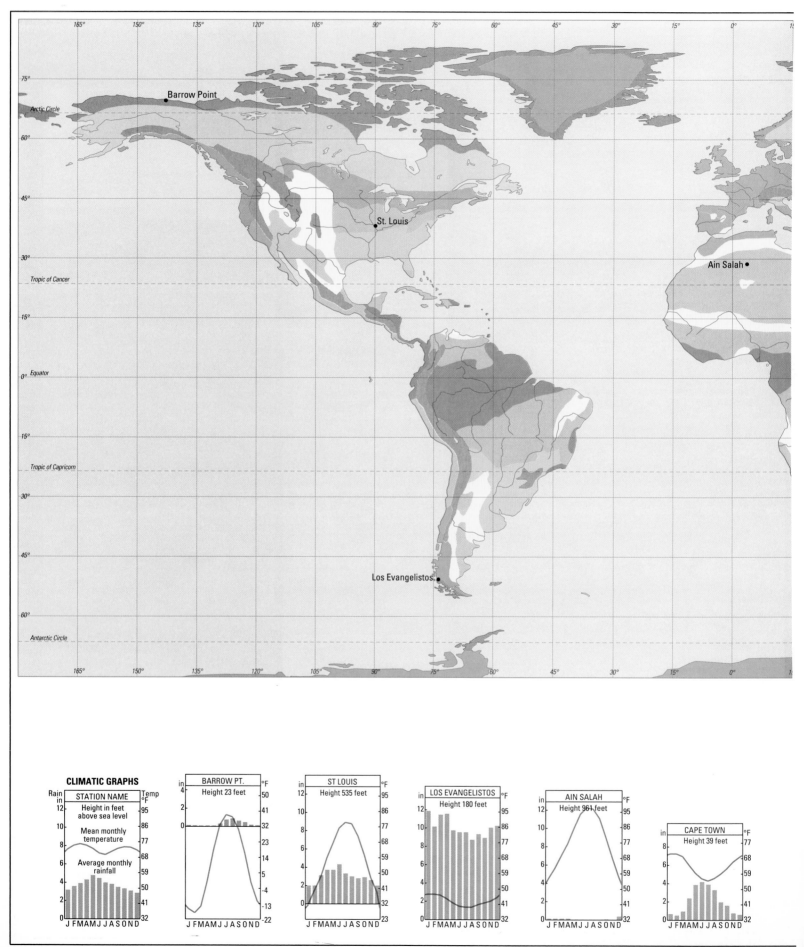

CLIMATIC GRAPHS

Rain in — STATION NAME — Temp °F
Height in feet above sea level
Mean monthly temperature
Average monthly rainfall

J F M A M J J A S O N D

BARROW PT.
Height 23 feet

ST LOUIS
Height 535 feet

LOS EVANGELISTOS
Height 180 feet

AIN SALAH
Height 961 feet

CAPE TOWN
Height 39 feet

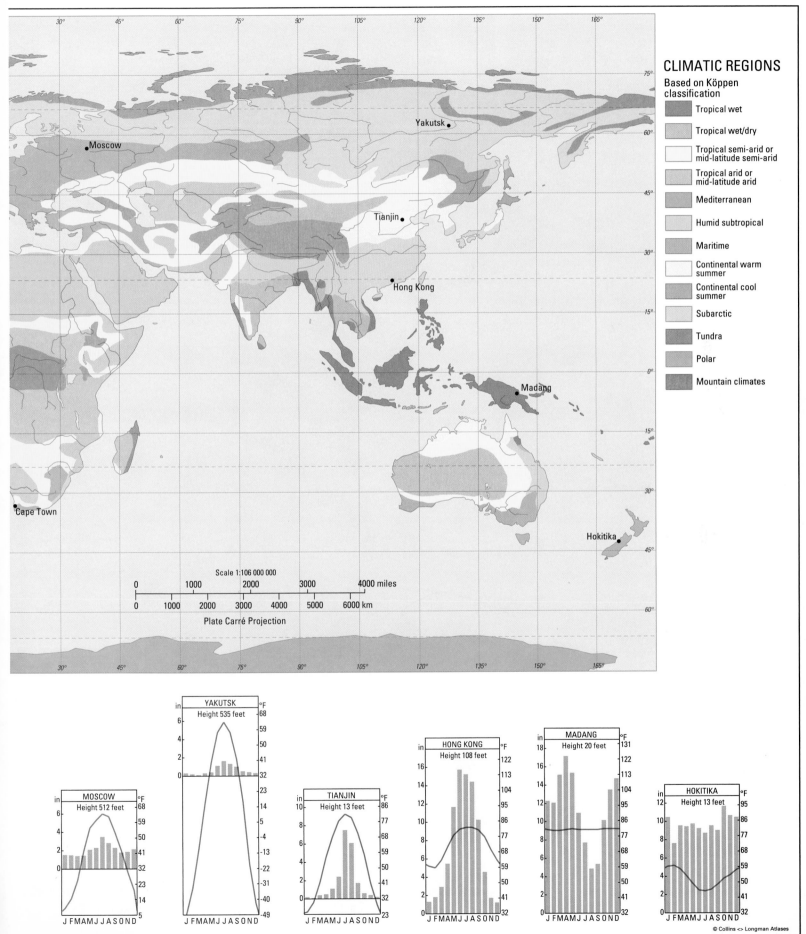

CLIMATIC REGIONS

Based on Köppen classification

- Tropical wet
- Tropical wet/dry
- Tropical semi-arid or mid-latitude semi-arid
- Tropical arid or mid-latitude arid
- Mediterranean
- Humid subtropical
- Maritime
- Continental warm summer
- Continental cool summer
- Subarctic
- Tundra
- Polar
- Mountain climates

Scale 1:106 000 000

| 0 | 1000 | 2000 | 3000 | 4000 miles |

| 0 | 1000 | 2000 | 3000 | 4000 | 5000 | 6000 km |

Plate Carré Projection

YAKUTSK
Height 535 feet

MOSCOW
Height 512 feet

TIANJIN
Height 13 feet

HONG KONG
Height 108 feet

MADANG
Height 20 feet

HOKITIKA
Height 13 feet

© Collins <> Longman Atlases

Space and Place

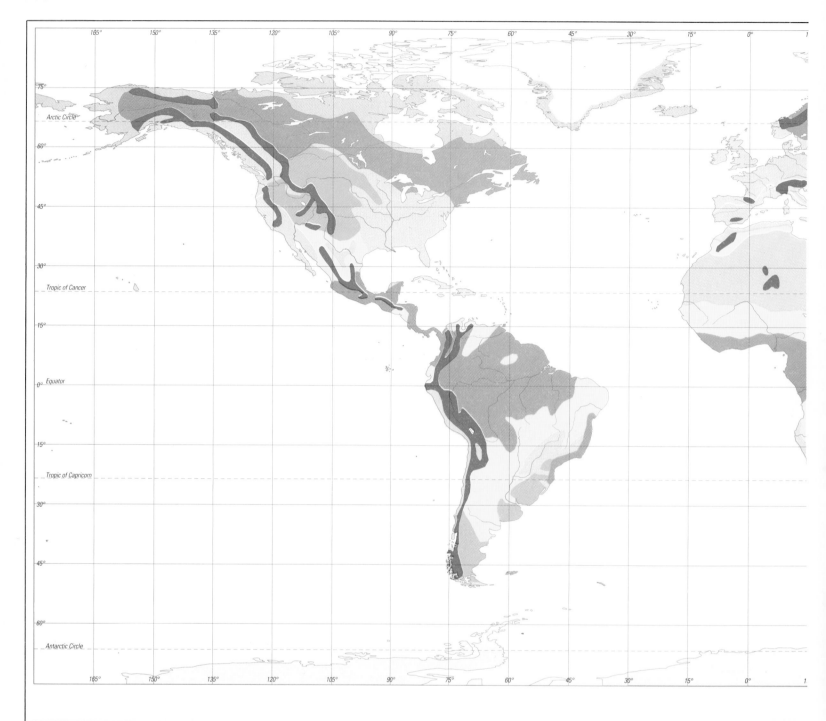

Ice cap, Antarctica

Tundra, Norway

Coniferous forest, Canada

Temperate deciduous forest, UK

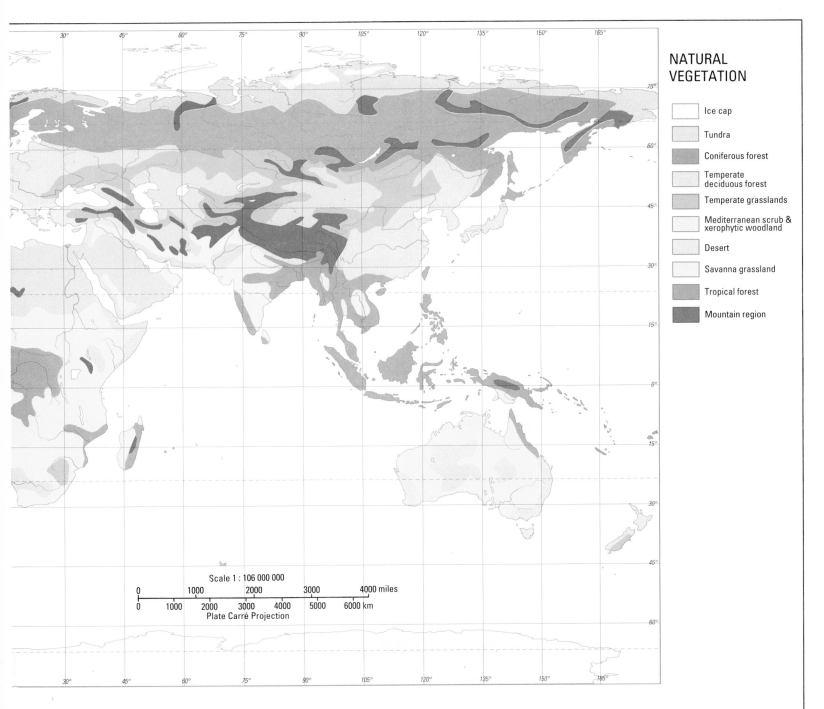

NATURAL VEGETATION

- [ ] Ice cap
- [ ] Tundra
- [ ] Coniferous forest
- [ ] Temperate deciduous forest
- [ ] Temperate grasslands
- [ ] Mediterranean scrub & xerophytic woodland
- [ ] Desert
- [ ] Savanna grassland
- [ ] Tropical forest
- [ ] Mountain region

Scale 1 : 106 000 000

| 0 | 1000 | 2000 | 3000 | 4000 miles |

| 0 | 1000 | 2000 | 3000 | 4000 | 5000 | 6000 km |

Plate Carré Projection

Desert, Iran

Savanna grassland, Nigeria

Tropical forest, Malaysia

Mountain region, Nepal

Space and Place

Plate boundaries, Earthquakes, and Volcanoes

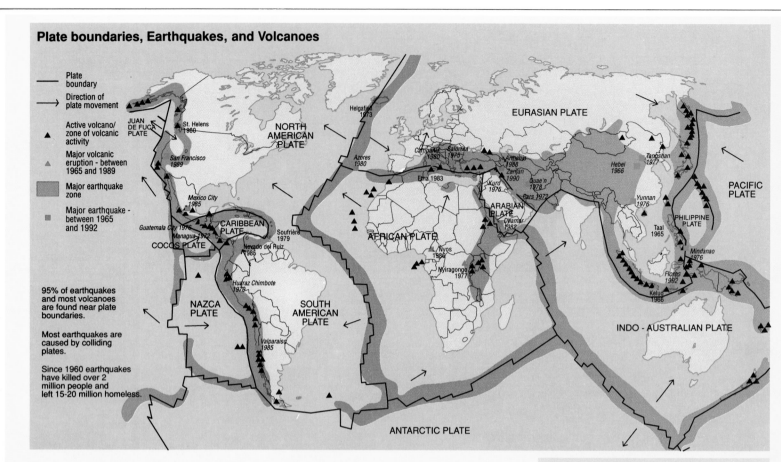

Legend:

— Plate boundary

→ Direction of plate movement

▲ Active volcano/ zone of volcanic activity

▲ Major volcanic eruption - between 1965 and 1989

Major earthquake zone

■ Major earthquake - between 1965 and 1992

95% of earthquakes and most volcanoes are found near plate boundaries.

Most earthquakes are caused by colliding plates.

Since 1960 earthquakes have killed over 2 million people and left 15-20 million homeless.

Map labels: JUAN DE FUCA PLATE, NORTH AMERICAN PLATE, EURASIAN PLATE, PACIFIC PLATE, PHILIPPINE PLATE, AFRICAN PLATE, ARABIAN PLATE, CARIBBEAN PLATE, COCOS PLATE, NAZCA PLATE, SOUTH AMERICAN PLATE, INDO - AUSTRALIAN PLATE, ANTARCTIC PLATE

Locations: St. Helens 1980, San Francisco 1989, Mexico City 1985, Guatemala City 1976, Managua 1972, Nevado del Ruiz 1985, Soufrière 1979, Huaraz Chimbote 1978, Valparaiso 1985, Helgafjell 1973, Azores 1980, Campania 1980, Salonika 1975, Etna 1983, Kurd 1976, Armenia 1988, Zanjan 1990, Quae'n 1978, Pars 1972, Dhamar 1982, Nyos 1986, Nyiragongo 1977, Hebei 1966, Tangshan 1977, Yunnan 1976, Taal 1965, Mindanao 1976, Flores 1992, Kelud 1966

The Structure of the Earth

The earth's surface or crust forms a rigid layer of rock which varies in thickness from 4 miles to 25 miles. Beneath the crust is a zone of semimolten rock known as the asthenosphere. Together with the upper mantle this reaches down to a depth of about 435 miles, below which there is the lower mantle and the core.

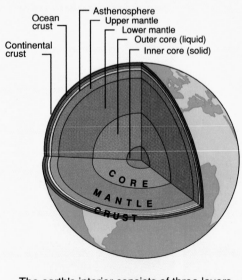

Ocean crust
Asthenosphere
Upper mantle
Lower mantle
Outer core (liquid)
Inner core (solid)
Continental crust

CORE
MANTLE
CRUST

The earth's interior consists of three layers - the crust on the surface, the mantle under-neath and the core at the center.

Types of Plates

The crust is broken into huge plates which fit together like the parts of a giant jigsaw. These float on the semimolten rock below. The boundaries between the plates are the site of many volcanoes and earthquakes.

There are three types of boundaries:-
Diverging plates. When two plates move away from each other, molten rock wells up from the earth's core creating a ridge, e.g. the ridge in the Atlantic Ocean from Iceland to Antarctica.

Converging plates. When two plates move towards each other a trench is formed as one slides beneath the other. It was a movement of this kind which created the Himalayas.

Shearing plates. Sometimes neighboring plates move horizontally in opposite directions from one another, e.g. the San Andreas Fault in California.

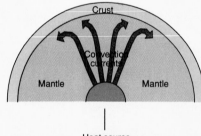

Crust
Convection currents
Mantle — Mantle

Heat source (Earth's core)

Convection and Plate Movement

Plate movements cause continents to drift at about 1 inch a year. They are carried by convection currents in the magma.

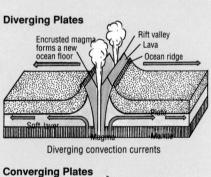

Diverging Plates

Encrusted magma forms a new ocean floor
Rift valley
Lava
Ocean ridge
Soft layer
Plate
Magma
Mantle

Diverging convection currents

Converging Plates

Volcanoes
Encrusted magma
Deep sea trenches

Converging convection currents

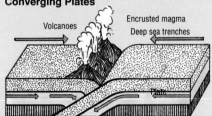

Shearing Plates

Encrusted magma
Plate
Plate

Currents moving past each other

Earthquakes

The shock from an earthquake spreads out from a point known as the epicenter. The amount of damage depends, among other things, on the depth of the epicenter.

The force of an earthquake is measured on a scale devised by an American, Dr Charles Richter in 1935. Each step on the scale represents a tenfold increase in intensity.

Parts of an earthquake

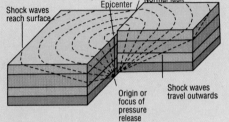

Major earthquakes since 1970

DATE	COUNTRY	FORCE (Richter scale)	DEATHS
31.5.70	Peru	7.7	66 800
23.12.72	Nicaragua	6.2	5 000
4.2.76	Guatemala	7.7	22 700
27.7.76	Tangshan, China	8.2	242 000
16.9.78	Iran	7.7	25 000
10.10.80	Algeria	7.5	2 600
23.11.80	Italy	6.8	3 000
13.12.82	Yemen	6.0	2 000
19.9.85	Mexico	8.1	25 000
7.12.88	Armenia	6.9	25 000
17.10.89	California, USA	6.9	300
21.6.90	Iran	7.5	40 000
12.12.92	Indonesia	7.5	2 000

Volcanoes

There are about 500 active volcanoes in the world. The majority of them are found in two main zones: a 'Ring of Fire' around the Pacific Ocean and an east-west belt from Europe to Indonesia.

Volcanic eruptions can cause terrible damage. Molten rock pours out of the vent over the surrounding area, and rock dust and gas are blown high into the atmosphere.

Mt. St. Helens Volcano

DATE: May 18, 1980
LOCATION: Washington, USA
EXTENT OF DEBRIS: 22,000 sq. miles
DEATHS: 60

The Mexican Earthquake Disaster

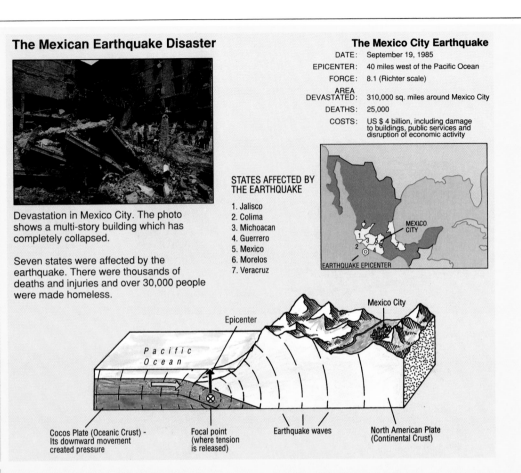

Devastation in Mexico City. The photo shows a multi-story building which has completely collapsed.

Seven states were affected by the earthquake. There were thousands of deaths and injuries and over 30,000 people were made homeless.

STATES AFFECTED BY THE EARTHQUAKE

1. Jalisco
2. Colima
3. Michoacan
4. Guerrero
5. Mexico
6. Morelos
7. Veracruz

Cocos Plate (Oceanic Crust) - Its downward movement created pressure

Focal point (where tension is released)

Earthquake waves

North American Plate (Continental Crust)

Epicenter

Mexico City

Pacific Ocean

The Mexico City Earthquake

DATE:	September 19, 1985
EPICENTER:	40 miles west of the Pacific Ocean
FORCE:	8.1 (Richter scale)
AREA DEVASTATED:	310,000 sq. miles around Mexico City
DEATHS:	25,000
COSTS:	US $ 4 billion, including damage to buildings, public services and disruption of economic activity

Mount St. Helens Eruption

The eruption of the Mount St. Helens in the state of Washington was one of the most dramatic in recent years. The explosion blew out of the side of the cone, and reduced the height of the mountain by 1280 feet, creating a vast new crater. The blast also flattened half a million trees over a radius of 15 miles and blew dust high into the stratosphere across all of North America.

The volcano was in a remote area so only a small number of people were affected. It gave scientists an opportunity to find out more about what the early earth looked like. Plant life returned quickly to the devastated areas. It seems that pockets survived in gulleys and under rocks enabling life to regenerate quickly.

How the volcano blew

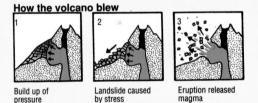

Build up of pressure

Landslide caused by stress

Eruption released magma

Results of the eruption

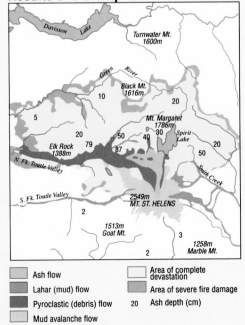

Ash flow	Area of complete devastation
Lahar (mud) flow	Area of severe fire damage
Pyroclastic (debris) flow	20 Ash depth (cm)
Mud avalanche flow	

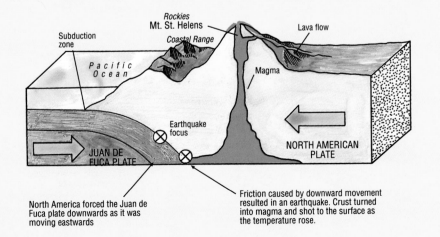

Subduction zone

Rockies
Mt. St. Helens

Coastal Range

Pacific Ocean

Lava flow

Magma

Earthquake focus

JUAN DE FUCA PLATE

NORTH AMERICAN PLATE

North America forced the Juan de Fuca plate downwards as it was moving eastwards

Friction caused by downward movement resulted in an earthquake. Crust turned into magma and shot to the surface as the temperature rose.

Space and Place

Many important towns and cities are built on rivers. The Nile, Indus, and Euphrates rivers supported some of the earliest civilizations. The needs of agriculture, communications, and trade have ensured that rivers remain important in the modern world. As population increases the demand on water resources is becoming greater. There is a pressing need for proper water management.

Major World Floods

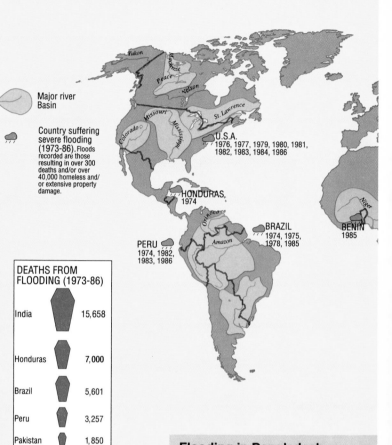

Major river Basin

Country suffering severe flooding (1973-86). Floods recorded are those resulting in over 300 deaths and/or over 40,000 homeless and/ or extensive property damage.

U.S.A. 1976, 1977, 1979, 1980, 1981, 1982, 1983, 1984, 1986

HONDURAS 1974

PERU 1974, 1982, 1983, 1986

BRAZIL 1974, 1975, 1978, 1985

BENIN 1985

Deforestation and Floods

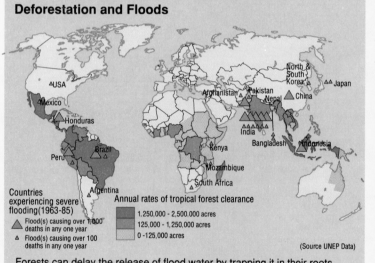

Countries experiencing severe flooding(1963-85)

△ Flood(s) causing over 1,000 deaths in any one year

△ Flood(s) causing over 100 deaths in any one year

Annual rates of tropical forest clearance

1,250,000 - 2,500,000 acres
125,000 - 1,250,000 acres
0 - 125,000 acres

(Source UNEP Data)

Forests can delay the release of flood water by trapping it in their roots. When the trees are cut down the result is often soil erosion and flooding.

DEATHS FROM FLOODING (1973-86)

India	15,658
Honduras	7,000
Brazil	5,601
Peru	3,257
Pakistan	1,850
China	1,550
Indonesia	1,501
Bangladesh	403
Japan	335
USA	305
Mozambique	300

(Source UNEP Data)

The Effects of Deforestation

FORESTED AREA

A) Heavy rain and water from melting snow runs down slopes and becomes trapped in the roots of trees.

B) Some of the water evaporates, forms clouds, and is carried on the wind to arid regions.

C) The water flows on towards the sea in a fairly steady flow, free of silt.

DEFORESTED AREA

1) Without trees to hold it back, flood water rushes down mountain slopes.

2) The swollen streams cut deep channels and carry away valuable top soil.

3) Further downstream the river channel becomes clogged with silt, causing floods.

Flooding in Bangladesh

In Bangladesh, the monsoon rains cause the rivers to flood each year. These floods are a normal part of life and help to renew the fertility of the soil. In recent years, however, the floods have become much more severe due to the clearance of forests in the Himalayas for fuel, farmland, and logging. These floods have caused serious damage and loss of life.

Severe flooding as a result of deforestation in the Himalayas is also a problem in India. Each year it spends over a million US$ on river defenses to control flooding.

SEPTEMBER 1987
671 dead
2 million homes washed away
4.3 million acres of land destroyed
3 million tons (10%) of rice and wheat crops lost

AUGUST 1988
Over 3,000 dead
75% of country flooded
250 bridges and 2,200 miles of road destroyed
3 million tons of rice and other crops destroyed

© BARTHOLOMEW

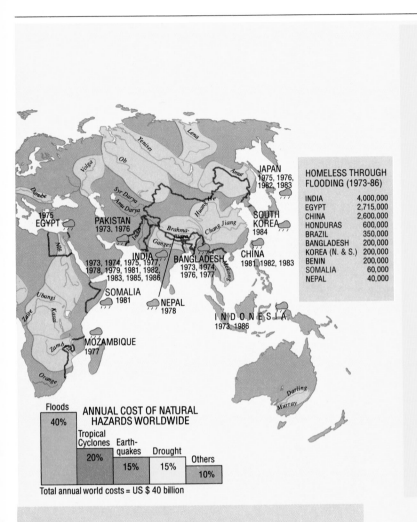

HOMELESS THROUGH FLOODING (1973-86)	
INDIA	4,000,000
EGYPT	2,715,000
CHINA	2,600,000
HONDURAS	600,000
BRAZIL	350,000
BANGLADESH	200,000
KOREA (N. & S.)	200,000
BENIN	200,000
SOMALIA	60,000
NEPAL	40,000

ANNUAL COST OF NATURAL HAZARDS WORLDWIDE

Floods 40%
Tropical Cyclones 20%
Earthquakes 15%
Drought 15%
Others 10%

Total annual world costs = US $ 40 billion

Flood Damage

Flooding causes more damage than any other environmental hazard.

While all countries in the world are affected by floods, the impact on people in developing countries is greater. The number of deaths and homes destroyed is often much higher. This is partly because they cannot afford to protect themselves, and partly because shortage of land forces them to live in vulnerable areas. In addition any loss of food crops, export crops, and employment can have a devastating effect.

Controlling Floods

Around the world there are plans for dams which will control floods and generate hydroelectric power.

Examples include:

Mekong dams on the Red River in Vietnam
Three Gorges Dam on the Chang Jiang in China
Narmada Dam in India

The problem with all these schemes is that they will flood large areas of land and attract industry which will put pressure on environmentally sensitive areas. Often local people do not benefit from them, foreign companies and banks taking most of the profits.

Many flood control measures only deal with the symptoms. The best solutions tackle the causes as well.

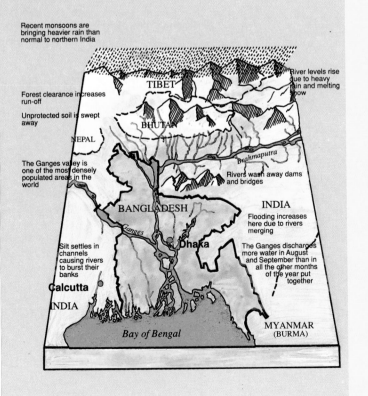

Space and Place

Tropical Storms

In tropical regions, intense storms form over the ocean in late summer and early autumn. The majority occur in the Northern Hemisphere. They are known as 'hurricanes' in either the North Atlantic Ocean or eastern Pacific Ocean, 'typhoons' in the western Pacific Ocean, and 'cyclones' in the Indian Ocean.

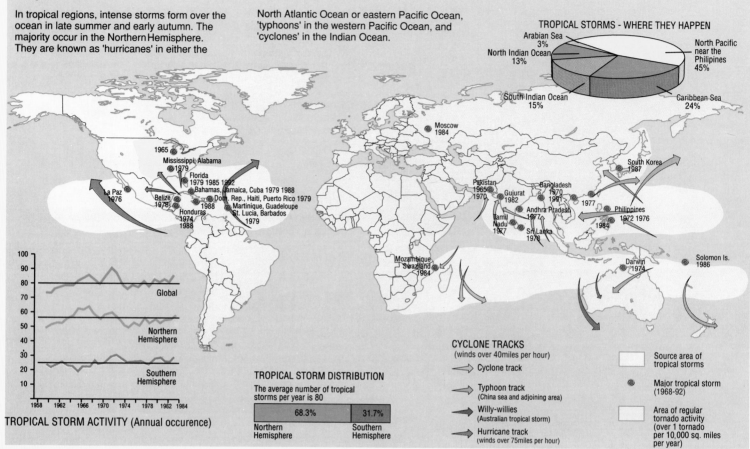

TROPICAL STORMS - WHERE THEY HAPPEN

Arabian Sea 3%
North Indian Ocean 13%
North Pacific near the Philipines 45%
South Indian Ocean 15%
Caribbean Sea 24%

TROPICAL STORM ACTIVITY (Annual occurence)

Global
Northern Hemisphere
Southern Hemisphere

TROPICAL STORM DISTRIBUTION
The average number of tropical storms per year is 80

68.3%	31.7%
Northern Hemisphere	Southern Hemisphere

CYCLONE TRACKS
(winds over 40miles per hour)

- Cyclone track
- Typhoon track (China sea and adjoining area)
- Willy-willies (Australian tropical storm)
- Hurricane track (winds over 75miles per hour)

- Source area of tropical storms
- Major tropical storm (1968-92)
- Area of regular tornado activity (over 1 tornado per 10,000 sq. miles per year)

The Life of a Tropical Storm

Tropical storms can only begin if sea temperatures rise to 80°F or more. This allows large quantities of moisture to evaporate into the atmosphere creating unsettled weather conditions. As the pressure drops, the storm begins to spin violently and is carried along by the trade winds. The storm sucks in more moisture as it passes over the warm ocean and becomes more intense. Eventually the storm moves to cooler areas, or passes over land, loses energy, and breaks up.

Structure of a Tropical Storm

At the center of a tropical storm there is an 'eye' of calm and cloudless skies. Around it, violent winds, often in excess of 100miles per hour, bring torrential rain that may last for several days.

Naming Tropical Storms

Since the Second World War, tropical storms have been named in alphabetical order during each year. This means you can tell from the initial letter how many there have been in a season. Typhoons often use the full range of the alphabet. Hurricanes, being less frequent, tend to only use the first half.

Structure of a Hurricane

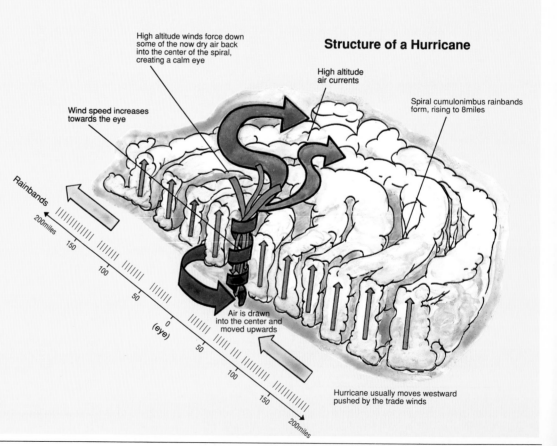

High altitude winds force down some of the now dry air back into the center of the spiral, creating a calm eye

High altitude air currents

Spiral cumulonimbus rainbands form, rising to 8miles

Wind speed increases towards the eye

Rainbands

Air is drawn into the center and moved upwards

Hurricane usually moves westward pushed by the trade winds

NORTH CAROLINA

SOUTH CAROLINA

GEORGIA

ATLANTIC OCEAN

Hurricane Hugo

First detected on September 9 as a cluster of storms off the west African coast, Hurricane Hugo developed into the strongest hurricane of 1989, sustaining wind speeds of 160miles per hour. Hurricane Hugo left a trail of destruction across a number of Caribbean islands and in both the states of North and South Carolina. The cost of the storm damage was estimated at 10 billion US dollars and 49 lives were lost.

False color satellite image showing Hurricane Hugo as it struck the eastern coast of the United States at South Carolina on September 22, 1989.

The Effect of Hurricanes in the Caribbean

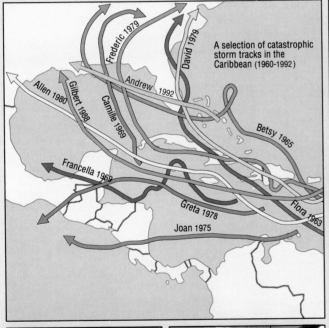

A selection of catastrophic storm tracks in the Caribbean (1960-1992)

Frederic 1979
David 1979
Andrew 1992
Allen 1980
Gilbert 1988
Camille 1969
Betsy 1965
Francella 1969
Greta 1978
Flora 1963
Joan 1975

Vehicles, caught in a hurricane in Houston, Texas, dodge live power lines.

Hurricane Camille caused severe flooding in the USA. More than 300 people were killed.

In 1988, Gilbert, the most powerful hurricane ever recorded, led to a national disaster being declared in Jamaica.

Hurricane David in 1979 caused widespread damage in Dominica. 1,300 people died and 100,000 were left homeless.

Hurricane Allen crossed Barbados and Jamaica causing death and destruction.

Hurricanes

Tropical storms can do terrible damage. Not only do the fierce winds tear buildings apart, but the low pressure can create a surge of seawater that floods coastal areas. The torrential rain adds to these problems.

In some parts of the world, special emergency services and hurricane warning systems have been set up. It is in poorer countries that most lives are lost and the damage is worst. Here many buildings are badly constructed and people can not afford to take precautions.

Tornadoes

Tornadoes are powerful, twisting wind storms associated with rain and thunderstorms. Usually about 100yards in width, and with only the most violent lasting longer than an hour. They are rotating funnel clouds that extend downward from a mass of dark clouds. Wind speeds at the center can reach over 180mph. At such high speed, tornadoes can cause loss of life and severe damage to property.

Tornadoes are particularly common in the United States especially in the Midwestern and Southern states where the warm humid air from the Gulf of Mexico meets the cool dry air from the north. They also occur, less frequently, in other parts of the world, including Australia and India.

Space and Place

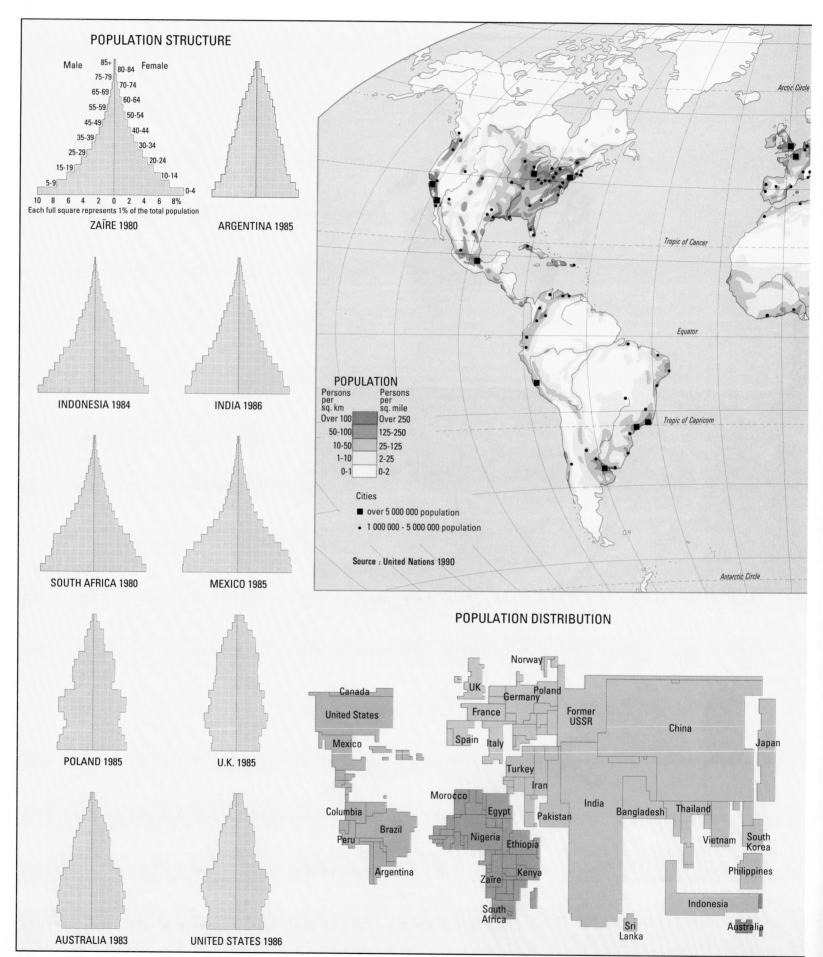

POPULATION STRUCTURE

Male   85+   Female
75-79   80-84
65-69   70-74
55-59   60-64
45-49   50-54
35-39   40-44
25-29   30-34
15-19   20-24
5-9   10-14
        0-4

10 8 6 4 2 0 2 4 6 8%
Each full square represents 1% of the total population

ZAÏRE 1980

ARGENTINA 1985

INDONESIA 1984

INDIA 1986

SOUTH AFRICA 1980

MEXICO 1985

POLAND 1985

U.K. 1985

AUSTRALIA 1983

UNITED STATES 1986

POPULATION

Persons per sq. km	Persons per sq. mile
Over 100	Over 250
50-100	125-250
10-50	25-125
1-10	2-25
0-1	0-2

Cities

■ over 5 000 000 population

• 1 000 000 - 5 000 000 population

Source : United Nations 1990

Arctic Circle

Tropic of Cancer

Equator

Tropic of Capricorn

Antarctic Circle

POPULATION DISTRIBUTION

Norway · UK · Poland · Germany · France · Former USSR · China · Japan · Spain · Italy · Canada · United States · Mexico · Turkey · Iran · India · Bangladesh · Thailand · Morocco · Egypt · Pakistan · Vietnam · South Korea · Columbia · Nigeria · Philippines · Brazil · Ethiopia · Peru · Zaïre · Kenya · Argentina · Indonesia · South Africa · Sri Lanka · Australia

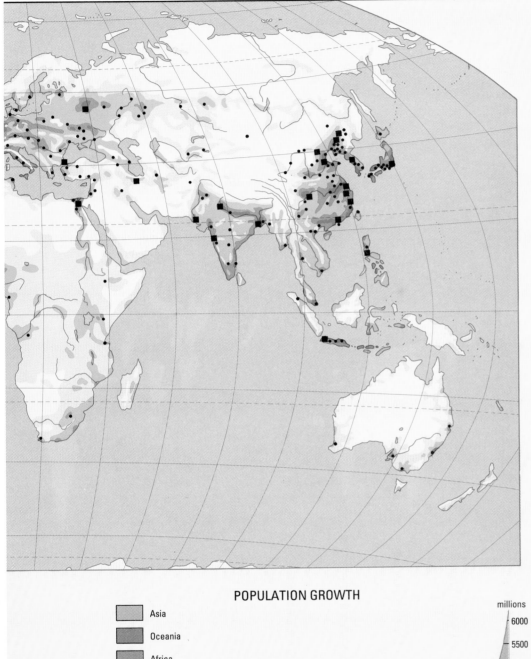

FACT*file* **Largest Cities**
Population figures in millions

AFRICA

Cairo	Egypt	9.0
Lagos	Nigeria	7.7
Alexandria	Egypt	3.7
Kinshasa	Zaïre	3.5
Casablanca	Morocco	3.2
Algiers	Algeria	3.0
Cape Town	South Africa	2.3
Abidjan	Côte d'Ivoire	2.2
Tripoli	Libya	2.1
Khartoum	Sudan	1.9

ASIA

Tokyo	Japan	18.1
Shanghai	China	13.4
Calcutta	India	11.8
Bombay	India	11.2
Seoul	South Korea	11.0
Beijing	China	10.8
Tianjin	China	9.4
Jakarta	Indonesia	9.3
Delhi	India	8.8
Manila	Philippines	8.5

EUROPE

Moscow	Russian Federation	8.8
Paris	France	8.5
London	United Kingdom	7.5
Milan	Italy	5.3
Madrid	Spain	5.2
St. Petersburg	Russian Federation	5.1
Naples	Italy	3.6
Barcelona	Spain	3.4
Athens	Greece	3.4
Katowice	Poland	3.4

NORTH AMERICA

Mexico City	Mexico	20.2
New York	United States	16.2
Los Angeles	United States	11.9
Chicago	United States	7.0
Philadelphia	United States	4.3
Detroit	United States	3.7
San Francisco	United States	3.7
Toronto	Canada	3.5
Dallas	United States	3.4
Guadalajara	Mexico	3.2

SOUTH AMERICA

São Paulo	Brazil	17.4
Buenos Aires	Argentina	11.5
Rio de Janeiro	Brazil	10.7
Lima	Peru	6.2
Santiago	Chile	4.7
Caracas	Venezuela	4.1
Belo Horizonte	Brazil	3.6
Porto Alegre	Brazil	3.1
Recife	Brazil	2.5
Salvador	Brazil	2.4

OCEANIA

Sydney	Australia	3.4
Melbourne	Australia	2.8
Brisbane	Australia	1.2
Perth	Australia	1.1

Note: Figures refer to urban agglomerations as defined by the U. N.

POPULATION GROWTH

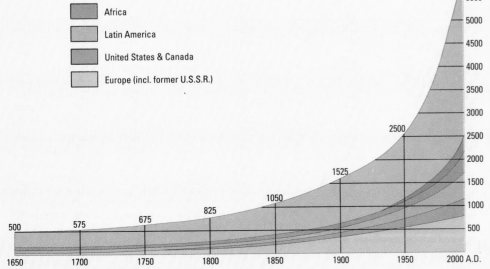

- Asia
- Oceania
- Africa
- Latin America
- United States & Canada
- Europe (incl. former U.S.S.R.)

millions: 6000, 5500, 5000, 4500, 4000, 3500, 3000, 2500, 2000, 1500, 1000, 500

2500, 1525, 1050, 825, 675, 575, 500

1650, 1700, 1750, 1800, 1850, 1900, 1950, 2000 A.D.

Environment and Society

Forests cover about one third of the world's land surface. Temperate and coniferous forests spread across areas of Europe, Asia, and North America. Further south, a band of tropical rain forests extending about ten degrees in latitude north and south of the equator, forms the richest habitat on earth.

Temperate and coniferous forests are generally carefully managed and are quick to regrow. Rain forests take longer to grow and occupy a more fragile environment. They are being destroyed at an alarming rate as people sell the wood and clear land for housing, crops, and industry.

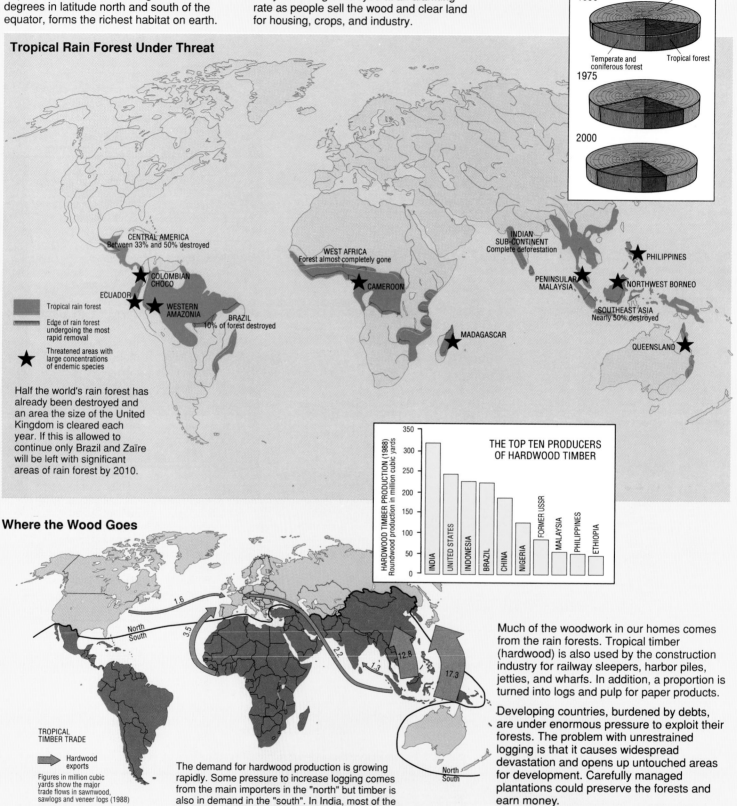

Shrinking Forests

1950

Rest of the earth

Temperate and coniferous forest

Tropical forest

1975

2000

Tropical Rain Forest Under Threat

CENTRAL AMERICA
Between 33% and 50% destroyed

COLOMBIAN CHOCO

ECUADOR

WESTERN AMAZONIA

BRAZIL
10% of forest destroyed

WEST AFRICA
Forest almost completely gone

CAMEROON

MADAGASCAR

INDIAN SUB-CONTINENT
Complete deforestation

PENINSULAR MALAYSIA

PHILIPPINES

NORTHWEST BORNEO

SOUTHEAST ASIA
Nearly 50% destroyed

QUEENSLAND

Tropical rain forest

Edge of rain forest undergoing the most rapid removal

Threatened areas with large concentrations of endemic species

Half the world's rain forest has already been destroyed and an area the size of the United Kingdom is cleared each year. If this is allowed to continue only Brazil and Zaïre will be left with significant areas of rain forest by 2010.

THE TOP TEN PRODUCERS OF HARDWOOD TIMBER

HARDWOOD TIMBER PRODUCTION (1988)
Roundwood production in million cubic yards

INDIA · UNITED STATES · INDONESIA · BRAZIL · CHINA · NIGERIA · FORMER USSR · MALAYSIA · PHILIPPINES · ETHIOPIA

Where the Wood Goes

North South

1.6

3.5

2.2

1.3

12.8

17.3

North South

TROPICAL TIMBER TRADE

Hardwood exports

Figures in million cubic yards show the major trade flows in sawnwood, sawlogs and veneer logs (1988)

The demand for hardwood production is growing rapidly. Some pressure to increase logging comes from the main importers in the "north" but timber is also in demand in the "south". In India, most of the 318 million yd³ produced is for domestic use as fuel.

Much of the woodwork in our homes comes from the rain forests. Tropical timber (hardwood) is also used by the construction industry for railway sleepers, harbor piles, jetties, and wharfs. In addition, a proportion is turned into logs and pulp for paper products.

Developing countries, burdened by debts, are under enormous pressure to exploit their forests. The problem with unrestrained logging is that it causes widespread devastation and opens up untouched areas for development. Carefully managed plantations could preserve the forests and earn money.

© BARTHOLOMEW

The Real Costs of Rain Forest Destruction

What we are losing?

People
In South America the rain forest is the home for tribal groups like the Yanomani. Rubber tappers also operate in many areas.

Plants
Many crops and medicines come from rain forest plants which are a unique and extremely valuable resource.

Creatures
The rain forests are the richest and densest habitat on earth. They contain over half the world's insects, birds, and animals.

The rain forests generally grow on very poor soils. The trees protect the soil from tropical storms and help to keep it moist during the dry season. Once the trees are cleared, the earth quickly washes away and the land, exposed to the hot sun, turns to desert.

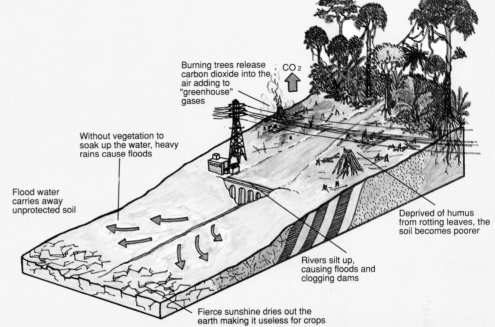

Burning trees release carbon dioxide into the air adding to "greenhouse" gases CO_2

Without vegetation to soak up the water, heavy rains cause floods

Flood water carries away unprotected soil

Deprived of humus from rotting leaves, the soil becomes poorer

Rivers silt up, causing floods and clogging dams

Fierce sunshine dries out the earth making it useless for crops

Deforestation in Amazonia

About a third of the world's rain forest is in Amazonia. This area mostly belongs to Brazil, but also covers parts of neighboring countries.

Many Brazilians want to open up Amazonia and exploit its riches. They see this as a way of developing industry and paying off debts. However, many projects take little account of the destruction which causes priceless areas of rain forest to literally go up in smoke.

DEFORESTATION AND ECONOMIC DEVELOPMENT IN BRAZILIAN AMAZONIA

BRAZIL

Brazilian Amazonia

Macapá
Belém
Manaus
Amazon
Santarém
São Luís
NORTE PROJECT
CALHA
GRANDE CARAJÁS PROGRAM
Trans Amazonian Highway
Pôrto Velho
Recife
POLONOROESTE
B R A Z I L
Brasilia
Rio de Janeiro
São Paulo
Pôrto Alegre

- Extent of Brazilian Amazonia
- Tropical rain forest
- Vegetation other than rain forest dominant
- Severe deforestation : areas where over 50% of the rain forest has been lost
- Main roads through Amazonia
- Roads under construction
- Major development project - (see text for details)

A huge area along the northern border of Brazil has been set aside for the Calha Norte Project. Here companies have been granted mining concessions and permission to explore for oil. Hydroelectric power stations are being built to provide power for industrial development. The dams for these schemes will flood large areas of land, threatening the homes of fifty thousand Indians.

Further south, the Grand Carajás Program involves a massive iron ore mine which will be linked by rail to a special port. Huge tracts of forest will also be cleared for a bauxite mine, cash crop plantations, and cattle ranches.

In the west, the Polonoroeste Development Project has allowed thousands of immigrants to move into the area. Originally it was intended to open up the area for agriculture, but the soil is so poor it cannot sustain crops.

DEMANDS ON LAND IN BRAZILIAN AMAZONIA

	10^3 miles^2	% total
Already cleared	130	10%
Area to be flooded for HEP development	60	4.4%
Forest reserves maintained for timber produ	190	15%
Colonized (up to 1989)	170	13%
Total officially earmarked for development	810	63.5%

Environment and Society

What is Desertification?

Desertification, or the spread of deserts, threatens over a third of the world's land surface. Severe deterioration and loss of soil can turn productive land into desert. Every year, an area the size of the United Kingdom is either lost or severely degraded. In some cases deserts appear to invade good land from the outside, but in fact it is deterioration of soil in the border regions which causes them to expand. By the year 2000, the situation is likely to become critical especially in the Sahel in Africa, the Andes in South America, and parts of South Asia.

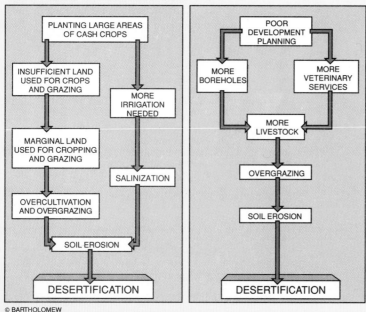

At one time lush trees and shrubs surrounded this Nile valley village.

The Causes

Desertification often begins when people decide or are forced to use land in dry areas too intensively. Overcultivation, overgrazing and the clearance of trees for fuel combine to degrade the soil. In other places, badly damaged irrigation schemes can make the land so salty it can no longer grow crops. The diagram below shows two ways in which desertification is triggered. Once desertification is started, natural factors, such as drought accelerate the process.

Where is Desertification Taking Place?

Fertile areas on the edge of existing deserts are most at risk. Here, harsh conditions mean that the land is only just able to grow crops and needs particularly careful management. Some 850 million people live in desert border regions and the population is growing rapidly.

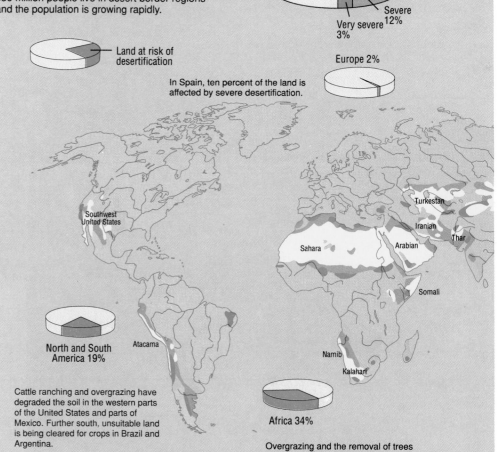

WORLD LAND AT RISK

Other land 66%
Existing desert 6%
Moderate 13%
Severe 12%
Very severe 3%

Land at risk of desertification

Europe 2%

In Spain, ten percent of the land is affected by severe desertification.

North and South America 19%

Cattle ranching and overgrazing have degraded the soil in the western parts of the United States and parts of Mexico. Further south, unsuitable land is being cleared for crops in Brazil and Argentina.

Africa 34%

Overgrazing and the removal of trees threaten the Sahel, Mediterranean coast, and southern Africa.

Two Models of Desertification

```
PLANTING LARGE AREAS
OF CASH CROPS
        │
        ▼
INSUFFICIENT LAND
USED FOR CROPS ──► MORE
AND GRAZING        IRRIGATION
        │          NEEDED
        ▼            │
MARGINAL LAND        ▼
USED FOR CROPPING  SALINIZATION
AND GRAZING          │
        │            │
        ▼            │
OVERCULTIVATION      │
AND OVERGRAZING      │
        │            │
        ▼            ▼
      SOIL EROSION
        │
        ▼
   DESERTIFICATION
```

```
        POOR
     DEVELOPMENT
      PLANNING
      │      │
      ▼      ▼
MORE        MORE
BOREHOLES   VETERINARY
      │     SERVICES
      │      │
      ▼      ▼
      MORE
      LIVESTOCK
        │
        ▼
    OVERGRAZING
        │
        ▼
    SOIL EROSION
        │
        ▼
   DESERTIFICATION
```

Effects of Desertification

Effects on People

Desertification is slow and insidious. Developing countries suffer most. Here, rural communities become trapped in a cycle of poverty which forces them to exploit the land beyond its capacity. This makes them very vulnerable to natural hazards, such as drought.

As crops fail and water sources dry up, people have no alternative but to leave the land. One sixth of the population of Burkina fled the country in the drought of the early 1970 s. In India and Brazil many victims of desertification have gone to live in the big cities, swelling the urban population.

Effects on Climate

Desertification can have a significant effect on the climate. The increase in dust prevents air from rising freely and forming clouds. In addition, the loss of vegetation reduces the amount of moisture in the air and allows temperatures to rise. Both these factors tend to make droughts worse.

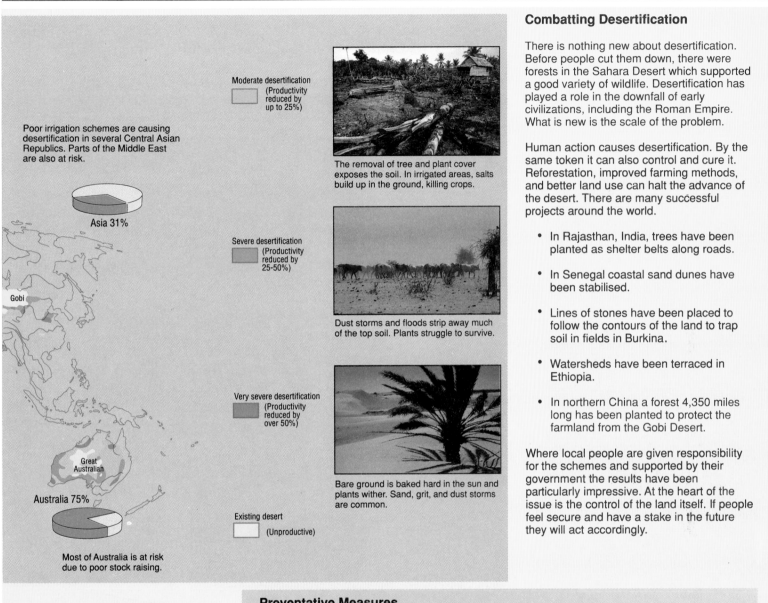

Poor irrigation schemes are causing desertification in several Central Asian Republics. Parts of the Middle East are also at risk.

Asia 31%

Gobi

Great Australian

Australia 75%

Most of Australia is at risk due to poor stock raising.

Moderate desertification
(Productivity reduced by up to 25%)

The removal of tree and plant cover exposes the soil. In irrigated areas, salts build up in the ground, killing crops.

Severe desertification
(Productivity reduced by 25-50%)

Dust storms and floods strip away much of the top soil. Plants struggle to survive.

Very severe desertification
(Productivity reduced by over 50%)

Bare ground is baked hard in the sun and plants wither. Sand, grit, and dust storms are common.

Existing desert
(Unproductive)

Combatting Desertification

There is nothing new about desertification. Before people cut them down, there were forests in the Sahara Desert which supported a good variety of wildlife. Desertification has played a role in the downfall of early civilizations, including the Roman Empire. What is new is the scale of the problem.

Human action causes desertification. By the same token it can also control and cure it. Reforestation, improved farming methods, and better land use can halt the advance of the desert. There are many successful projects around the world.

- In Rajasthan, India, trees have been planted as shelter belts along roads.

- In Senegal coastal sand dunes have been stabilised.

- Lines of stones have been placed to follow the contours of the land to trap soil in fields in Burkina.

- Watersheds have been terraced in Ethiopia.

- In northern China a forest 4,350 miles long has been planted to protect the farmland from the Gobi Desert.

Where local people are given responsibility for the schemes and supported by their government the results have been particularly impressive. At the heart of the issue is the control of the land itself. If people feel secure and have a stake in the future they will act accordingly.

Africa - Population Affected by Desertification

Mediterranean Africa 8.5 million

Sahel 28.5 million

1 million people

Africa South of the Sahel 25 million

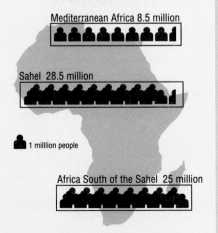

During the 1960s and 1970s the Sahara Desert spread 60 miles further south, forcing millions of people to leave their homes.

Preventative Measures

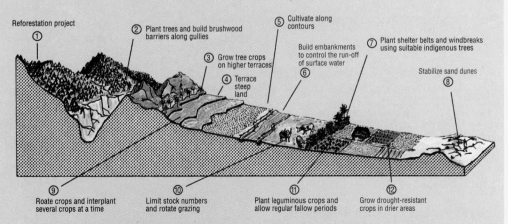

Reforestation project ①

② Plant trees and build brushwood barriers along gullies

③ Grow tree crops on higher terraces

④ Terrace steep land

⑤ Cultivate along contours

⑥ Build embankments to control the run-off of surface water

⑦ Plant shelter belts and windbreaks using suitable indigenous trees

⑧ Stabilize sand dunes

⑨ Roate crops and interplant several crops at a time

⑩ Limit stock numbers and rotate grazing

⑪ Plant leguminous crops and allow regular fallow periods

⑫ Grow drought-resistant crops in drier areas

Although we know how to halt desertification, we are not winning the battle against it. Too little money is spent on preventative measures and there is a lack of long-term planning. Many people are at risk and a massive effort will be needed to avoid famine in the years ahead.

Environment and Society

What is Pollution?

All damage to the environment is known as pollution. Some pollution comes from natural sources. Volcanoes, for example, release poisonous gases into the atmosphere. Most pollution, however, is caused by people. As the population of the world increases and the number of industries grows, pollution problems become more severe.

Air Pollution

The earth is covered by a layer of air which extends far into space. Only the lowest few miles can support life. As more and more wastes enter the atmosphere important changes begin to occur. If people continue polluting the atmosphere, the earth will eventually become uninhabitable.

Ozone Destruction

The earth is surrounded by a layer of ozone, O_3, in the stratosphere about 15miles above the surface. The ozone layer filters out harmful ultraviolet rays from the sun which can cause skin cancer. Recently scientists have noticed that the ozone layer is getting thinner. They were alarmed to discover a hole in the ozone over Antarctica each spring.

Ozone destruction is caused by gases known as *chlorofluorocarbons* (CFCs). These are used in foams, refrigerants, and aerosols. In 1987 many countries undertook to reduce their use of CFCs by signing an agreement called the Montreal Protocol.

The expanding hole in the ozone layer

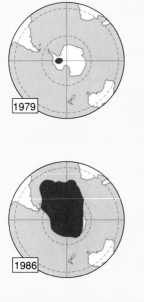

Each year the hole in the ozone layer over Antarctica gets larger. Places as far away as Australia and New Zealand are affected by the reduction in the ozone layer.

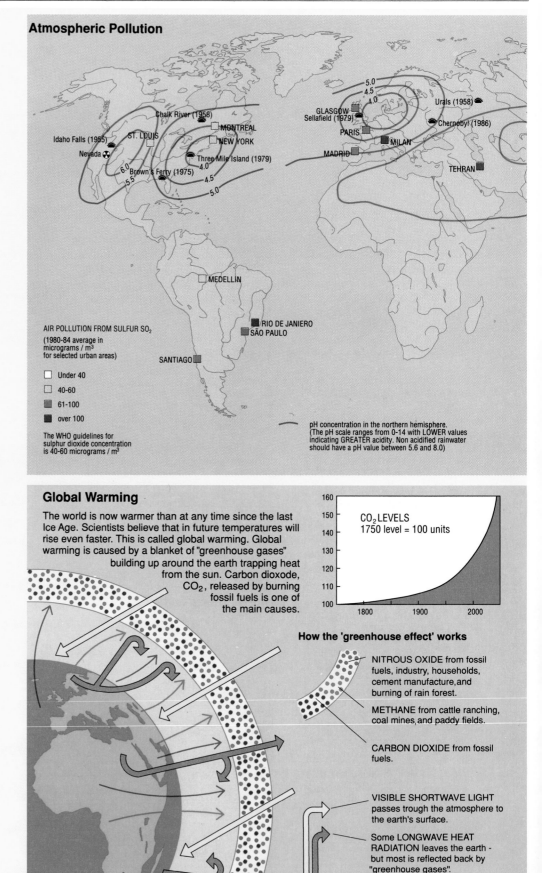

Atmospheric Pollution

AIR POLLUTION FROM SULFUR SO_2
(1980-84 average in micrograms / m^3 for selected urban areas)

- ☐ Under 40
- ☐ 40-60
- ◼ 61-100
- ◼ over 100

The WHO guidelines for sulphur dioxide concentration is 40-60 micrograms / m^3

pH concentration in the northern hemisphere. (The pH scale ranges from 0-14 with LOWER values indicating GREATER acidity. Non acidified rainwater should have a pH value between 5.6 and 8.0)

Global Warming

The world is now warmer than at any time since the last Ice Age. Scientists believe that in future temperatures will rise even faster. This is called global warming. Global warming is caused by a blanket of "greenhouse gases" building up around the earth trapping heat from the sun. Carbon dioxode, CO_2, released by burning fossil fuels is one of the main causes.

CO_2 LEVELS
1750 level = 100 units

How the 'greenhouse effect' works

NITROUS OXIDE from fossil fuels, industry, households, cement manufacture, and burning of rain forest.

METHANE from cattle ranching, coal mines, and paddy fields.

CARBON DIOXIDE from fossil fuels.

VISIBLE SHORTWAVE LIGHT passes trough the atmosphere to the earth's surface.

Some LONGWAVE HEAT RADIATION leaves the earth - but most is reflected back by "greenhouse gases".

Acid Rain

Coal and oil release a mixture of gases as they burn. These gases combine with water vapor, sunlight, and oxygen to form sulfuric acid and nitric acid which fall back to earth as acid rain. The effects of acid rain vary greatly, but areas with poor soil suffer most, especially in spring when melting snow pours contaminated water into rivers and lakes. One way of reducing the problem is to fit catalytic converters to cars and build filters for industrial smokestacks. It would also help if people used energy more efficiently to reduce their consumption of fuel.

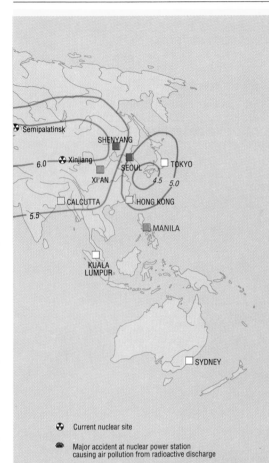

Semipalatinsk
SHENYANG
6.0 Xinjiang
XI'AN. SEOUL TOKYO
4.5 5.0
CALCUTTA HONG KONG
5.5
MANILA
KUALA LUMPUR
SYDNEY

☢ Current nuclear site

☢ Major accident at nuclear power station causing air pollution from radioactive discharge

Acid rain in Europe

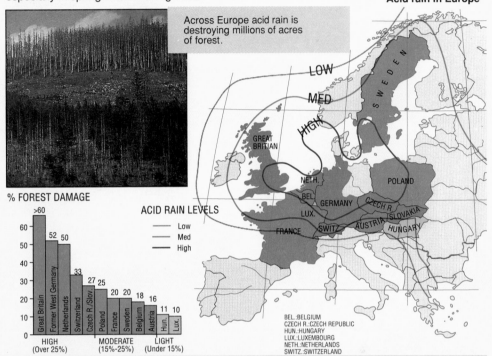

Across Europe acid rain is destroying millions of acres of forest.

% FOREST DAMAGE

	%
Great Britain	>60
Former West Germany	52
Netherlands	50
Switzerland	33
Czech R./Slov.	27
Poland	25
France	20
Sweden	20
Belgium	18
Austria	16
Hun.	11
Lux.	10

HIGH (Over 25%)   MODERATE (15%-25%)   LIGHT (Under 15%)

ACID RAIN LEVELS
— Low
— Med
— High

LOW
MED
HIGH
SWEDEN
GREAT BRITIAN
NETH.
BEL
LUX. GERMANY CZECH R. SLOVAKIA
FRANCE SWITZ. AUSTRIA HUNGARY
POLAND

BEL.:BELGIUM
CZECH R.:CZECH REPUBLIC
HUN.:HUNGARY
LUX.:LUXEMBOURG
NETH.:NETHERLANDS
SWITZ.:SWITZERLAND

What might happen if the earth's surface temperature increased, on average, by 2°F

In an attempt to tackle the problem of global warming, the European Community has agreed to freeze emissions of carbon dioxide at the current levels by the year 2000.

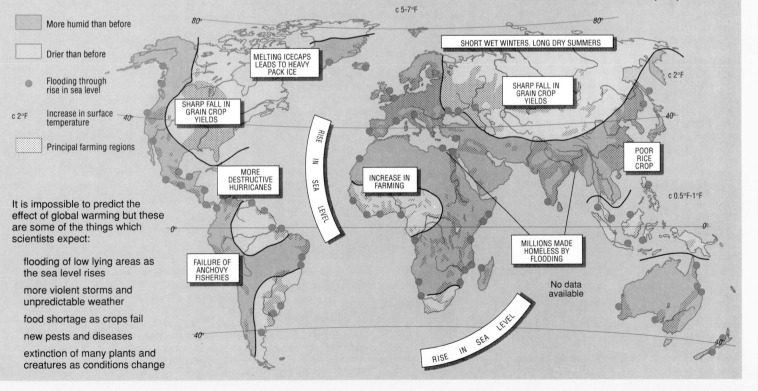

■ More humid than before

□ Drier than before

● Flooding through rise in sea level

c 2°F Increase in surface temperature

▒ Principal farming regions

It is impossible to predict the effect of global warming but these are some of the things which scientists expect:

flooding of low lying areas as the sea level rises

more violent storms and unpredictable weather

food shortage as crops fail

new pests and diseases

extinction of many plants and creatures as conditions change

c 5-7°F
c 2°F
c 0.5°F-1°F

MELTING ICECAPS LEADS TO HEAVY PACK ICE

SHORT WET WINTERS. LONG DRY SUMMERS

SHARP FALL IN GRAIN CROP YIELDS

SHARP FALL IN GRAIN CROP YIELDS

POOR RICE CROP

RISE IN SEA LEVEL

MORE DESTRUCTIVE HURRICANES

INCREASE IN FARMING

MILLIONS MADE HOMELESS BY FLOODING

FAILURE OF ANCHOVY FISHERIES

No data available

RISE IN SEA LEVEL

Environment and Society

Hazardous Waste - Production and Trade

Hazardous and toxic waste damages the environment and poisons people and animals. Most toxic waste comes from the chemical industry. It is produced in increasing quantities each year.

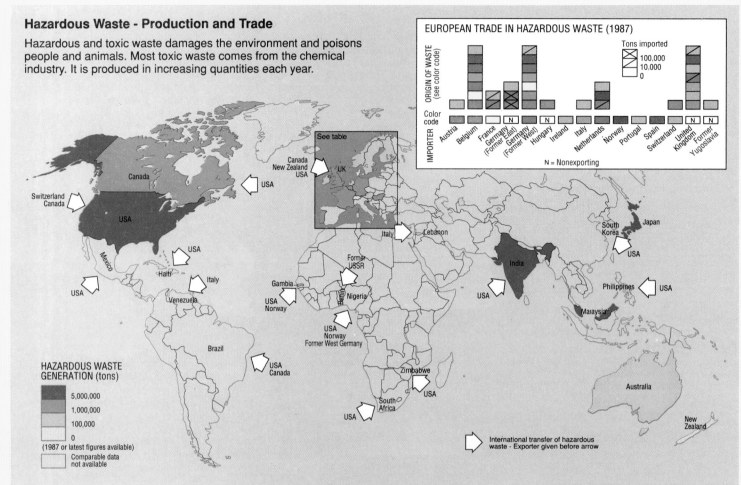

EUROPEAN TRADE IN HAZARDOUS WASTE (1987)

N = Nonexporting

HAZARDOUS WASTE GENERATION (tons)

5,000,000
1,000,000
100,000
0
(1987 or latest figures available)
Comparable data not available

International transfer of hazardous waste - Exporter given before arrow

Toxic Trade

It is very expensive to dispose of toxic waste properly so industrialized nations are looking for cheap solutions. At the moment, large quantities of waste are shipped to developing countries, often illegally. In 1988, for example, 10,000 drums of hazardous waste from Italy were discovered in a yard in the port of Koko, Nigeria. They were leaking acid and poisonous chemicals but local people had no idea what they contained. Nearly forty countries have now banned toxic waste imports but the regulations are difficult to enforce.

Waste Dumping

Some 350 million tons of hazardous waste are produced each year and there are over 70,000 different chemicals in regular use. Many of them have never been tested for their effect on the environment and nobody knows what happens when the chemicals are mixed together.

For years toxic waste has been dumped in landfill sites. If these are unlined, dangerous chemicals can seep into the soil and contaminate water supplies. The problem of indiscriminate dumping affects most industrialized countries and there are thousands of sites which need to be cleaned up.

DILUTE AND DISPERSE LANDFILL DISPOSAL

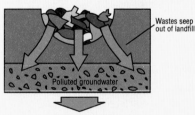

Wastes seep out of landfill

Polluted groundwater

Polluted streams and water supply

Toxic waste dump, Czech Republic

© BARTHOLOMEW

% WASTE DISPOSAL BY LANDFILL
(selected countries - 1987 or latest figures available)

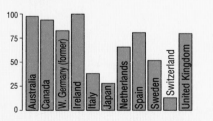

In Britain toxic waste is mixed with domestic rubbish in the controversial "dilute and disperse" method. Many other countries favor the opposite approach and concentrate their most dangerous waste in specific places. Incineration is also increasingly favored.

The best way of solving the problem of toxic waste is not to produce it in the first place. It is estimated that over the next decade industry could cut its production by a third. More waste could also be recycled or reused.

Agrochemicals

Around the world farmers are putting more and more chemicals on their land. This has led to great increases in crop yields but has also brought environmental problems. Nutrients from fertilizers are polluting rivers and lakes, while residues from pesticides have been detected in crops and drinking water. In addition, pesticides are losing their effectiveness as insects develop immunity to them. In the future, agrochemicals will need to be used much more selectively.

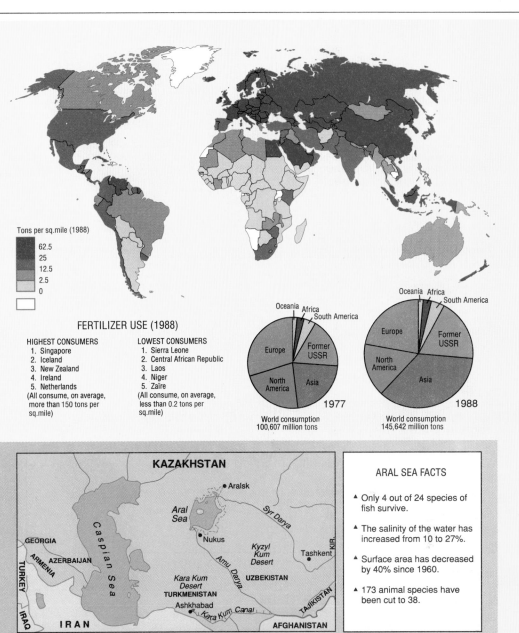

Tons per sq.mile (1988)
- 62.5
- 25
- 12.5
- 2.5
- 0

NEW INSECTICIDES AND RESISTANT SPECIES

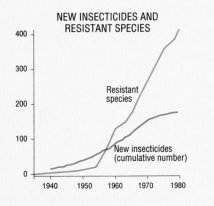

Resistant species

New insecticides (cumulative number)

FERTILIZER USE (1988)

HIGHEST CONSUMERS
1. Singapore
2. Iceland
3. New Zealand
4. Ireland
5. Netherlands
(All consume, on average, more than 150 tons per sq.mile)

LOWEST CONSUMERS
1. Sierra Leone
2. Central African Republic
3. Laos
4. Niger
5. Zaïre
(All consume, on average, less than 0.2 tons per sq.mile)

1977
World consumption 100,607 million tons

1988
World consumption 145,642 million tons

The Aral Sea Disaster

The Aral Sea in Southwestern Asia used to be the fourth biggest lake in the world. It supported a thriving fishing industry, mixed agriculture, and many species of plants and animals. Now the Aral Sea is drying up as more and more water is diverted to irrigate cotton crops. Unless something is done the sea could disappear completely over the next thirty years.

Environmental Consequences

The dry sea bed has become a desert, poisoned by salt and residues from the chemicals sprayed on the cotton crop. Huge dust storms sweep up the contaminated soil and dump it back on the fields. Deposits have been found up to 2,000 mls. away on the shores of the Arctic Ocean.

The climate of the region has also begun to change. The Aral Sea used to act as a battery, storing heat in the summer and releasing it in the winter. Now temperatures have become more extreme and there is less rainfall.

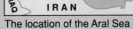

The location of the Aral Sea

The effect on the surrounding communities has been disastrous. Towns which used to depend on fishing are now up to 25 miles from the shore. Diseases and illnesses have increased among adults and one in ten babies die before their first birthday.

ARAL SEA FACTS

▲ Only 4 out of 24 species of fish survive.

▲ The salinity of the water has increased from 10 to 27%.

▲ Surface area has decreased by 40% since 1960.

▲ 173 animal species have been cut to 38.

What could be done?

At present most of the irrigation canals leak. If they were lined with plastic or concrete, it would save large amounts of water. Also, the acreage under cotton could be reduced to cut down the need for irrigation. It will take massive changes to halt the present process and the Aral Sea will probably never be restored properly.

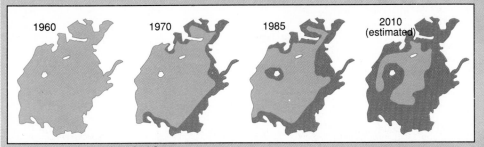

1960 1970 1985 2010 (estimated)

The changing shape of the Aral Sea

Aralsk, Kazakhstan - rusting boats lie in the wasteland that was once part of the Aral Sea.

Environment and Society

The Water Budget

Seventy percent of the earth's surface is covered by water. However, fresh water represents only 2.5% of the total. The rest is found in the oceans where the presence of salt makes it difficult to use.

Most of the fresh water lies deep underground or is frozen in the polar ice caps. Only a small proportion is freely available. Nevertheless there is enough to meet people's needs. The problem is that supplies are unevenly distributed around the world.

Fresh Water 2.5%

97.5% Salt Water

Water Pollution

Water pollution is a worldwide problem. Waste from factories, farms, and cities is poisoning rivers and seeping into groundwater. Lakes are particularly at risk as they allow pollutants to build up. Coastlines and shallow seas are highly vulnerable. The discharge of oil from tanker accidents and ships that wash out their tanks illegally is another problem. It is estimated that several million tons of oil are put into the sea each year.

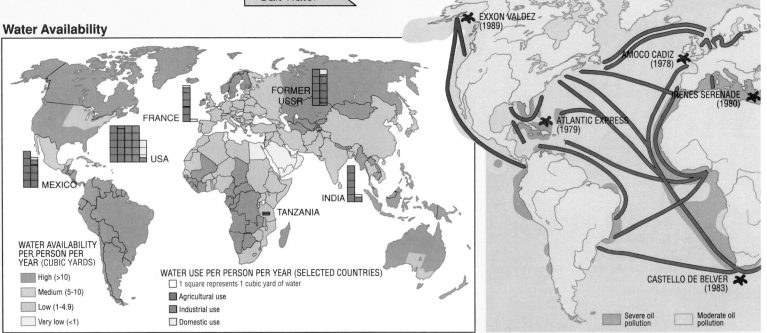

EXXON VALDEZ (1989)

AMOCO CADIZ (1978)

IRENES SERENADE (1980)

ATLANTIC EXPRESS (1979)

CASTELLO DE BELVER (1983)

Severe oil pollution

Moderate oil pollution

Water Availability

FORMER USSR

FRANCE

USA

MEXICO

INDIA

TANZANIA

WATER AVAILABILITY PER PERSON PER YEAR (CUBIC YARDS)
- High (>10)
- Medium (5-10)
- Low (1-4.9)
- Very low (<1)

WATER USE PER PERSON PER YEAR (SELECTED COUNTRIES)
- ☐ 1 square represents 1 cubic yard of water
- Agricultural use
- Industrial use
- ☐ Domestic use

Pollution in the North Sea

North Sea Facts
- Average water depth 300 ft.
- Rich variety of flora and fauna, including commercial fish stocks.
- 150 oil and gas platforms.
- 5,000 ships operating at any one time.
- Water replaced every 18 months on average

B - BELGIUM
N - NETHERLANDS
D - DENMARK

NORWAY

North Sea

IRELAND UK

GERMANY

The North Sea receives much of the pollution that is generated in northwestern Europe. Some is dumped directly into the water or absorbed from the atmosphere. Rivers are the single biggest source of pollution and contribute nearly half of the total.

Pollution has begun to have a serious effect on the ecology of the North Sea. Heavy metals from industry, sewage from towns, and oil from ships have all added to the problem. In 1988, large numbers of seals were killed by a mystery virus. Countries bordering the North Sea have now agreed on various measures to control pollution. A lot more still needs to be done and many people would like to see stricter controls.

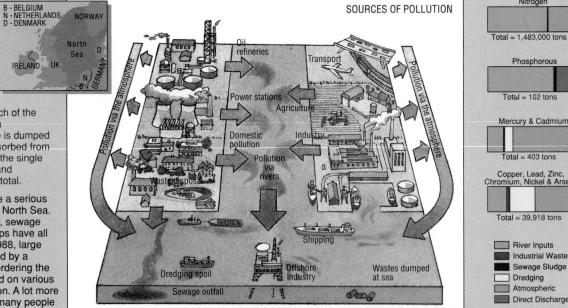

SOURCES OF POLLUTION

Pollution via the atmosphere

Oil refineries

Transport

Power stations

Agriculture

Domestic pollution

Industry

Pollution via rivers

Waste disposal

Shipping

Dredging spoil

Offshore industry

Wastes dumped at sea

Sewage outfall

SOURCES OF POLLUTION (1985)

Nitrogen
Total = 1,483,000 tons

Phosphorous
Total = 102 tons

Mercury & Cadmium
Total = 403 tons

Copper, Lead, Zinc, Chromium, Nickel & Arsenic
Total = 39,918 tons

- River Inputs
- Industrial Waste
- Sewage Sludge
- ☐ Dredging
- Atmospheric
- Direct Discharge

Source - North Sea Quality Status Report 1987

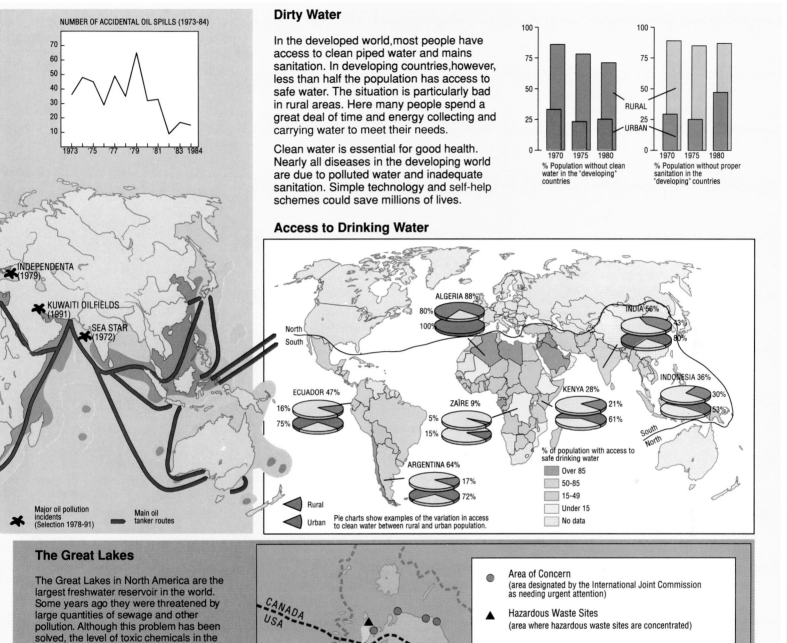

NUMBER OF ACCIDENTAL OIL SPILLS (1973-84)

INDEPENDENTA
(1979)

KUWAITI OILFIELDS
(1991)

SEA STAR
(1972)

✸ Major oil pollution incidents (Selection 1978-91)

━━ Main oil tanker routes

Dirty Water

In the developed world, most people have access to clean piped water and mains sanitation. In developing countries, however, less than half the population has access to safe water. The situation is particularly bad in rural areas. Here many people spend a great deal of time and energy collecting and carrying water to meet their needs.

Clean water is essential for good health. Nearly all diseases in the developing world are due to polluted water and inadequate sanitation. Simple technology and self-help schemes could save millions of lives.

RURAL
URBAN

1970 1975 1980
% Population without clean water in the "developing" countries

1970 1975 1980
% Population without proper sanitation in the "developing" countries

Access to Drinking Water

ALGERIA 88%
80%
100%

North
South

INDIA 56%
43%
80%

ECUADOR 47%
16%
75%

ZAÏRE 9%
5%
15%

KENYA 28%
21%
61%

INDONESIA 36%
30%
53%

South
North

ARGENTINA 64%
17%
72%

◣ Rural
◣ Urban

% of population with access to safe drinking water
- Over 85
- 50-85
- 15-49
- Under 15
- No data

Pie charts show examples of the variation in access to clean water between rural and urban population.

The Great Lakes

The Great Lakes in North America are the largest freshwater reservoir in the world. Some years ago they were threatened by large quantities of sewage and other pollution. Although this problem has been solved, the level of toxic chemicals in the water is now causing concern.

The chemicals come from a variety of sources. They are discharged into rivers, seep into the water from waste dumps, fall from the sky as acid rain, and wash off fields treated with fertilizers and pesticides. Sediments in some areas are so toxic they are unsafe to dredge. More than 360 chemicals have been identified in the Great Lakes which are the source of drinking water for 35 million people.

The International Joint Commission, which manages the Great Lakes, has designated forty two "areas of concern" which need urgent attention. While this will help, it will not stop pollution from happening. In the longer term, people need to alter their lifestyles so that they use fewer chemicals.

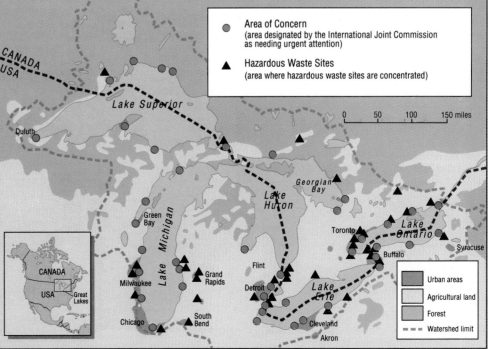

● Area of Concern
(area designated by the International Joint Commission as needing urgent attention)

▲ Hazardous Waste Sites
(area where hazardous waste sites are concentrated)

CANADA
USA

Lake Superior

Duluth

0   50   100   150 miles

Georgian Bay

Lake Huron

Green Bay

Lake Michigan

Grand Rapids

Toronto

Lake Ontario

Buffalo

Syracuse

Flint

Milwaukee

Detroit

Lake Erie

Cleveland

Chicago

South Bend

Akron

CANADA
USA
Great Lakes

- Urban areas
- Agricultural land
- Forest
- - - Watershed limit

Environment and Society

What are Natural Resources?

Minerals, water, plants, and animals are all natural resources. Human beings depend on using them for their survival.

For thousands of years people only used natural resources in small quantities. With the growth of industry and population, the demand has escalated. The world now uses three times the amount of minerals that it did in 1950. This is causing people to be concerned about whether there will always be enough.

Renewable Resources

When people use resources they sometimes consume them completely. Many machines, for instance, burn up gasoline in order to generate energy. Resources which are used in this way are said to be nonrenewable. They include oil, chemicals, and a variety of metals.

Other sources can be replaced. Timber, for example, is sometimes grown on plantations which are harvested at regular intervals. It is a renewable resource.

Renewable resources hold the key to the future. Sooner or later all the nonrenewable resources will be used up. By contrast, we can go on using renewable resources for ever.

Exploitation of Natural Resources

Natural resources are unevenly distributed around the world. Large countries such as the United States, former USSR, China, and Australia are rich in resources. Some smaller countries also have big reserves. Jamaica and Guinea, for example, have important bauxite mines which provide the raw material for aluminum.

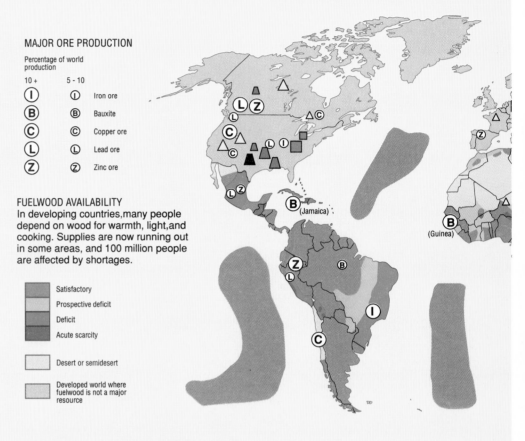

MAJOR ORE PRODUCTION

Percentage of world production

10 +	5 - 10	
Ⓘ	ⓘ	Iron ore
Ⓑ	ⓑ	Bauxite
Ⓒ	ⓒ	Copper ore
Ⓛ	ⓛ	Lead ore
Ⓩ	ⓩ	Zinc ore

FUELWOOD AVAILABILITY

In developing countries, many people depend on wood for warmth, light, and cooking. Supplies are now running out in some areas, and 100 million people are affected by shortages.

- Satisfactory
- Prospective deficit
- Deficit
- Acute scarcity
- Desert or semidesert
- Developed world where fuelwood is not a major resource

Environmental Issues in Mining

Mining is having a greater and greater effect on the environment. Ugly slag heaps and open pits have left scars in areas of scenic beauty. Even more serious is the damage done to rivers as poisonous metals are washed into the water. For example, this is a cause of concern in Brazil where prospectors are panning for gold in the tributaries of the Amazon.

Many countries have laws to control mining. Some old quarries have been restored to farmland or flooded to create attractive lakes.

The environmental damage caused by extensive mining.

Uranium Mining in Australia

Australia possesses about one third of the world's reserves of uranium. This mineral has become imporant in the present century because it is the raw material for nuclear power stations and nuclear weapons. Most of its reserves are concentrated in the Northern Territory. The decision to use the reserves was highly controversial.

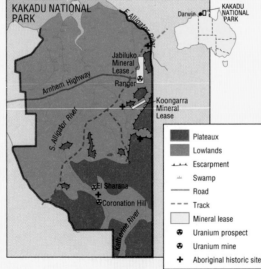

	Plateaux
	Lowlands
⊥⊥⊥	Escarpment
	Swamp
—	Road
- - -	Track
	Mineral lease
✪	Uranium prospect
✪	Uranium mine
✚	Aboriginal historic site

Arguments in favor

- The mines earn money and provide employment
- Nuclear power can help solve the world's energy crisis
- Strict safeguards control how the uranium is used

Arguments against

- Nuclear power stations are not safe
- The uranium could fall into the hands of terrorists
- The mines threatened a beautiful area where aborigines live

In 1977 the Australian government decided to go ahead with the mines. At the same time it created a National Park in the surrounding area and agreed to give some of the profits to the aborigines. Despite this compromise many people are still not satisfied.

NATURAL RESOURCES FROM THE OCEANS

There are large quantities of minerals deep beneath the ocean floor. Unfortunately these are difficult to get at and exploit.

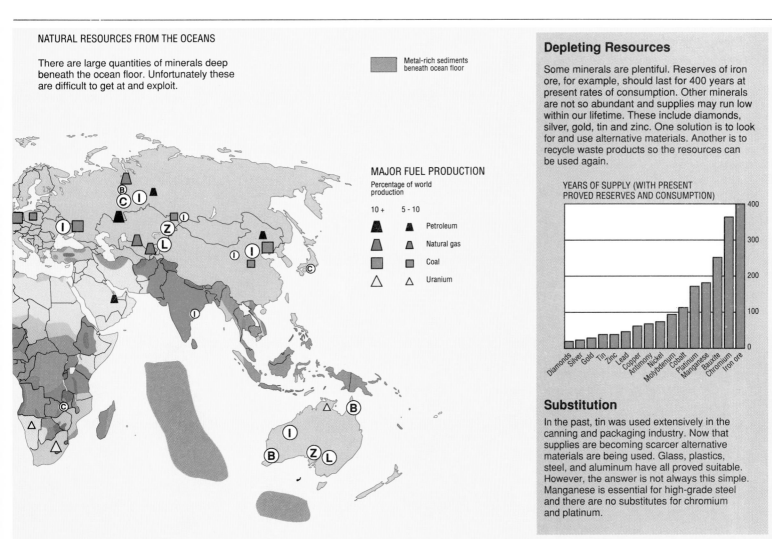

Metal-rich sediments beneath ocean floor

MAJOR FUEL PRODUCTION

Percentage of world production

10 +	5 - 10	
▲	▲	Petroleum
▲	▲	Natural gas
■	■	Coal
△	△	Uranium

Depleting Resources

Some minerals are plentiful. Reserves of iron ore, for example, should last for 400 years at present rates of consumption. Other minerals are not so abundant and supplies may run low within our lifetime. These include diamonds, silver, gold, tin and zinc. One solution is to look for and use alternative materials. Another is to recycle waste products so the resources can be used again.

YEARS OF SUPPLY (WITH PRESENT PROVED RESERVES AND CONSUMPTION)

Diamonds, Silver, Gold, Tin, Zinc, Lead, Copper, Antimony, Nickel, Molybdenum, Cobalt, Platinum, Manganese, Bauxite, Chromium, Iron ore

Substitution

In the past, tin was used extensively in the canning and packaging industry. Now that supplies are becoming scarcer alternative materials are being used. Glass, plastics, steel, and aluminum have all proved suitable. However, the answer is not always this simple. Manganese is essential for high-grade steel and there are no substitutes for chromium and platinum.

Recycling

Most waste products can be recycled. On a domestic level, many people now sort out paper and glass from their household rubbish. In industry, scrap metal provides almost half the iron needed for steelmaking.

Recycling not only reduces the demand on natural resources, it saves energy, conserves water, and reduces pollution. It also helps to solve the problem of waste disposal.

Recycling has enormous scope. As individuals we can all play our part, but nations also need to help by putting taxes on pollution and encouraging conservation.

ENVIRONMENTAL BENEFITS OF RECYCLING
(Percentage reduction)

	ALUMINUM	PAPER	GLASS
REDUCTION IN ENERGY USE	90-97	23-24	4-32
REDUCTION IN AIR POLLUTION	95	74	20
REDUCTION IN WATER POLLUTION	97	35	-
REDUCTION IN WATER USE	-	58	50

Recycling Aluminum Cans

Aluminum cans are cheap and easy to recycle. It takes twenty times more energy to make new aluminum from bauxite than to use scrap.

RECYCLING PROCESS

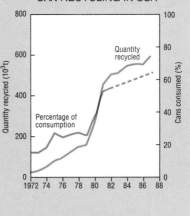

Collection Point

Used cans

Reprocess

Cans in use

New cans

In the United States nearly 80% of aluminum cans are recycled. Other countries, especially in Europe, are beginning to follow suit.

TRENDS IN ALUMINUM CAN RECYCLING IN USA

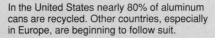

Quantity recycled (10³t)

Cans consumed (%)

Quantity recycled

Percentage of consumption

1972 74 76 78 80 82 84 86 88

Environment and Society

The Energy Problem

We depend on energy for almost everything that we do. Factories, farms, houses, and vehicles all need power to make them work.

It was the discovery of new sources of power - chiefly wind, water, and coal - which caused the Industrial Revolution. Since 1945 the boom in world economic activity has been based on oil.

Fossil fuels - coal, oil, and gas - provide most of the world's energy. Consumption is very uneven. The United States, Western Europe, and Japan use nearly three quarters of the total. Africa and South Asia use only small quantities.

Fumes from fossil fuels contribute to many pollution problems and are major factors in acid rain and global warming. This is one reason why plans to save energy are receiving so much attention. Wiser use of energy would also help to conserve supplies.

WORLD ENERGY PRODUCTION

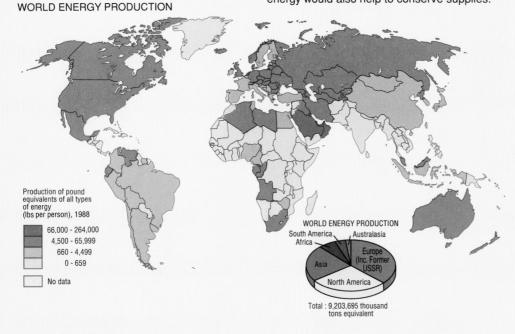

Production of pound equivalents of all types of energy
(lbs per person), 1988

- 66,000 - 264,000
- 4,500 - 65,999
- 660 - 4,499
- 0 - 659
- No data

WORLD ENERGY PRODUCTION

South America
Africa
Asia
North America
Australasia
Europe (Inc. Former USSR)

Total : 9,203,695 thousand tons equivalent

WORLD ENERGY CONSUMPTION

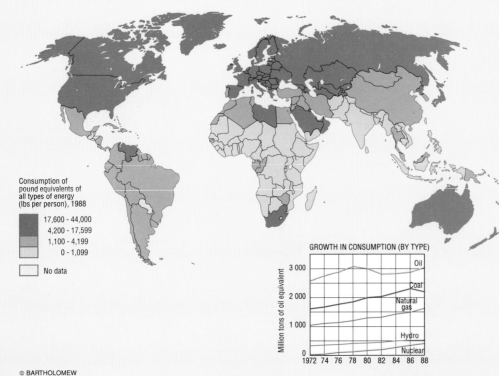

Consumption of pound equivalents of all types of energy
(lbs per person), 1988

- 17,600 - 44,000
- 4,200 - 17,599
- 1,100 - 4,199
- 0 - 1,099
- No data

GROWTH IN CONSUMPTION (BY TYPE)

Oil
Coal
Natural gas
Hydro
Nuclear

Million tons of oil equivalent
3 000
2 000
1 000
0
1972 74 76 78 80 82 84 86 88

Fuel Reserves

Fossil fuels will not last forever. It took a million years to create the fuel people now burn every twelve months. At present rates of consumption, the known supplies of oil will be used up in about 45 years. Coal is much more plentiful and will last for several centuries.

WORLD RESERVES (BY TYPE), 1989

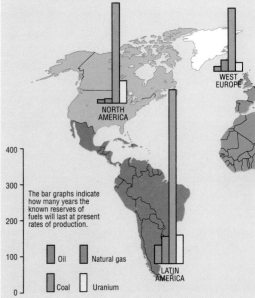

WEST EUROPE

NORTH AMERICA

LATIN AMERICA

400
300
200
100
0

The bar graphs indicate how many years the known reserves of fuels will last at present rates of production.

- Oil
- Coal
- Natural gas
- Uranium

Nuclear Energy

At one time nuclear power appeared to offer almost limitless supplies of cheap and clean electricity. However, there have always been doubts. There is the problem of disposing of nuclear waste and there is the risk of accidents. The catastrophe of Chernobyl in 1986, which spread radiation across the whole of Europe, made such dangers abundantly clear. It is now known that electricity from nuclear power is more expensive than electricity from coal.

In1989 there were 426 commercial nuclear reactors producing one sixth of the world's electricity. The map shows the number of reactors in the European Community. Countries like the United Kingdom have invested heavily in nuclear power.Others, like Denmark, Ireland and Greece have never become involved.

NUCLEAR POWER IN THE EC

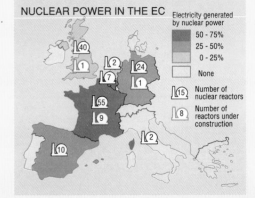

Electricity generated by nuclear power

- 50 - 75%
- 25 - 50%
- 0 - 25%
- None

15 Number of nuclear reactors

8 Number of reactors under construction

The search for new supplies will almost certainly result in valuable new finds. In addition, developments in technology will make it possible to make use of reserves that are currently uneconomical. The disadvantage is that many of these are likely to be in remote areas and difficult to extract.

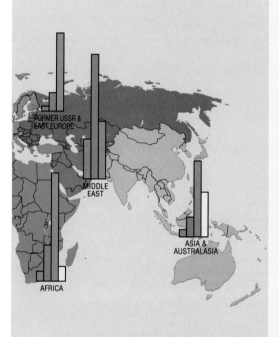

Renewable Energy

Fossil fuels are likely to become more expensive as they get scarcer, and nuclear power is surrounded by questions. The alternative is to harness renewable energy from natural sources. This has the added advantage of avoiding the problem of air pollution.

Hydroelectric Power

Hydroelectric power works by storing water in dams to drive turbines. It now provides more than a fifth of the world's electricity. One of the drawbacks of hydroelectric power is that the dams flood good farmland and in hot countries encourage the spread of waterborne diseases.

Solar Power

The simplest way of using the sun's rays is to use flat-plate collectors to heat water and buildings. Solar power can be converted into electricity using reflectors. The most promising areas are in the tropics where solar radiation is highest.

Solar panels for powering a borehole pump, Somali Republic.

Geothermal Power

Hot rocks beneath the earth's surface are a valuable source of energy. Most houses in Iceland are heated with steam from underground reservoirs. In the United Kingdom experiments are being undertaken in Cornwall and Southampton.

Wind Power *see below*

Wave Power

The motion of the waves can be used to generate electricity. It is estimated that half the United Kingdom's supplies could come from an area off northwest Scotland. Much more research is needed but the world's first wave power scheme is operating off the coast of Norway.

A tidal barrage on the River Rance, Brittany, France.

Tidal Power

Dams can trap sea water as it rises and falls with the tide. Estuaries make the best sites as they have a large tidal range. A dam on the Severn estuary could generate 5% of the United Kingdom's electricity but would cause ecological problems.

Biomass Power

Rotting waste matter from plants and animals produces methanol which can be collected in tanks and used as fuel. In some places special power stations run on crop waste. India, Malaysia, the Philippines and the United States, for example, have power stations which burn rice husks.

Wind Power in the United Kingdom

LOCATION OF UNITED KINGDOM WIND DEVELOPMENTS

- ● Turbines connected to the grid
- ● Turbines under construction
- ● Possible wind farm locations

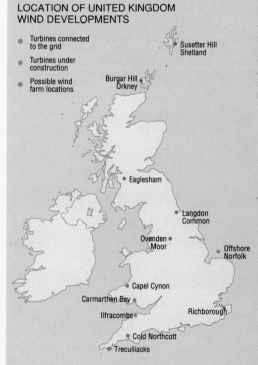

Modern wind turbines can harness the power of the wind, much as windmills did in the past. Coasts and mountains are the best sites as the turbines need winds of over 15miles per hour to make them work. Unfortunately, as shown on the map, these coincide with many of the United Kingdom's most scenic areas. Offshore locations might provide a better solution.

A wind turbine in operation at Burgar Hill, Orkney.

Ovenden Moor Wind Farm

At Ovenden Moor in West Yorkshire, a local company plans to build a wind farm with 35 turbines. The turbines will be about 100 feet high and painted so they blend in with the landscape. The site is on windy moorland remote from towns and villages.

Some people are worried about how the scheme will affect the landscape. They are also concerned about the disruption to a peaceful part of the country. A proposed wind farm in mid Wales has met with similar objections.

LOCATION MAP OF PROPOSED SITE

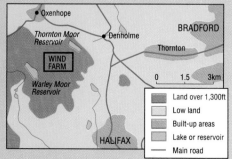

- ■ Land over 1,300ft
- □ Low land
- Built-up areas
- Lake or reservoir
- — Main road

Environment and Society

The Growth of Cities

Cities were first built in the Middle East about 8,000 years ago. Here, the development of settled agriculture provided enough surplus food to support an urban population.

Today cities play a crucial role in human affairs. Athens, Rome, and Venice, for example, are famous for their contributions to European civilization and culture. Administration and government is also organized from cities which explains their political importance.

The largest cities have vast populations. About 18 million people live in New York and Mexico City has over 20 million inhabitants. By the year 2000, over half the world's population will be living in urban areas. This rapid expansion of cities in the developing world is causing a crisis.

% CHANGE IN URBAN POPULATION (1976-87)

- Over 100
- 50 - 100
- 25 - 50
- 0 - 25
- No data

RATE OF URBANIZATION

The World's Largest Cities

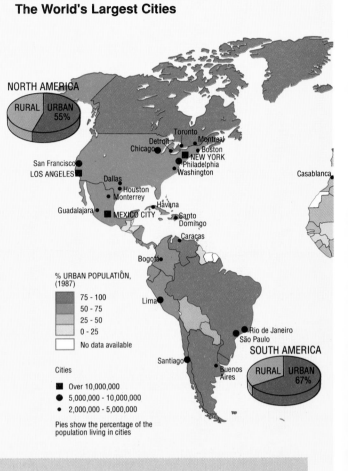

NORTH AMERICA

RURAL | URBAN 55%

% URBAN POPULATION, (1987)

- 75 - 100
- 50 - 75
- 25 - 50
- 0 - 25
- No data available

Cities

- ■ Over 10,000,000
- ● 5,000,000 - 10,000,000
- • 2,000,000 - 5,000,000

Pies show the percentage of the population living in cities

SOUTH AMERICA

RURAL | URBAN 67%

Planned Growth?

Developing World : Jakarta

Jakarta is one of the largest cities in the world. Almost half the people have no real jobs but survive by providing services for others. This has created an underclass of people living in miserable shanties that sprawl along the surrounding roads. The population increases by approximately a million every three years. Coping with such huge numbers is an immense challenge for the city authorities.

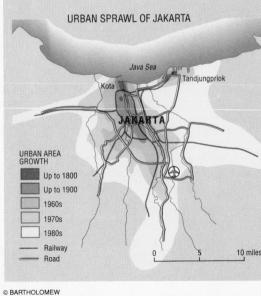

URBAN SPRAWL OF JAKARTA

URBAN AREA GROWTH

- Up to 1800
- Up to 1900
- 1960s
- 1970s
- 1980s
- Railway
- Road

Developed World : Paris

Paris is another large city. It suffers from overcrowding, traffic congestion, and poor housing. To tackle these problems, new buildings have been put up in the historic center, satellite towns established round the edge, and public transportation systems improved. These measures have helped to protect the city and maintain the quality of life of the people who live there.

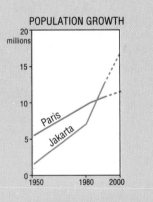

POPULATION GROWTH

20 millions

15

10

5

Paris

Jakarta

1950   1980   2000

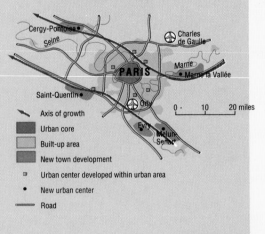

URBAN GROWTH PLAN FOR PARIS

- Axis of growth
- Urban core
- Built-up area
- New town development
- Urban center developed within urban area
- New urban center
- Road

Sprawling slums of suburban Jakarta

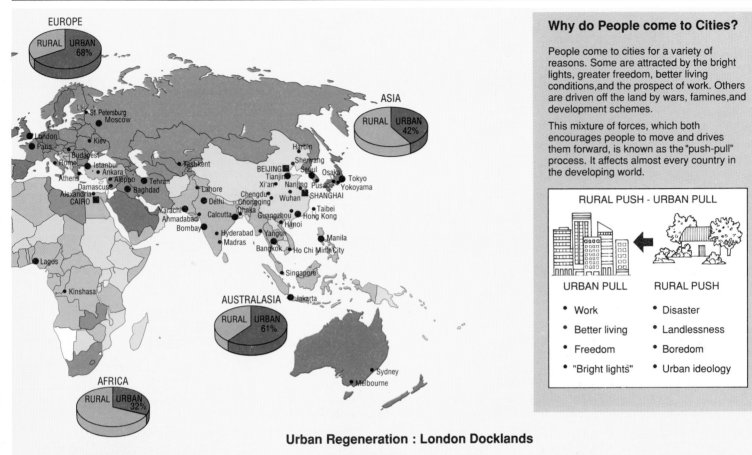

EUROPE
RURAL | URBAN 68%

ASIA
RURAL | URBAN 42%

AUSTRALASIA
RURAL | URBAN 61%

AFRICA
RURAL | URBAN 32%

Why do People come to Cities?

People come to cities for a variety of reasons. Some are attracted by the bright lights, greater freedom, better living conditions,and the prospect of work. Others are driven off the land by wars, famines,and development schemes.

This mixture of forces, which both encourages people to move and drives them forward, is known as the "push-pull" process. It affects almost every country in the developing world.

RURAL PUSH - URBAN PULL

URBAN PULL	RURAL PUSH
• Work	• Disaster
• Better living	• Landlessness
• Freedom	• Boredom
• "Bright lights"	• Urban ideology

Urban Problems

Since 1950 the number of people living in cities has almost tripled.

Housing
All big cities have homeless people. In the developing world,over half the city dwellers live in shanties where dirty water and poor sanitation cause disease. A quarter of all slum children die before the age of five.

Transport
Cities are busy, congested places and it is difficult to get about. In Athens,traffic fumes are eroding the historic buildings.

Waste
New York produces so much garbage it has run out of places to dispose of it. Human sewage has helped make the Mediterranean one of the dirtiest seas in the world.

Resources
As they grow, cities cover valuable farmland, and make huge demands on the surrounding countryside for food, water,and energy. Due to the shortage of firewood, Delhi is supplied from forests 450 miles away.

Welfare
Overcrowding, noise,and stress can have an adverse effect on the health of city dwellers. The number of violent crimes tends to be high.

Careful planning can help to provide better housing and services for city dwellers. Governments around the world could take a lead in tackling these issues.

Urban Regeneration : London Docklands

The London Docklands stretch down the Thames River from Tower Bridge. A large community depended on the docks, but during the 1960s trade began to decline. This was due, to some extent to changing patterns of trade, larger ships, labor disputes, and poor management. By 1981, all the docks had closed.

People had different ideas about what to do. One suggestion was to try and halt the job losses. The alternative, adopted by the government, was to attract new companies to the area. An airport and public railway to the center of London were built to encourage new businesses.

The population of the area has now begun to increase. Fifteen thousand new homes have been built and a major office center opened at Canary Wharf. This may benefit newcomers but local people question if it has helped the old community.

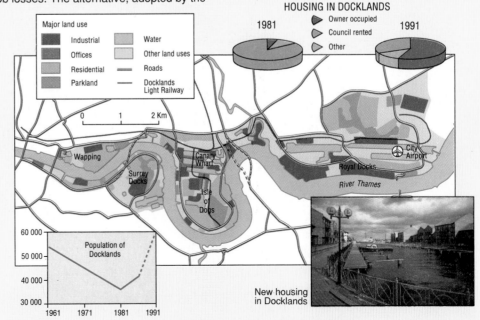

HOUSING IN DOCKLANDS

1981 — Owner occupied / Council rented / Other — 1991

Major land use
- Industrial
- Offices
- Residential
- Parkland
- Water
- Other land uses
- Roads
- Docklands Light Railway

Population of Docklands

New housing in Docklands

Spatial Dynamics and Connections

Ways of Travelling

For centuries the speed of travel depended on human effort or horse power. The Industrial Revolution changed all this. In the nineteenth century, railways revolutionized land travel, linking in hours places which had previously been days apart. Now modern jet aircraft fly around the world at 600 miles per hour. At this speed, it takes less than 24 hours to reach the other side of the earth.

Some people have better access to travel than others. In industrialized countries, extensive communications networks ensure that most of the people can move quickly from one place to another. In poorer countries, many people do not have access to these facilities. There are also big variations between sections of the population. Men, for example, are more likely to drive cars than women. Children and the elderly also tend to be disadvantaged.

In general people are making more journeys than ever before. Some travel voluntarily for vacations. Others are forced to travel in search of work or to escape war and famine. This increase in mobility is having a profound effect on social customs and values.

Major International Migrations

Much of world history is the story of the migration of people from one place to another. Many of these movements have been marked by battles and conflicts. They have also tended to occur in waves over a period of time, rather than as single events.

The map shows how Europe's expansion in the past has affected many parts of the world. In the present century, poverty, war, and famine have led to an unprecedented movement of people. As a result, many countries now have significant immigrant populations.

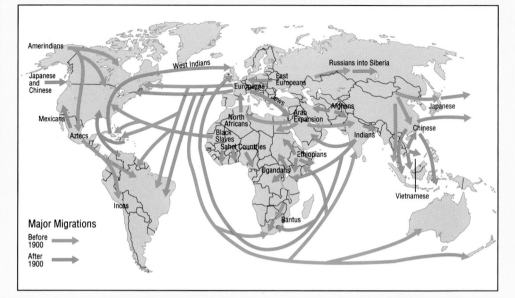

Car Culture

There are about 400 million cars in the world. Most of them are in industrialized countries. The United States, with 140 million, is still the home of the car culture.

The number of cars in the world has doubled in the last twenty years. Car making is the largest industry in the world economy. It is dominated by a handful of powerful international companies.

TOTAL NUMBER OF CARS PER COUNTRY
- 10,000,000
- 1,000,000
- 100,000
- 25,000
- 0
- No data

1988 or latest figures available

Cars may be convenient, but they cause widespread environmental damage. They are expensive to build, consume scarce resources, and are difficult to dispose of when they wear out. In addition, car fumes make a major contribution to acid rain and greenhouse gases. About a third of the land in towns and cities is devoted to roads and car parking. Around the world, a quarter of a million people die each year in car accidents.

Many people believe that the car culture needs to be better controlled. In the United Kingdom, for example, traffic is expected to double over the next thirty years. The government is planning a massive road-building program. Yet new roads gobble up valuable land and quickly attract more vehicles. One solution is to have more efficient public transport. The use of catalytic converters and lead free petroleum is a positive trend because it reduces air pollution.

CAR TRAVEL IN THE USA

Population	246,330,000
Area	3,619,000 sq.miles
Total number of cars	140,655,000
Car ownership (per 1,000 people)	571
Total length of road network	3,873,303 miles
Total length of motorways	51,087 miles
Road density	0.26 sq.miles
Annual fuel consumption	353,094,000 tons of petroleum
Average distance travelled per person per year	7,770 miles

CAR TRAVEL IN ITALY

Population	57,440,000
Area	113,500 sq.miles
Total number of cars	25,490,000
Car ownership (per 1,000 people)	444
Total length of road network	187,564 miles
Total length of motorways	3,726 miles
Road density	0.4 sq.miles
Annual fuel consumption	12,249,000 tons of petroleum
Average distance travelled per person per year	3,015 miles

The Impact of Tourism

The Alps form a chain of mountains 600 miles long. The snowy peaks, glaciers, and beautiful alpine scenery are major tourist attractions. Every year 50 million people visit the Alps for their vacations, two thirds of them for winter skiing.

The tourism boom has led to tree clearance to make room for ski resorts, and encouraged development on steep and unsuitable slopes. As a result, the risk of floods and avalanches has substantially increased. Areas above 6,500 feet are particularly at risk as their environment is delicately balanced.

Tourism and industry have caused an enormous increase in motor traffic and road building. Seven million vehicles cross the Alps each year contributing significantly to noise and air pollution. Acid rain affects 60% of the trees. Attempts are now being made to control vehicle fumes, replant trees, and restore damaged landscapes. If there is enough public pressure, much can be done to protect the Alps.

Around the world, tourism is on the increase. It creates jobs for local people, brings new community facilities, and helps to preserve cultural and natural heritage. But it also puts pressure on the environment, undermines traditional values, and tends to spoil the landscape. Careful planning can help to maximize the benefits and minimize the disturbance.

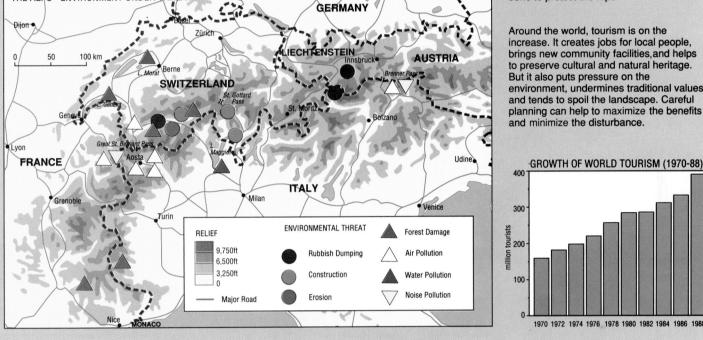

THE ALPS - ENVIRONMENT UNDER THREAT

RELIEF
- 9,750ft
- 6,500ft
- 3,250ft
- 0
- Major Road

ENVIRONMENTAL THREAT
- Rubbish Dumping
- Construction
- Erosion
- Forest Damage
- Air Pollution
- Water Pollution
- Noise Pollution

GROWTH OF WORLD TOURISM (1970-88)

million tourists

1970 1972 1974 1976 1978 1980 1982 1984 1986 1988

Refugees

There are about fifteen million refugees in the world. They are the victims of a variety of different forces. These include:

war and conflict
violence between different ethnic and religious groups
government repression
natural disasters such as floods, drought, and earthquakes

Poor people tend to be affected the most as they do not have the means to protect themselves. The majority of refugees are women and children.

Refugee camp in Ethiopia

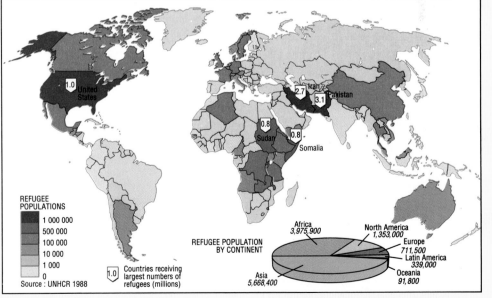

REFUGEE POPULATIONS
- 1 000 000
- 500 000
- 100 000
- 10 000
- 1 000
- 0

1.0 Countries receiving largest numbers of refugees (millions)

Source : UNHCR 1988

REFUGEE POPULATION BY CONTINENT

Africa 3,975,900
North America 1,353,000
Europe 711,500
Latin America 339,000
Oceania 91,800
Asia 5,668,400

Pakistan has the largest refugee population in the world. It accommodates over three million refugees who fled from the Afghan War during the 1980s. In 1990 and 1991, the Gulf Crisis caused the displacement of thousands of migrant workers, Kurds, and other minorities from Iraq.

Although some refugees go to live permanently in Western Europe and North America, governments are often unwilling to accept large numbers of displaced people. The United Nations High Commission for Refugees (UNHCR) provides valuable international assistance. In the long term the best solution is for refugees to return to their homelands.

Spatial Dynamics and Connections

What is Development?

Countries with a high standard of living such as the United States, Japan, and those in Western Europe are generally said to be "developed". They belong to the industrialized parts of the world where many people work in service industries and material possessions are plentiful. Countries which have not been industrialized are said to be economically "developing". Here the majority of the people are poor in material terms and earn their living by working on the land.

There are many different ways of measuring development. The first map below shows the percentage of income generated by service industries in each country. The second shows the quality of life based on life expectancy, infant mortality, and literacy. The maps need to be interpreted with care. People's need's are not the same in all environments for example, and there may well be big differences in wealth within a country whatever the average may be.

One World or Two?

In 1980 a group of political and economic experts published a report on the differences in wealth around the world. Known as the Brandt Report, it drew attention to the contrast between the rich, developed countries of the "North" and the poor, developing countries of the "South". The report argued that the countries of the North had a moral duty to help the South, and close the gap between them.

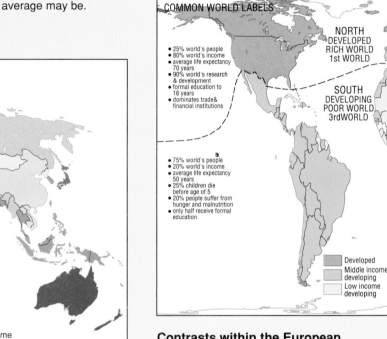

SERVICE INDUSTRY

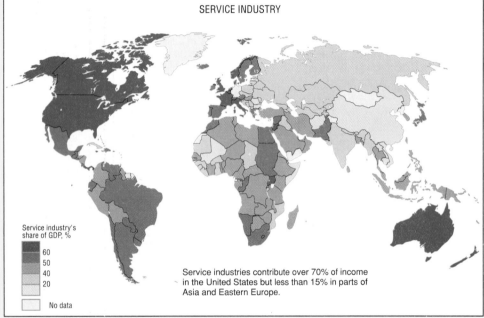

Service industry's share of GDP, %

60
50
40
20

No data

Service industries contribute over 70% of income in the United States but less than 15% in parts of Asia and Eastern Europe.

Contrasts within the European Community

There are wide variations in living standards within the European Community. In the central area, Germany, France, Luxembourg, and Denmark form a group of countries where people have the highest incomes. Many international companies and government departments have their headquarters here.

QUALITY OF LIFE

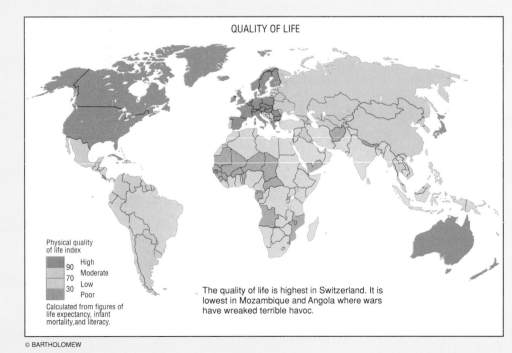

Physical quality of life index

90 High
70 Moderate
30 Low
Poor

Calculated from figures of life expectancy, infant mortality, and literacy.

The quality of life is highest in Switzerland. It is lowest in Mozambique and Angola where wars have wreaked terrible havoc.

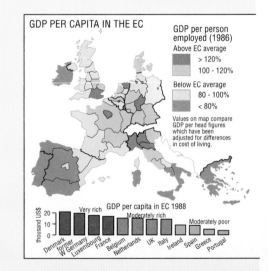

GDP PER CAPITA IN THE EC

GDP per person employed (1986)

Above EC average
> 120%
100 - 120%

Below EC average
80 - 100%
< 80%

Values on map compare GDP per head figures which have been adjusted for differences in cost of living.

Unequal Development in South Africa

Nowadays the terms "North" and "South" are used as a kind of shorthand. Like all generalizations they conceal big differences. The countries of the South are not all equally poor, nor is the North universally rich. In addition, conditions are always changing. Recent events in Eastern Europe and the Soviet Union, for example, have shown that these countries are much less "developed" than previously thought.

For many years South Africa has had a policy of segregating black and white people, known as apartheid. Homelands have been created as national states for the black population. These cover less than a fifth of the country although blacks form the majority of the population. Apartheid is the main cause of poverty in the black population of South Africa.

Blacks earn much lower wages than whites for doing exactly the same job. Most people think it is wrong to discriminate against people because of the color of their skin. Recently the laws have begun to change. However, it seems likely that white South Africans will continue to earn more and receive better services for many years to come.

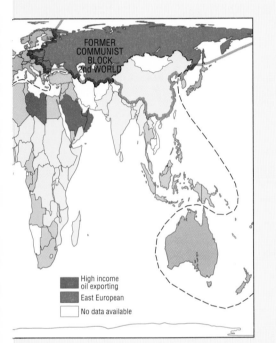

High income oil exporting

East European

No data available

APARTHEID IN SOUTH AFRICA

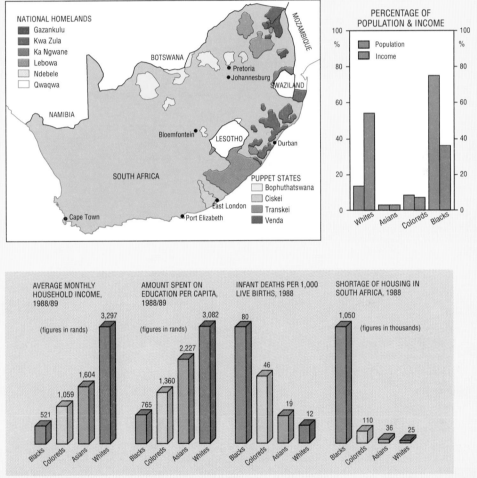

NATIONAL HOMELANDS
- Gazankulu
- Kwa Zula
- Ka Ngwane
- Lebowa
- Ndebele
- Qwaqwa

PUPPET STATES
- Bophuthatswana
- Ciskei
- Transkei
- Venda

PERCENTAGE OF POPULATION & INCOME
- Population
- Income

AVERAGE MONTHLY HOUSEHOLD INCOME, 1988/89 (figures in rands): Blacks 521, Coloreds 1,059, Asians 1,604, Whites 3,297

AMOUNT SPENT ON EDUCATION PER CAPITA, 1988/89 (figures in rands): Blacks 765, Coloreds 1,360, Asians 2,227, Whites 3,082

INFANT DEATHS PER 1,000 LIVE BIRTHS, 1988: Blacks 80, Coloreds 46, Asians 19, Whites 12

SHORTAGE OF HOUSING IN SOUTH AFRICA, 1988 (figures in thousands): Blacks 1,050, Coloreds 110, Asians 36, Whites 25

Around this core there are a number of moderately rich countries such as the United Kingdom, Belgium, the Netherlands, and Italy. They have good communications with the center but are not so prosperous. Further afield, Spain, Portugal, Ireland, and Greece form a third group of poorer countries.

UNEMPLOYMENT IN THE EC

Unemployment rate by region, 1987
Above EC average
- > 12.5%
- 10.7 - 12.5%
Below EC average
- 8.5 - 10.6%
- < 8.5%

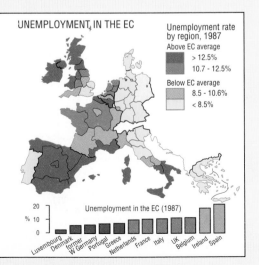

Unemployment in the EC (1987): Luxembourg, Denmark, former W Germany, Portugal, Greece, Netherlands, France, Italy, UK, Belgium, Ireland, Spain

Modern flats and offices in Nairobi, Kenya

Rural housing near Kakamega, Kenya.

There are often striking differences of wealth even within the same country.

Spatial Dynamics and Connections

The Roots of Modern Trade

Modern trade dates back to the sixteenth century when European explorers began to make journeys to India and the Americas. It developed dramatically in the eighteenth and nineteenth centuries. By then Europe had extensive overseas colonies and the Industrial Revolution was gathering pace. These two factors created a world economic system with European needs and interests at its core. Present patterns of trade continue to reflect this. The income of many developing countries still depends on exporting products such as copper, coffee, and tea. Manufacturing industries, by contrast, are concentrated in the developed countries of the "North". Machines, chemicals, and consumer goods are produced here in large volumes. This accounts for the huge disparity in the value of trade between countries.

VALUE OF EXPORTS, 1988

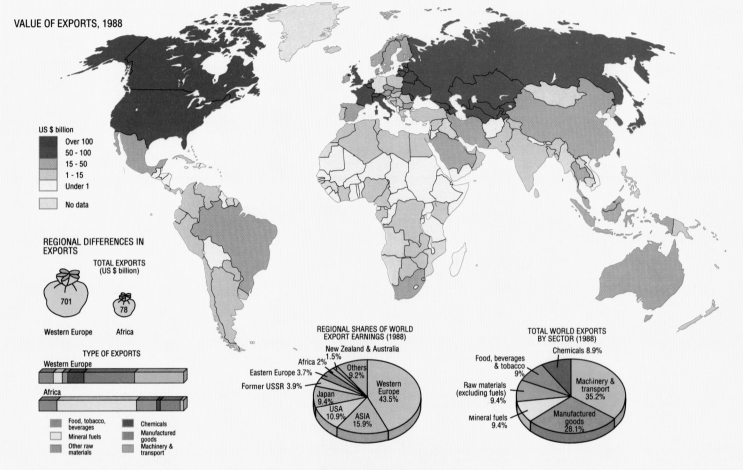

US $ billion
- Over 100
- 50 - 100
- 15 - 50
- 1 - 15
- Under 1
- No data

REGIONAL DIFFERENCES IN EXPORTS

TOTAL EXPORTS (US $ billion)

701 — Western Europe
78 — Africa

TYPE OF EXPORTS

Western Europe

Africa

- Food, tobacco, beverages
- Mineral fuels
- Other raw materials
- Chemicals
- Manufactured goods
- Machinery & transport

REGIONAL SHARES OF WORLD EXPORT EARNINGS (1988)
- New Zealand & Australia 1.5%
- Africa 2%
- Eastern Europe 3.7%
- Former USSR 3.9%
- Others 9.2%
- Western Europe 43.5%
- Japan 9.4%
- USA 10.9%
- ASIA 15.9%

TOTAL WORLD EXPORTS BY SECTOR (1988)
- Chemicals 8.9%
- Food, beverages & tobacco 9%
- Machinery & transport 35.2%
- Raw materials (excluding fuels) 9.4%
- Mineral fuels 9.4%
- Manufactured goods 28.1%

The Terms of Trade

One of the problems facing countries which export raw materials is that commodity prices fluctuate considerably. This is partly due to changing weather conditions. A bumper crop, for example, causes a glut and forces prices down.

The graph below shows how the terms of trade have changed. Between 1975 and 1983 most commodities halved their value in comparison with oil. Since then prices have to some extent recovered, but many producers are still struggling to recover from heavy losses in the early 1980s.

OIL BARRELS BOUGHT BY ONE TON OF COMMODITY, 1975, 1983 and 1988

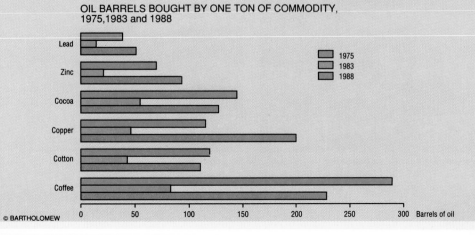

- 1975
- 1983
- 1988

Commodities: Lead, Zinc, Cocoa, Copper, Cotton, Coffee

Barrels of oil: 0, 50, 100, 150, 200, 250, 300

© BARTHOLOMEW

TERMS OF TRADE OF SELECTED COUNTRY GROUPINGS 1980-1989

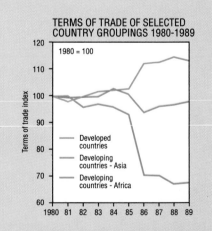

1980 = 100

Terms of trade index: 60, 70, 80, 90, 100, 110, 120

- Developed countries
- Developing countries - Asia
- Developing countries - Africa

1980 81 82 83 84 85 86 87 88 89

Africa has been particularly hard hit by changes in the terms of trade. During the 1980s, the value of its goods fell by a third. This has forced governments to borrow money, reducing economic and political independence.

Trade Dependency

Many developing countries depend on exporting one or two products which puts them in a very vulnerable position. Uganda, for example, earns 92% of its income from coffee. If the crops fails the results are disasterous. Also, the countries of the "North" are often able to push prices down by playing one producer off against another.

To stop this from happening, producers have formed themselves into associations called cartels. These have been largely unsuccessful, apart from OPEC (Organization of Petroleum Exporting Countries) which managed to quadruple oil prices during the 1973 Middle East War.

Diversifying Production

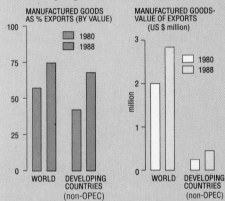

MANUFACTURED GOODS AS % EXPORTS (BY VALUE)

- 1980
- 1988

MANUFACTURED GOODS-VALUE OF EXPORTS (US $ million)

- 1980
- 1988

Developing countries are trying to diversify their economies to reduce trade dependency. More than half now have important manufacturing industries. As the graphs show, over the last decade the percentage of income from manufacturing has increased faster in the developing countries than in the rest of the world. In financial terms, however, these industries continue to be dwarfed by the developed countries of the "North".

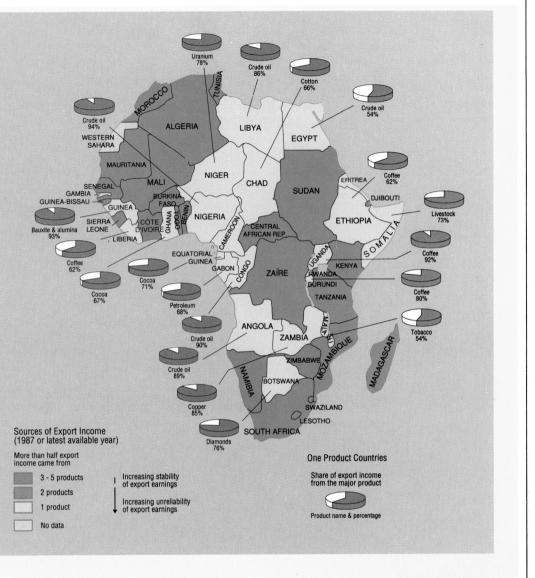

Sources of Export Income (1987 or latest available year)

More than half export income came from
- 3 - 5 products
- 2 products
- 1 product
- No data

Increasing stability of export earnings
Increasing unreliability of export earnings

One Product Countries

Share of export income from the major product

Product name & percentage

The Debt Crisis

Unequal patterns of trade have driven many developing countries into debt. Repayments on loans often consume all their income.

As they struggle for survival, developing countries have to exploit their environment. Forests are cut down and the soil impoverished for short-term gains.

One solution is to cancel all debts. Another is to exchange them for environmentally sound policies. It is clear that in many developing countries economic well-being and protection of the environment are inseparable.

Repayment as a percentage of exports (1988)
- Over 40
- 30 - 40
- 20 - 30
- 10 - 20
- Under 10
- No data

INTERNATIONAL DEBT: REPAYMENTS AS A PERCENTAGE OF EXPORTS

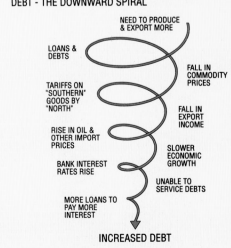

DEBT - THE DOWNWARD SPIRAL

- NEED TO PRODUCE & EXPORT MORE
- LOANS & DEBTS
- FALL IN COMMODITY PRICES
- TARIFFS ON "SOUTHERN" GOODS BY "NORTH"
- FALL IN EXPORT INCOME
- RISE IN OIL & OTHER IMPORT PRICES
- SLOWER ECONOMIC GROWTH
- BANK INTEREST RATES RISE
- UNABLE TO SERVICE DEBTS
- MORE LOANS TO PAY MORE INTEREST
- INCREASED DEBT

Regions

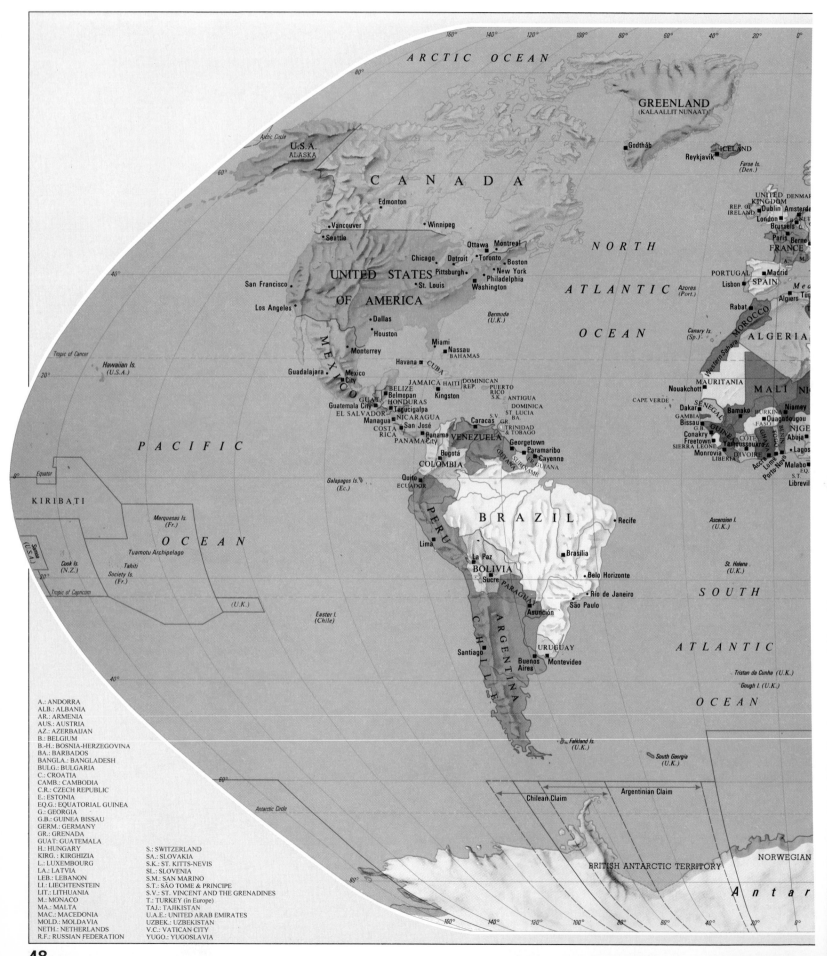

ARCTIC OCEAN

GREENLAND
(KALAALLIT NUNAAT)

Godthåb

Reykjavík ICELAND

Faroe Is.
(Den.)

Arctic Circle

U.S.A.
ALASKA

C A N A D A

UNITED DENMARK
KINGDOM
REP. OF
IRELAND
Dublin Amsterdam
London
Brussels
Paris Berne
FRANCE

Edmonton

Vancouver · Winnipeg
· Seattle

Chicago Detroit Ottawa Montreal
Toronto
Boston
UNITED STATES Pittsburgh New York
San Francisco OF AMERICA St. Louis Philadelphia
Washington

N O R T H

A T L A N T I C

O C E A N

PORTUGAL Madrid
Lisbon SPAIN Me
Azores
(Port.)
Algiers Tu

Los Angeles

Rabat
MOROCCO
ALGERIA

Dallas
Houston

Monterrey
Tropic of Cancer
Hawaiian Is.
(U.S.A.)

Bermuda
(U.K.)

Miami
Nassau
BAHAMAS

Havana CUBA

Guadalajara Mexico
MEXICO City

Canary Is.
(Sp.)

CAPE VERDE

Western Sahara

MAURITANIA
Nouakchott

MALI NI

JAMAICA HAITI DOMINICAN
REP.
PUERTO
RICO
S.K. ANTIGUA
DOMINICA
ST. LUCIA
BA.

BELIZE
Belmopan
Guatemala City HONDURAS
Kingston

Dakar SENEGAL Bamako BURKINA Niamey
GAMBIA Ouagadougou FASO
Bissau G.B. Conakry GUINEA Abuja NIGE
EL SALVADOR Tegucigalpa
GUAT. Freetown Yamoussoukro
Managua NICARAGUA
COSTA San José S.V. Caracas TRINIDAD
RICA GR. & TOBAGO
PANAMA Panama City VENEZUELA
Bogotá Georgetown
COLOMBIA Paramaribo
Cayenne
GUYANA FR.
SURINAME GUIANA
Quito
ECUADOR

SIERRA LEONE
Monrovia LIBERIA
CÔTE
D'IVOIRE Accra Lomé
Lagos
Porto-Novo
Malabo
E.G.
Librevil

Galapagos Is.
(Ec.)

PACIFIC

KIRIBATI

Marquesas Is.
(Fr.)

Samoa
(U.S.A.)

O C E A N

Cook Is.
(N.Z.)
Tahiti
Society Is.
(Fr.)

Tuamotu Archipelago

Tropic of Capricorn

(U.K.)

Equator

Easter I.
(Chile)

PERU
Lima

B R A Z I L

La Paz
BOLIVIA
Sucre

Recife

Brasília

Belo Horizonte

Rio de Janeiro
São Paulo

PARAGUAY
Asunción

CHILE
Santiago ARGENTINA
Buenos
Aires

URUGUAY
Montevideo

Ascension I.
(U.K.)

St. Helena
(U.K.)

S O U T H

A T L A N T I C

Tristan da Cunha (U.K.)
Gough I. (U.K.)

O C E A N

Falkland Is.
(U.K.)

South Georgia
(U.K.)

A.: ANDORRA
ALB.: ALBANIA
AR.: ARMENIA
AUS.: AUSTRIA
AZ.: AZERBAIJAN
B.: BELGIUM
B.-H.: BOSNIA-HERZEGOVINA
BA.: BARBADOS
BANGLA.: BANGLADESH
BULG.: BULGARIA
C.: CROATIA
CAMB.: CAMBODIA
C.R.: CZECH REPUBLIC
E.: ESTONIA
EQ.G.: EQUATORIAL GUINEA
G.: GEORGIA
G.B.: GUINEA BISSAU
GERM.: GERMANY
GR.: GRENADA
GUAT: GUATEMALA
H.: HUNGARY
KIRG.: KIRGHIZIA
L.: LUXEMBOURG
LA.: LATVIA
LEB.: LEBANON
LI.: LIECHTENSTEIN
LIT.: LITHUANIA
M.: MONACO
MA.: MALTA
MAC.: MACEDONIA
MOLD.: MOLDAVIA
NETH.: NETHERLANDS
R.F.: RUSSIAN FEDERATION

S.: SWITZERLAND
SA.: SLOVAKIA
S.K.: ST. KITTS-NEVIS
SL.: SLOVENIA
S.M.: SAN MARINO
S.T.: SÃO TOME & PRINCIPE
S.V.: ST. VINCENT AND THE GRENADINES
T.: TURKEY (in Europe)
TAJ.: TAJIKISTAN
U.A.E.: UNITED ARAB EMIRATES
UZBEK.: UZBEKISTAN
V.C.: VATICAN CITY
YUGO.: YUGOSLAVIA

Antarctic Circle

Chilean Claim Argentinian Claim

BRITISH ANTARCTIC TERRITORY NORWEGIAN

Antar

48

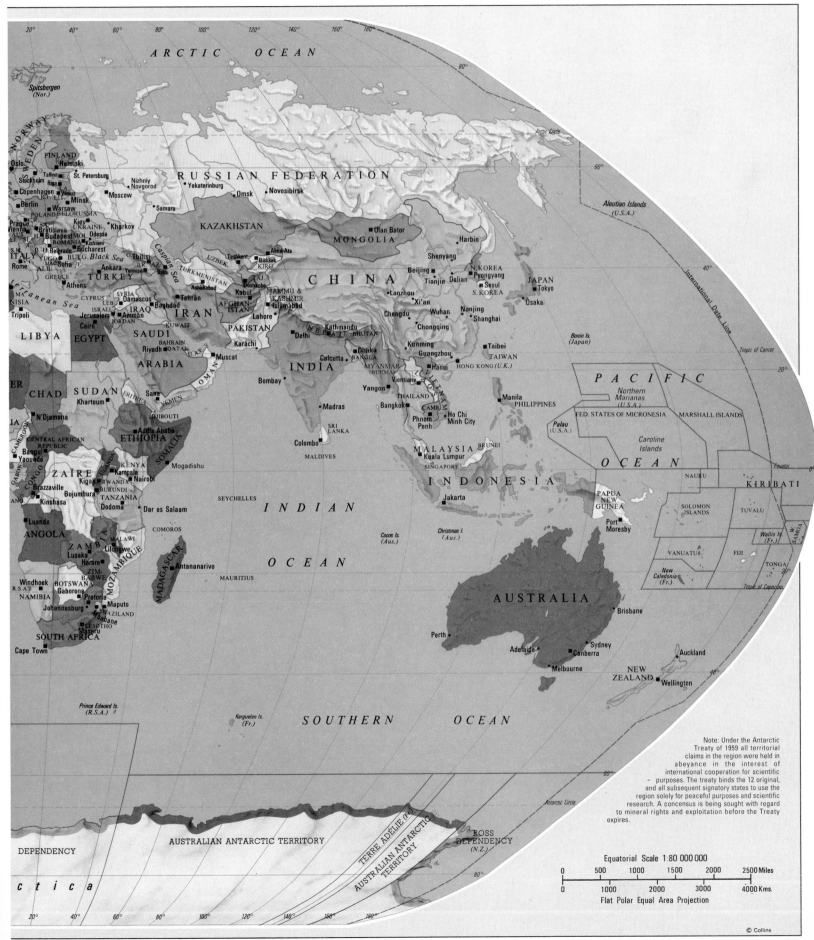

ARCTIC OCEAN

Spitsbergen
(Nor.)

Arctic Circle

RUSSIAN FEDERATION

International Date Line

NORWAY
SWEDEN
Oslo
FINLAND
Helsinki
Stockholm
Tallinn
St. Petersburg
Copenhagen
Riga
Vilnius
Minsk
Nizhniy
Novgorod
Yekaterinburg
Omsk
Novosibirsk
Aleutian Islands
(U.S.A.)
Berlin
Warsaw
Moscow
Samara
POLAND
BELORUSSIA
Prague
Kiev
UKRAINE
Kharkov
Vienna
Bratislava
Budapest
Odessa
Kishinev
KAZAKHSTAN
MONGOLIA
Ulan Bator
Harbin
ITALY
Belgrade
Bucharest
ROMANIA
BULG.
Black Sea
Sofia
Tbilisi
Shenyang
N.KOREA
Pyongyang
JAPAN
Rome
GREECE
Ankara
TURKEY
Yerevan
Baku
AZ.
TURKMENISTAN
Tashkent
UZBEK.
Bishkek
KIRG.
Alma-Ata
Beijing
Tianjin
Dalian
S.KOREA
Seoul
Tokyo
Athens
CYPRUS
SYRIA
Damascus
IRAQ
Ashkhabad
Dushanbe
TAJ.
CHINA
Lanzhou
Xi'an
Osaka
ISRAEL
LEB.
Baghdad
Tehran
Kabul
AFGHAN-
ISTAN
JAMMU &
KASHMIR
Islamabad
Chengdu
Wuhan
Nanjing
Shanghai
Jerusalem
Amman
JORDAN
IRAN
Lahore
PAKISTAN
Delhi
NEPAL
Kathmandu
BHUTAN
Chongqing
Bonin Is.
(Japan)
Tropic of Cancer
LIBYA
EGYPT
SAUDI
KUWAIT
BAHRAIN
QATAR
Riyadh
U.A.E.
Muscat
OMAN
Karachi
INDIA
Calcutta
Dhaka
BANGLA.
Kunming
Guangzhou
Taibei
TAIWAN
HONG KONG (U.K.)
PACIFIC
ARABIA
CHAD
SUDAN
ERITREA
Sana
YEMEN
DJIBOUTI
Bombay
MYANMAR
(BURMA)
Yangon
VIETNAM
Hanoi
Vientiane
Northern
Marianas
(U.S.A.)
N'Djamena
CENTRAL AFRICAN
REPUBLIC
Khartoum
Addis Ababa
ETHIOPIA
Madras
SRI
LANKA
THAILAND
Bangkok
CAMB.
Phnom
Penh
Ho Chi
Minh City
Manila
PHILIPPINES
FED. STATES OF MICRONESIA
MARSHALL ISLANDS
CAMEROON
Bangui
Yaounde
GABON
CONGO
Brazzaville
ZAIRE
Kampala
KENYA
Nairobi
RWANDA
BURUNDI
Bujumbura
TANZANIA
Dodoma
Mogadishu
SOMALIA
Colombo
MALDIVES
MALAYSIA
Kuala Lumpur
SINGAPORE
BRUNEI
Palau
(U.S.A.)
Caroline
Islands
OCEAN
Kinshasa
SEYCHELLES
INDIAN
INDONESIA
NAURU
KIRIBATI
ANGOLA
Luanda
ZAMBIA
Lusaka
MALAWI
Lilongwe
Harare
MOZAMBIQUE
COMOROS
MADAGASCAR
Antananarivo
Dar es Salaam
OCEAN
Cocos Is.
(Aus.)
Christmas I.
(Aus.)
Jakarta
PAPUA
NEW
GUINEA
Port
Moresby
SOLOMON
ISLANDS
TUVALU
Wallis Is.
(Fr.)
W.SAMOA
Windhoek
NAMIBIA
R.S.A.
BOTSWANA
Gaborone
ZIM-
BABWE
MAURITIUS
VANUATU
New
Caledonia
(Fr.)
FIJI
TONGA
Pretoria
Johannesburg
SWAZILAND
Mbabane
LESOTHO
Maseru
Maputo
AUSTRALIA
Brisbane
SOUTH AFRICA
Cape Town
Perth
Adelaide
Sydney
Canberra
Auckland
Melbourne
NEW
ZEALAND
Wellington
Tropic of Capricorn
Prince Edward Is.
(R.S.A.)
Kerguelen Is.
(Fr.)
SOUTHERN
OCEAN

DEPENDENCY
AUSTRALIAN ANTARCTIC TERRITORY
TERRE ADÉLIE (Fr.)
AUSTRALIAN ANTARCTIC
TERRITORY
ROSS
DEPENDENCY
(N.Z.)
ctica

Antarctic Circle

Equatorial Scale 1:80 000 000

0   500   1000   1500   2000   2500 Miles
0   1000   2000   3000   4000 Kms.
Flat Polar Equal Area Projection

© Collins

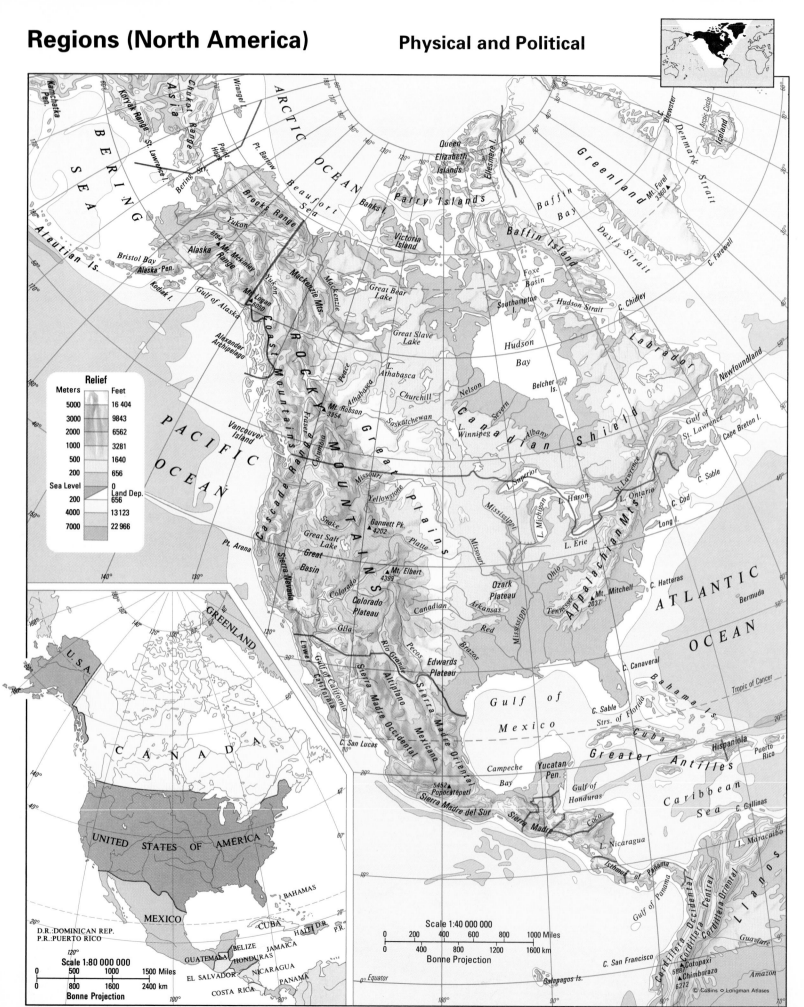

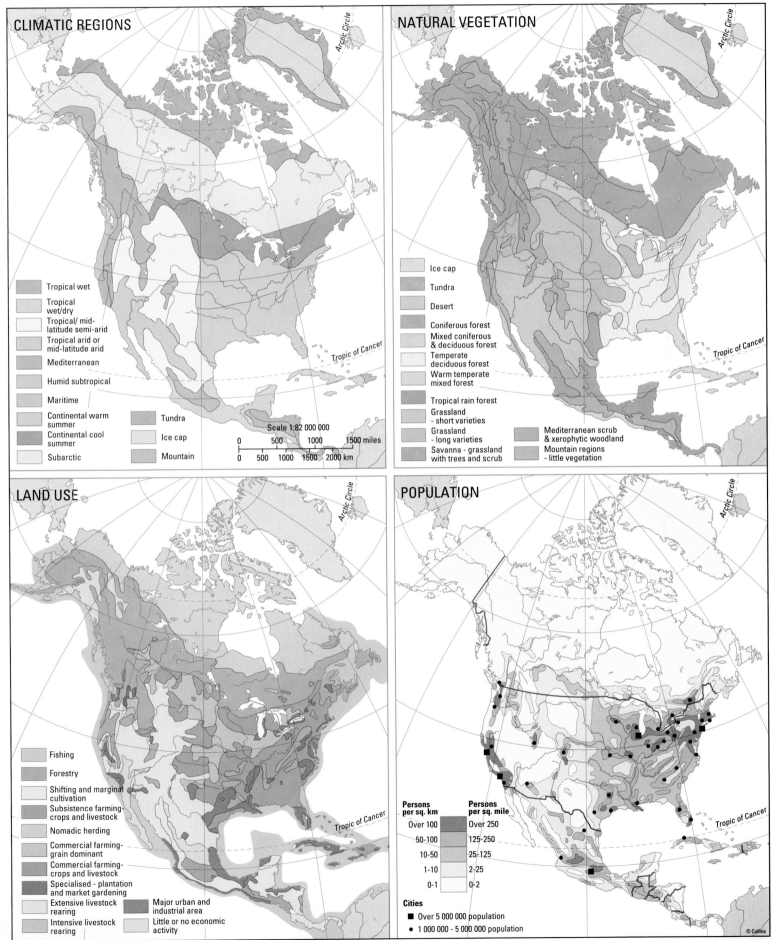

CLIMATIC REGIONS

- Tropical wet
- Tropical wet/dry
- Tropical/mid-latitude semi-arid
- Tropical arid or mid-latitude arid
- Mediterranean
- Humid subtropical
- Maritime
- Continental warm summer
- Continental cool summer
- Subarctic
- Tundra
- Ice cap
- Mountain

Scale 1:82 000 000

0   500   1000   1500 miles

0   500   1000   1500   2000 km

NATURAL VEGETATION

- Ice cap
- Tundra
- Desert
- Coniferous forest
- Mixed coniferous & deciduous forest
- Temperate deciduous forest
- Warm temperate mixed forest
- Tropical rain forest
- Grassland - short varieties
- Grassland - long varieties
- Savanna - grassland with trees and scrub
- Mediterranean scrub & xerophytic woodland
- Mountain regions - little vegetation

LAND USE

- Fishing
- Forestry
- Shifting and marginal cultivation
- Subsistence farming - crops and livestock
- Nomadic herding
- Commercial farming - grain dominant
- Commercial farming - crops and livestock
- Specialised - plantation and market gardening
- Extensive livestock rearing
- Intensive livestock rearing
- Major urban and industrial area
- Little or no economic activity

POPULATION

Persons per sq. km	Persons per sq. mile
Over 100	Over 250
50-100	125-250
10-50	25-125
1-10	2-25
0-1	0-2

Cities
- ■ Over 5 000 000 population
- ● 1 000 000 - 5 000 000 population

© Collins

51

Regions (North America)

Relief

Feet		Meters
16 404		5000
9 843		3000
6 562		2000
3 281		1000
1 640		500
656		200
0		Sea Level
Land Dep.		
656		200
13 123		4000
22 966		7000

Scale 1 : 17 000 000

| 0 | 100 | 200 | 300 | 400 | 500 Miles |

| 0 | 100 | 200 | 300 | 400 | 500 | 600 | 700 | 800 Kms. |

Bonne Projection

Canada

© Collins ◇ Longman Atlases

Regions (North America)

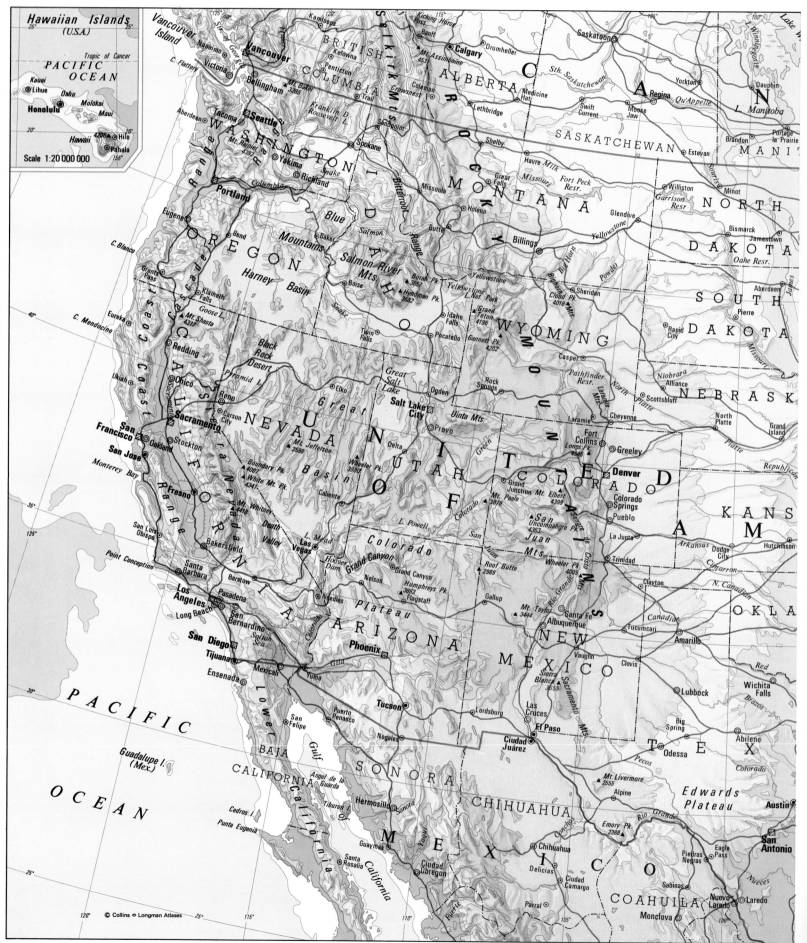

Conterminous United States

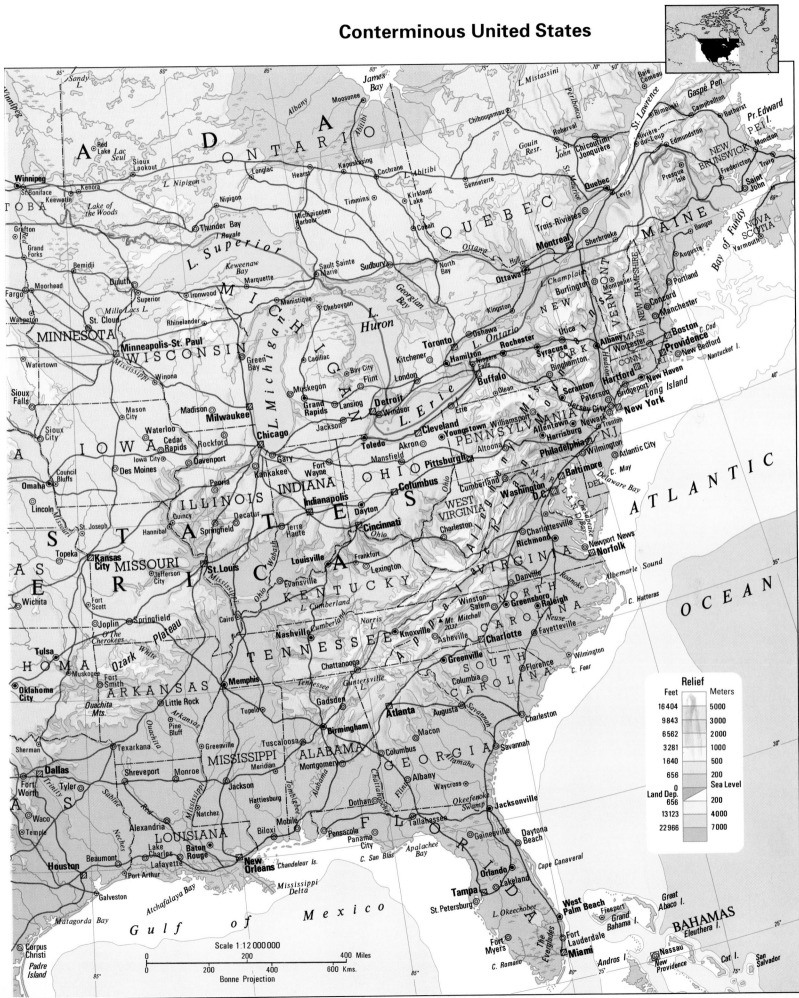

Regions (North America)

Guam, American Samoa, Micronesia

US OUTLYING AREAS

RUSSIAN FEDERATION

Sea of Okhotsk

Bering Sea

ALASKA
Arctic Circle
Anchorage

Gulf of Alaska

CANADA

Hudson Bay

Edmonton

CHINA
Vladivostok
Beijing
N. KOREA
S. KOREA
JAPAN
Tokyo
Shanghai
Taibei
TAIWAN
Manila
PHILIPPINES
GUAM

PACIFIC

OCEAN

International Date Line

Midway Is. (U.S.A.)
Tropic of Cancer

HAWAII
Johnston (U.S.A.)

Wake (U.S.A.)

NORTHERN MARIANAS
MARSHALL IS.
FEDERATED STATES OF MICRONESIA
PALAU

Vancouver
Winnipeg
Seattle

UNITED STATES

San Francisco
Los Angeles
Houston
Monterrey
Guadalajara

Detroit
Toronto
Washington

Boston
New York
Philadelphia

ATLANTIC

OCEAN

Miami
Gulf of Mexico
Mexico City
BELIZE
HONDURAS
GUATEMALA
EL SALVADOR
NICARAGUA
Havana
DOM. REP.
HAITI
PUERTO RICO

MEXICO

Palmyra Is. (U.S.A.)
Howland (U.S.A.)
Baker (U.S.A.)
Jarvis U.S.A.
Equator

NAURU

PAPUA NEW GUINEA
INDONESIA
SOLOMON IS.
TUVALU
WEST SAMOA
AMERICAN SAMOA
AUSTRALIA
KIRIBATI
Cook Is.

	U.S. States
	U.S. Commonwealths
	U.S. Territories
	Countries in a Compact of Free Association with U.S.
	U.S. Trust Territory of the Pacific Island

PALAU
1:1 000 000
0   5 miles
0 10 kms

Konrei
Arekalong Pen.
Ngardmau Bay
Ngardmau
Pkulagalid Pt
Gulitel
200 Keklau
218 Makelulu
Namai Bay
Melekeiok
Babelthuap
Mukeru
Koror
Malakal
134°30'
Garusuun

GUAM
1:1 000 000

Ritidian Pt.
Pati Pt.
262
Tumon Bay
Tamuning
13°30'
Dededo
Piti 330 Agana
Orote Pen.
Apra Heights
Pago Bay
Agat
405 Santa Rita
Talofofo
Facpi Pt.
Lamlam
378
Inarajan
Merizo
144°45'

SAIPAN & TINIAN
(NORTHERN MARIANAS)
1:1 000 000

Sabaneta Pt.
Tanapag
Garapan
Kalabera
465
Mt. Tagpochau
Chalan Kanoa
Saipan
Tahgong Pt.
Saipan Channel
Naftan Pt.
15°
Diablo Pt.
Tinian
Tachungnya
178
Carolinas Pt.
145°40'

TUTUILA
(AMERICAN SAMOA)
1:1 000 000
170°40'

Vatia
C. Matatula
Pago Pago
Fagasa
Aua
Tula
652
Pago Pago Harbor
Amanave
Nu'uuli
14°20'
Leone
Tafuna
Steps Pt.
170°40'

MANUA
(AMERICAN SAMOA)
1:1 000 000
169°30'

484
639
Ofu
Olosega
14°10'
Luma
931
Ta'u
169°30'

MICRONESIA
Scale 1:20 000 000
0   200   400 miles
0   200 400 600 miles

Farallon de Pajaros
Maug Is.
Asuncion
Agrihan
Pagan
Alamagan
Guguan
Sarigan
Anatahan
Farallon de Medinilla
Garapan
Saipan
Tinian
Rota
Agana

NORTHERN

MARIANAS

GUAM

Mariana Trench

PACIFIC   OCEAN

20°N
Wake I. (U.S.A)
20°N

Taongi
15°N
15°N

MARSHALL ISLANDS

Enewetak
Bikini
Rongerik
Bikar
Rongelap
Ailuk
Likiep
Ujelang
Kwajalein
Wotje
Ujae
Erikub
Namu
Dalap-Uliga-Darrit
Alinglapalap
Majuro
Ratak Chain
Ralik Chain

10°N
10°N

Ulithi
Fais
Yap Is.
Ngulu
Sorol
Gaferut
Namonuito
Fayu
Hall Is.
Faraulep
West Fayu
Woleai
Olimarao
Pulap
Truk Is.
Eauripik
Ifalik
Lamotrek
Puluwat
Pulusuk
Losap
Pakin
Pohnpei
Palikir
Mokil

FEDERATED STATES

OF MICRONESIA

Kosrae
Satawan
Jaluit
Mili

Babelthuap
Palau Is.
Angaur

Caroline   Islands

Sonsorol Is.
Pulo Anna
Merir
Nukuoro
Ebon
5°N
5°N

PALAU

Tobi

Butaritari

Abaiang
Tarawa
Maiana
Abemama
KIRIBATI

Kapingamarangi
Equator
INDONESIA
140°E
PAPUA NEW GUINEA
160°E
NAURU Yaren
170°E
Gilbert Islands
Aranuka
0°

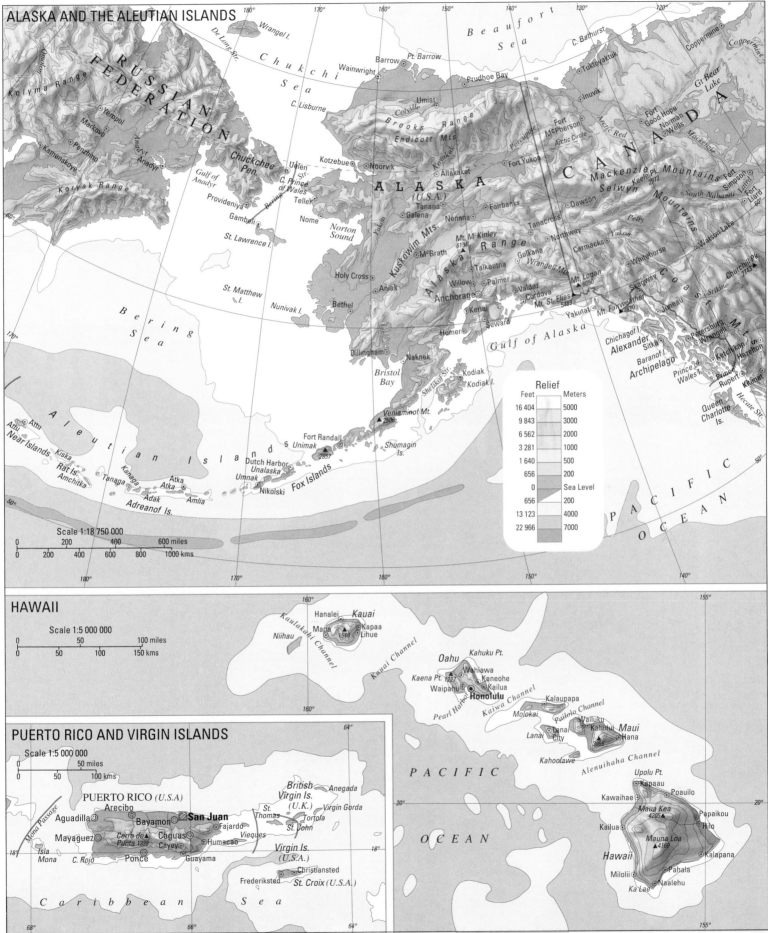

ALASKA AND THE ALEUTIAN ISLANDS

RUSSIAN FEDERATION

Beaufort Sea

Chukchi Sea

CANADA

ALASKA (U.S.A.)

Kolyma Range
Koryak Range
Chuckchee Pen.
Brooks Range
Endicott Mts.
Mackenzie Mountains
Coast Mountains

Wrangel I.
De Long Str.
Pt. Barrow
Barrow
Wainwright
Prudhoe Bay
C. Bathurst
Coppermine
Gt Bear Lake
Tuktoyaktuk
Inuvik
Fort Good Hope
Fort Norman
Fort Wells
Fort Simpson
Fort Liard
South Nahanni
Latrd

Keele Pk. 2972
Selwyn Mountains
Churchill Pk. 2743

Mt. Logan 6050
Mt. St. Elias 5489
Mt. Fairweather 4670

Anadyr'
Anadyr
Providéniya
Gambeli
Teller
Nome
Uelen
C. Prince of Wales
Bering Str.
Kotzebue
Noorvik
Allakaket
Fort Yukon
Dawson
Carmacks
Whitehorse
Watson Lake

Gulf of Anadyr
St. Lawrence I.
Norton Sound
Yukon
Tanana
Galena
Fairbanks
Nenana
Tanacross
Northway
Yukon
Petty

Holy Cross
Aniak
McGrath
Mt. McKinley 6194
Willow
Talkeetna
Gulkana
Wrangell Mts.
Skagway
Juneau

Bethel
Anchorage
Palmer
Valdez
Cordova
Yakutat

Homer
Kenai
Seward
Gulf of Alaska

Dillingham
Naknek
Shelikof Str.
Kodiak
Kodiak I.

Chichagof I.
Alexander Archipelago
Sitka
Baranof I.
Petersburg
Wrangell
Ketchikan
Hazelton

Bristol Bay
Veniaminof Mt. 2506
Fort Randall
Unimak 2857
Shumagin Is.

Prince of Wales I.
Prince Rupert
Kitimat
Queen Charlotte Is.
Hecate Str.

Bering Sea

Attu
Attu
Near Islands
Kiska
Rat Is.
Amchitka
Tanaga
Kanaga
Adak
Adreanof Is.
Amlia
Amukta
Atka
Atka
Nikolski
Umnak
Unalaska
Dutch Harbor
Fox Islands

Aleutian Islands

St. Matthew I.
Nunivak I.
St. Lawrence I.

Relief

Feet	Meters
16 404	5000
9 843	3000
6 562	2000
3 281	1000
1 640	500
656	200
0	Sea Level
656	200
13 123	4000
22 966	7000

PACIFIC OCEAN

Scale 1:18 750 000

0   200   400   600 miles
0 200 400 600 800 1000 kms

HAWAII

Scale 1:5 000 000

0   50   100 miles
0 50 100 150 kms

Kauai
Hanalei
Kapaa
Lihue
Mana
Niihau
Kaulakahi Channel

Oahu
Kahuku Pt.
Wahiawa
Kaneohe
Kaena Pt. 1227
Waipahu
Kailua
Honolulu
Pearl Harbor
Kauai Channel
Kaiwi Channel

Molokai
Kalaupapa
Lanai City
Lanai
Pailolo Channel
Wailuku
Kahului
Maui
Hana

Kahoolawe
Alenuihaha Channel

PACIFIC OCEAN

Upolu Pt.
Kapaau
Poauilo
Kawaihae
Kawaihae
Mauna Kea 4205
Papaikou
Kailua
Hilo
Mauna Loa 4169
Kalapana
Hawaii
Milolii
Pahala
Ka Lae
Naalehu

PUERTO RICO AND VIRGIN ISLANDS

Scale 1:5 000 000

0   50 miles
0 50 100 kms

PUERTO RICO (U.S.A)
Arecibo
Aguadilla
Bayamon
San Juan
Mayaguez
Cerro de Punta 1338
Caguas
Cayey
Isla Mona
C. Rojo
Ponce
Guayama
Humacao

Mona Passage

British Virgin Is. (U.K.)
Anegada
Virgin Gorda
St. Thomas
Tortola
St. John
Vieques
Virgin Is. (U.S.A.)
Fajardo

Christiansted
Frederiksted
St. Croix (U.S.A.)

Caribbean Sea

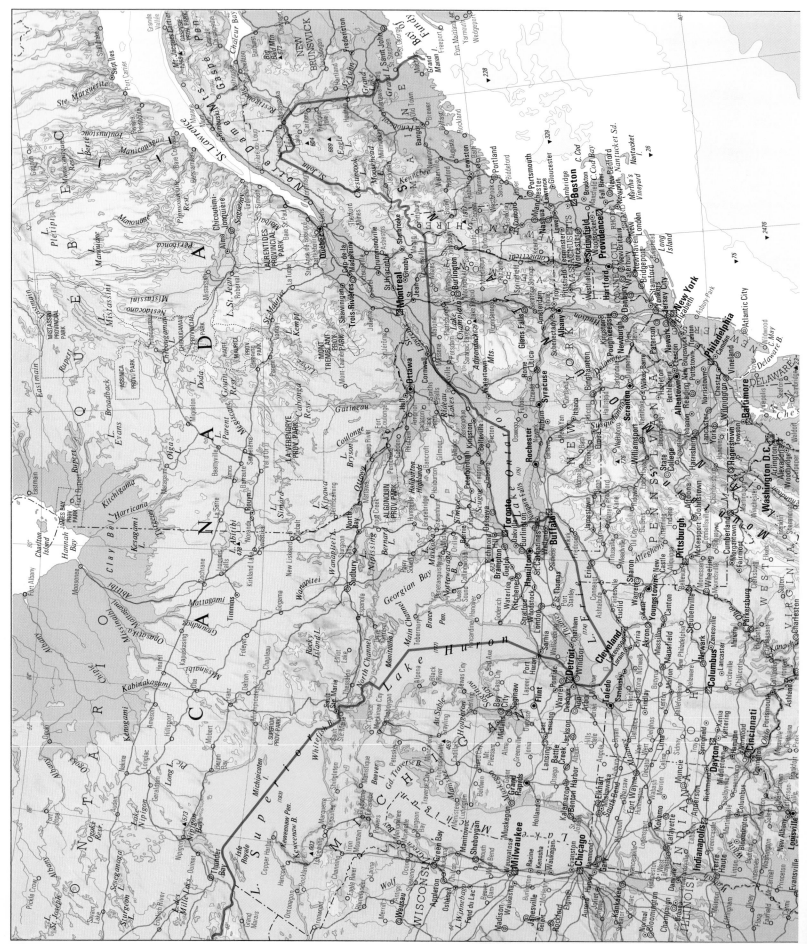

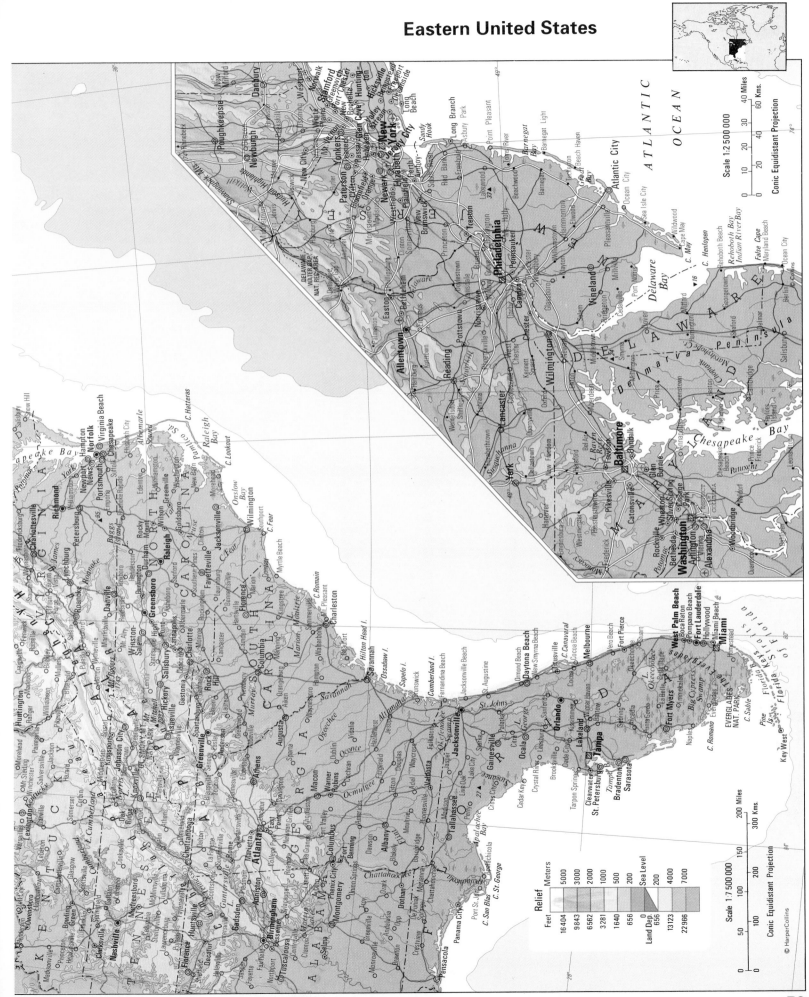

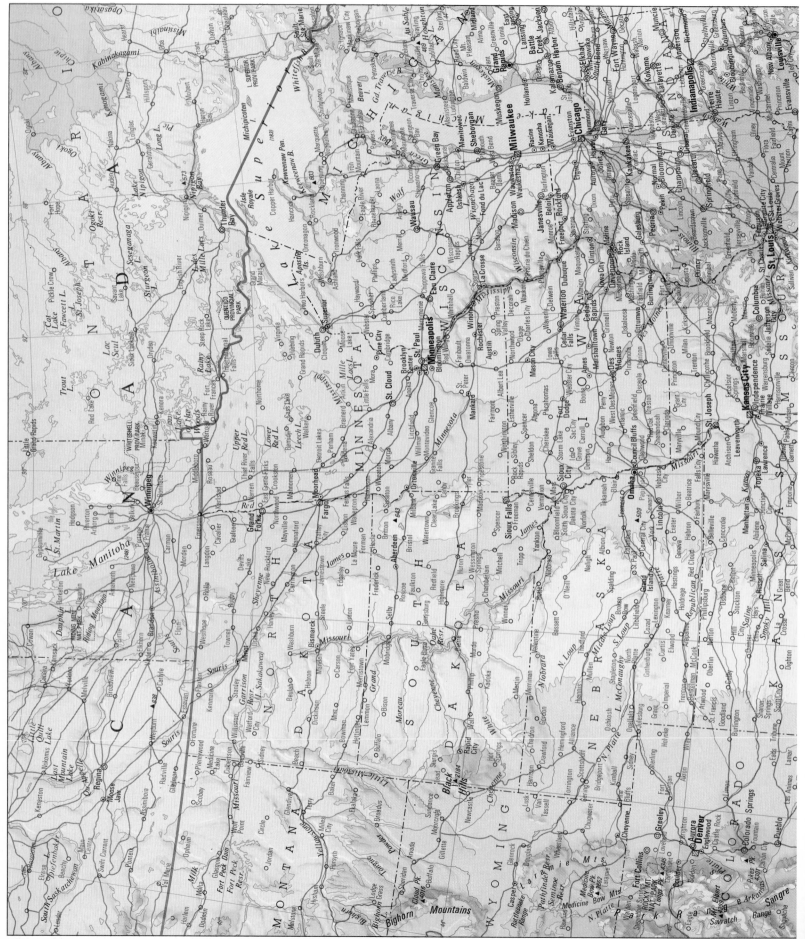

Middle United States

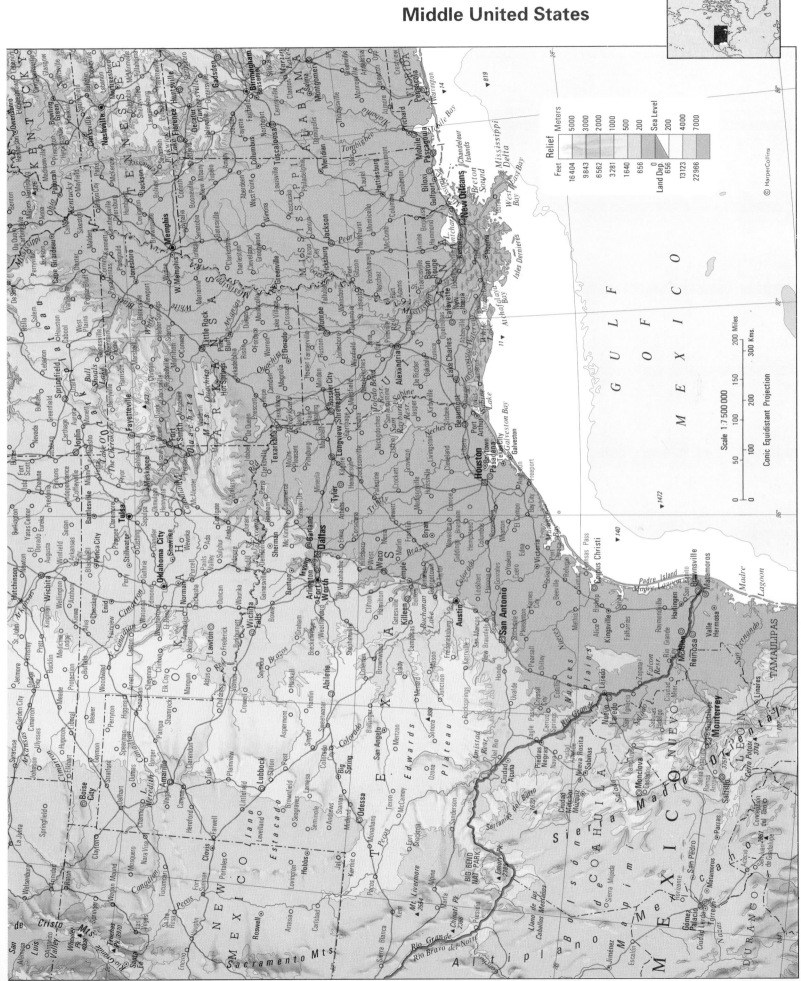

Regions (North America)

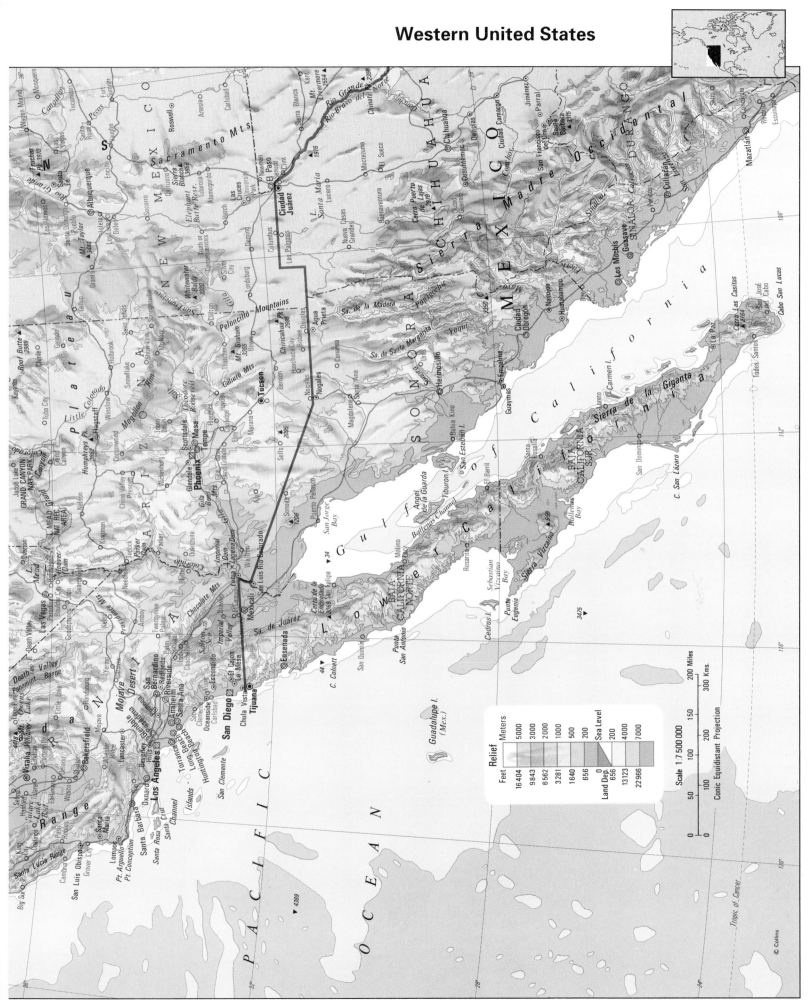

Relief

Feet	Meters
16404	5000
9843	3000
6562	2000
3281	1000
1640	500
656	200
0	Sea Level
	200
	Land Dep.
656	
13123	4000
22966	7000

Scale 1:7 500 000

200 Miles
300 Kms.

Conic Equidistant Projection

© Collins

Regions (North America)

Mexican States numbered on map
1. AGUASCALIENTES
2. DISTRICT FEDERAL
3. TLAXCALA

Relief
Feet		Meters
16404		5000
9843		3000
6562		2000
3281		1000
1640		500
656		200
0		Sea Level
Land Dep.		
656		200
13123		4000
22966		7000

Scale 1:12 500 000

0 100 200 300 400 Miles

0 100 200 300 400 500 600 Kms.

Conic Equal Area Projection

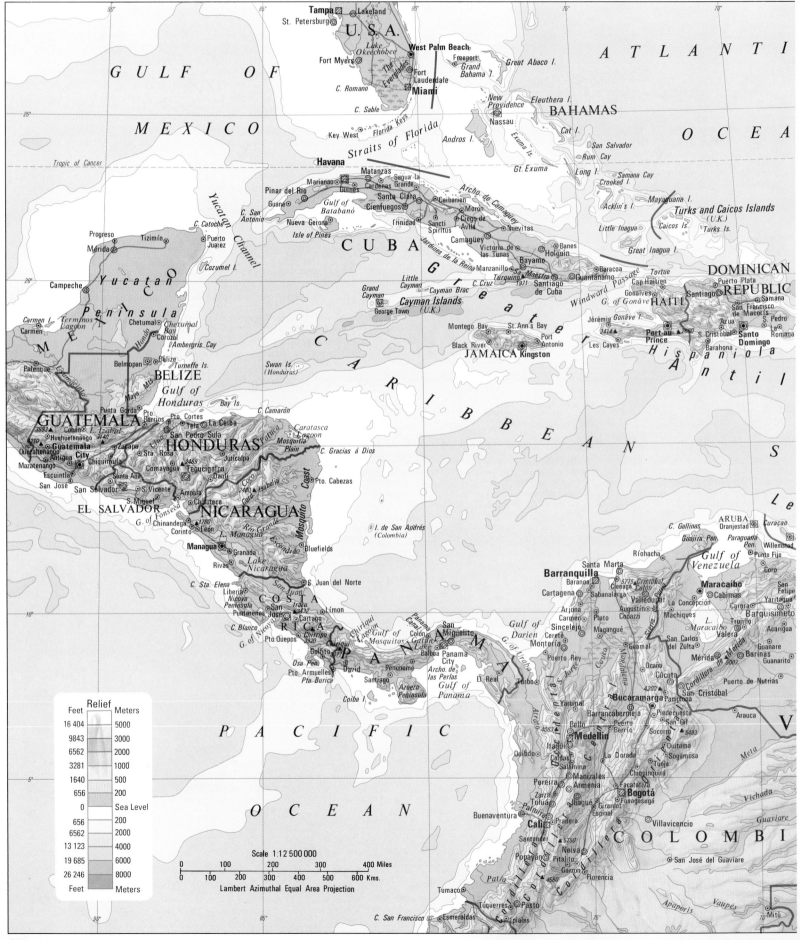

Relief

Feet		Meters
16 404		5000
9843		3000
6562		2000
3281		1000
1640		500
656		200
0		Sea Level
656		200
6562		2000
13 123		4000
19 685		6000
26 246		8000
Feet		Meters

Scale 1:12 500 000

0   100   200   300   400 Miles

0   100   200   300   400   500   600 Kms.

Lambert Azimuthal Equal Area Projection

Central America and The West Indies

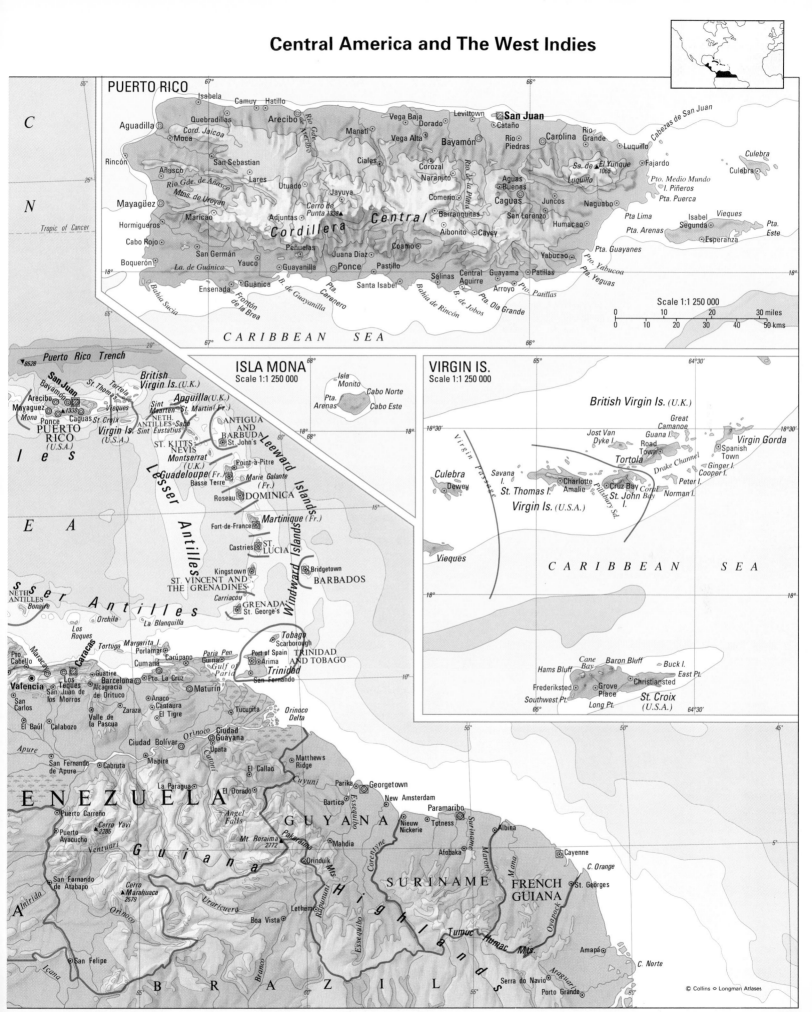

PUERTO RICO

Isabela · Camuy · Hatillo · Vega Baja · Levittown · San Juan · Cabezas de San Juan
Aguadilla · Quebradillas · Arecibo · Dorado · Cataño · Carolina · Rio Grande · Luquillo · Culebra
Cord. Jaicoa · Moca · Manati · Vega Alta · Bayamón · Río Piedras · Luquillo · Fajardo · Culebra
Rincón · San Sebastian · Ciales · Corozal · Aguas Buenas · Sa. de El Yunque 1065 · Pto. Medio Mundo · I. Piñeros
Añasco · Lares · Naranjito · Comerio · Caguas · Juncos · Naguabo · Pta. Puerca
Mayagüez · Rio Gde. de Añasco · Mtns. de Uroyan · Utuado · Jayuya · Cerro de Punta 1338 · Cordillera · Central · San Lorenzo · Humacao · Pta. Arenas · Isabel Segunda · Vieques · Pta. Este
Maricao · Adjuntas · Barranquitas · Aibonito · Cayey · Pta. Lima
Hormigueros · Peñuelas · Juana Diaz · Coamo · Yabucoa · Pta. Guayanes · Pta. Yeguas
Cabo Rojo · San Germán · Yauco · Pastillo · Salinas · Guayama · Patillas · Pto. Yabucoa · Esperanza
Boquerón · Guayanilla · Ponce · Santa Isabel · Central Aguirre · Arroyo · Pto. Patillas · Pta. Ola Grande
Ensenada · Guánica · B. de Guayanilla · Pta. Carenero · Frontón de la Brea · Bahía de Rincón · B. de Jobos

La. de Guánica · Bahia Sucia

CARIBBEAN SEA

Scale 1:1 250 000
0 10 20 30 miles
0 10 20 30 40 50 kms

Tropic of Cancer

C · N

Puerto Rico Trench
8528
San Juan · Bayamón · British Virgin Is. (U.K.)
Arecibo · St. Thomas · Tortola
Mayagüez · Vieques · Anguilla (U.K.)
Mona · Ponce · Caguas · St. Croix · Sint Maarten - St. Martin (Fr.)
PUERTO RICO (U.S.A.) · Virgin Is. (U.S.A.) · NETH. ANTILLES · Saba · Sint Eustatius
ANTIGUA AND BARBUDA · St. John's · Leeward Islands
ST. KITTS NEVIS · Montserrat (U.K.) · Point-à-Pitre
Guadeloupe (Fr.) · Marie Galante (Fr.)
Basse Terre · Roseau · DOMINICA
Lesser Antilles
Martinique (Fr.)
Fort-de-France
Castries · ST. LUCIA
Kingstown · Windward Islands · Bridgetown
ST. VINCENT AND THE GRENADINES · BARBADOS
Carriacou
NETH. ANTILLES · Bonaire · GRENADA · St. George's
Orchila · La Blanquilla · Grenadines
Los Roques · Tobago
Tortuga · Margarita I. · Scarborough
Caracas · Porlamar · Paria Pen. · Port of Spain · TRINIDAD AND TOBAGO
Pto. Cabello · Carúpano · Güiria · Arima
Cumaná · Gulf of Paria · Trinidad
Guatire · Pto. La Cruz · San Fernando
Valencia · Barcelona · Maturín
San Juan de los Morros · Altagracia de Orituco
San Carlos · Anaco · Cantaura · El Tigre
El Baúl · Calabozo · Zaraza · Valle de la Pascua · Tucupita · Orinoco Delta
E A · les · E A

ISLA MONA
Scale 1:1 250 000
Isla Monito
Pta. Arenas · Cabo Norte
Cabo Este

VIRGIN IS.
Scale 1:1 250 000

British Virgin Is. (U.K.)
Great Camanoe
Jost Van Dyke I. · Guana I. · Virgin Gorda
Culebra · Savana I. · Road Town · Spanish Town · Tortola · Drake Channel · Ginger I.
Dewey · St. Thomas I. · Cooper I.
Charlotte Amalie · Cruz Bay · Coral · Peter I.
Virgin Is. (U.S.A.) · St. John · Pillsbury Sd. · Bay · Norman I.
Vieques

CARIBBEAN SEA

Cane Bay · Baron Bluff · Buck I.
Hams Bluff · Christiansted · East Pt.
Frederiksted · Grove Place · St. Croix (U.S.A.)
Southwest Pt. · Long Pt.

Virgin Passage

VENEZUELA
Puerto Carreño · Cerro Yavi 2285
Ciudad Bolívar · Ciudad Guayana · Upata
Mapire · El Callao
San Fernando de Apure · Cabruta · La Paragua · El Dorado · Parika · Georgetown
Puerto Ayacucho · Angel Falls · GUYANA · Bartica · New Amsterdam · Paramaribo
Mt. Roraima 2772 · Mahdia · Nieuw Nickerie · Totness · Albina
Ventuari · Orinoco · Guiana · Afobaka · Maroni · Cayenne
San Fernando de Atabapo · Cerro Marahuaca 2579 · Oriduik · C. Orange
Atabapo · Uraricuera · SURINAME · FRENCH GUIANA · St. Georges
Inírida · Guiana Highlands · Lethem · Boa Vista · Mana · Ovapock
Orinoco · Branco · Tumuc Humac Mts. · Amapá
Isana · San Felipe · Serra do Navio · Porto Grande · C. Norte

B R A Z I L

© Collins ◊ Longman Atlases

Yucatan Channel
C u b a
Bahama Is.
Greater Antilles
Hispaniola
Puerto Rico
Leeward Is.
Yucatan Pen.
Gulf of Honduras
Jamaica
Sierra Madre
Caribbean Sea
Lesser Antilles
Windward Is.
C. Gallinas
Curaçao
Trinidad
L. Nicaragua
Isthmus of Panama
Gulf of Panama
L. Maracaibo
Llanos
Orinoco
Orinoco Delta
Meta
Orinoco
Roraima 2772
Guiana Highlands
Essequibo
Cordillera Occidental
Cordillera Central
Cordillera Oriental
Cotopaxi 5897
Chimborazo 6271
Japurá
Negro
Equator
Marañon
Javari
Juruá
Amazon
Selvas
Purús
Madeira
Tapajos
Xingu
C. São Roque
C. Negra
Ucayali
A N D E S
Huascaran 6768
Tocantins
Araguaia
Parnaiba
PACIFIC
OCEAN
Guaporé
Planalto do Mato Grosso
Brazilian
São Francisco
Atacama Desert
L. Titicaca
Paraguay
Highlands
L. Poopo
Agulhas Negras 2797
C. Frio
Gran Chaco
Filcomayo
Paraná
Tropic of Capricorn
Salado
Paraná
Uruguay
SOUTH
Aconcagua 6960
Pampas
Rio de la Plata
ATLANTIC
G. of S. Matias
Chiloe
Patagonia
ATLANTIC
OCEAN
Bahía Grande
Magellan's Str.
Falkland Is.
Tierra del Fuego
S. Georgia

POLITICAL
TRINIDAD & TOBAGO
VENEZUELA
GUYANA
FR. GUIANA
COLOMBIA
SURINAME
ECUADOR
PERU
B R A Z I L
BOLIVIA
PARAGUAY
CHILE
ARGENTINA
URUGUAY

Scale 1 : 80 000 000
0   500   1000   1500 Miles
0   1000   2000 Kms.

Falkland Islands

Scale 1:35 000 000
0   200   400   600   800   1000 Miles
0   500   1000   1500 Kms.
Lambert Azimuthal Equal Area Projection

© Collins ◦ Longman Atlases

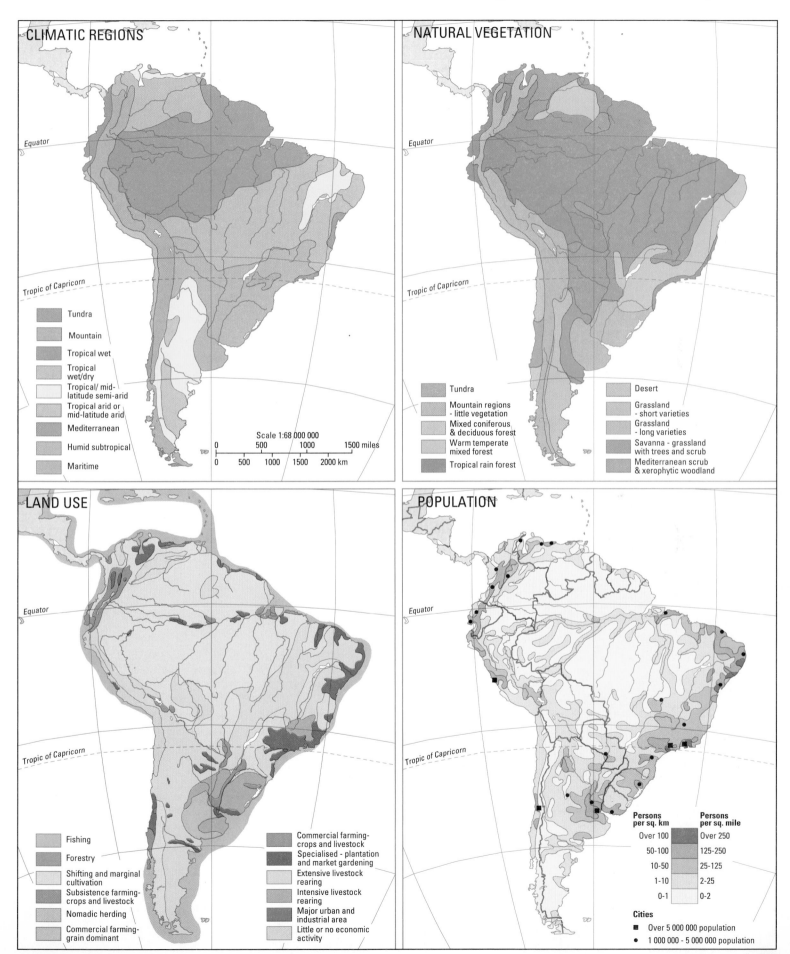

CLIMATIC REGIONS

Equator

Tropic of Capricorn

Scale 1:68 000 000

0   500   1000   1500 miles

0   500   1000   1500   2000 km

- Tundra
- Mountain
- Tropical wet
- Tropical wet/dry
- Tropical/ mid-latitude semi-arid
- Tropical arid or mid-latitude arid
- Mediterranean
- Humid subtropical
- Maritime

NATURAL VEGETATION

Equator

Tropic of Capricorn

- Tundra
- Mountain regions - little vegetation
- Mixed coniferous & deciduous forest
- Warm temperate mixed forest
- Tropical rain forest
- Desert
- Grassland - short varieties
- Grassland - long varieties
- Savanna - grassland with trees and scrub
- Mediterranean scrub & xerophytic woodland

LAND USE

Equator

Tropic of Capricorn

- Fishing
- Forestry
- Shifting and marginal cultivation
- Subsistence farming- crops and livestock
- Nomadic herding
- Commercial farming- grain dominant
- Commercial farming- crops and livestock
- Specialised - plantation and market gardening
- Extensive livestock rearing
- Intensive livestock rearing
- Major urban and industrial area
- Little or no economic activity

POPULATION

Equator

Tropic of Capricorn

Persons per sq. km	Persons per sq. mile
Over 100	Over 250
50-100	125-250
10-50	25-125
1-10	2-25
0-1	0-2

Cities

- ■ Over 5 000 000 population
- ● 1 000 000 - 5 000 000 population

69

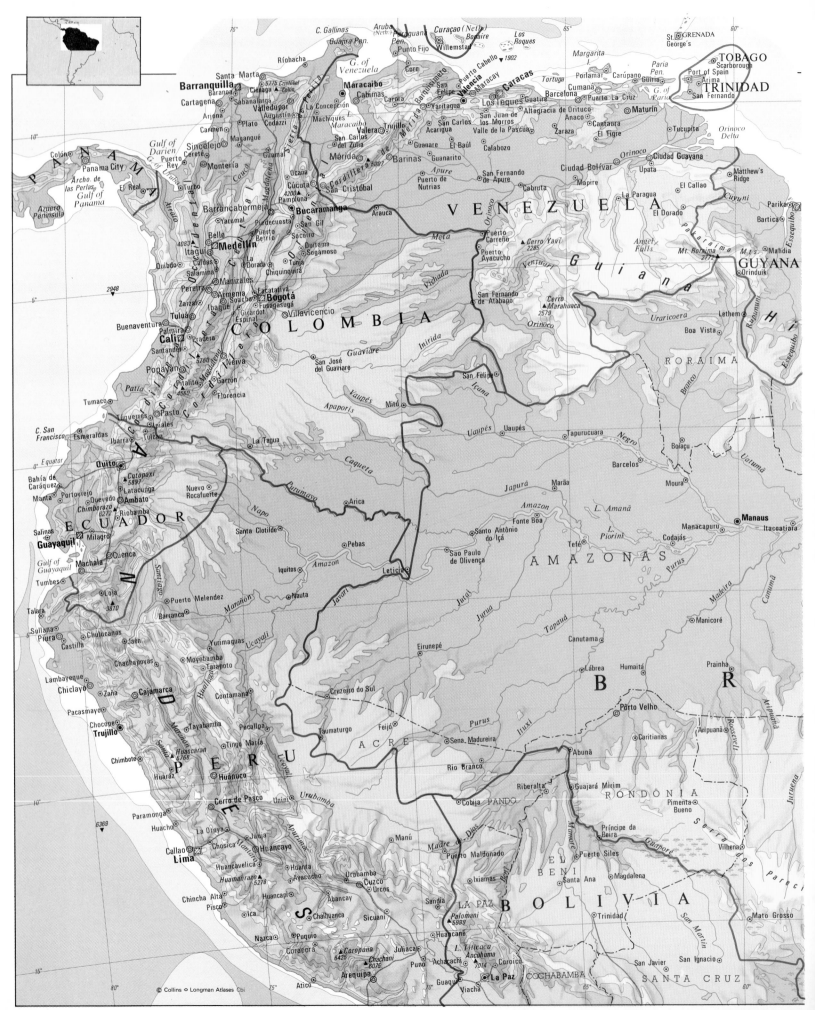

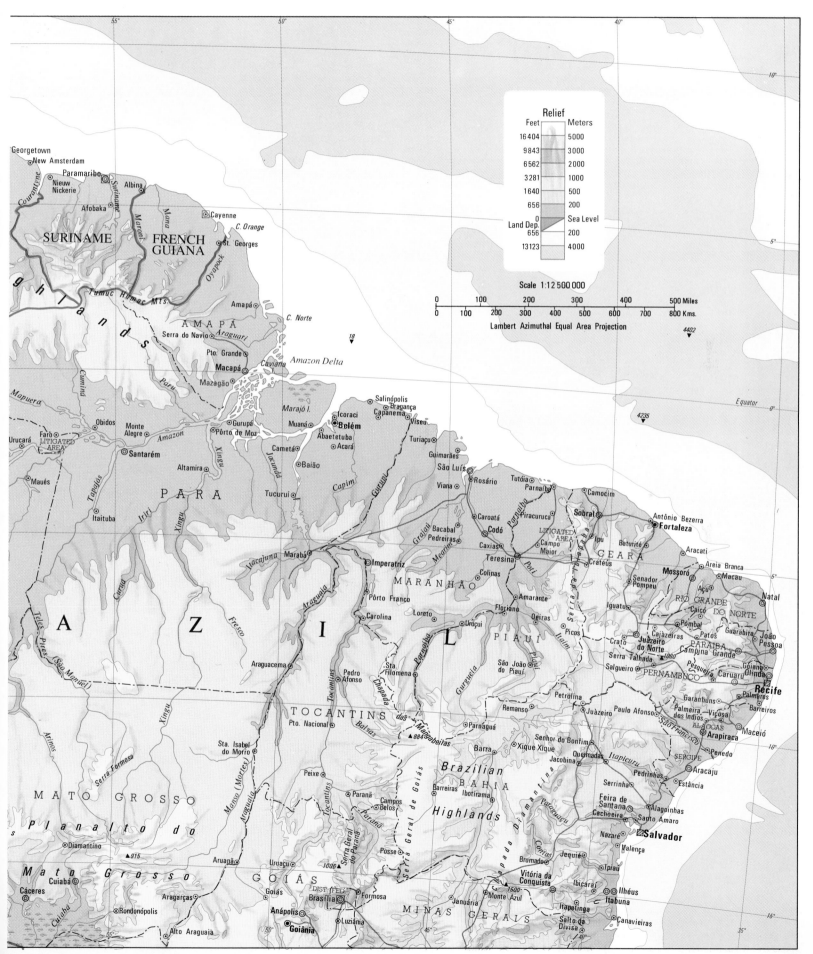

Relief

Feet		Meters
16 404		5000
9843		3000
6562		2000
3281		1000
1640		500
656		200
0		Sea Level
Land Dep.		
656		200
13 123		4000

Scale 1:12 500 000

100 200 300 400 500 Miles

100 200 300 400 500 600 700 800 Kms.

Lambert Azimuthal Equal Area Projection

Georgetown
New Amsterdam
Paramaribo
Nieuw Nickerie
Afobaka
Albina
SURINAME
FRENCH GUIANA
Courantyne
Suriname
Maroni
Nana
Cayenne
C. Orange
St. Georges
Oyapock
ghlands
Tumuc Humac Mts.
Amapá
AMAPÁ
C. Norte
Serra do Navio
Araguari
Pto. Grande
Macapá
Caviana
Amazon Delta
Mazagão
Marajó I.
Salinópolis
Bragança
Capanema
Icoraci
Viseu
Muaná
Belém
Mapuera
Obidos
Monte Alegre
Gurupá
Pôrto de Moz
Abaetetuba
Acará
Turiaçu
Guimarães
São Luís
Faro
Urucará
LITIGATED AREA
Amazon
Cametá
Baião
Viana
Rosário
Tutóia
Parnaíba
Camocim
Santarém
Altamira
Tucuruí
Capim
Gurupi
Grajaú
Bacabal
Pedreiras
Caroatá
Codó
Campo Maior
Piracuruca
Sobral
Ipu
Baturité
Antônio Bezerra
Fortaleza
Maués
Itaituba
Xingu
Iriri
Marabá
Imperatriz
Caxias
Teresina
Crateús
CEARÁ
Aracati
Areia Branca
PARÁ
Vacajuna
Megrine
Colinas
Pati
Senador Pompeu
Iguatu
Mossoró
Macau
Açu
Natal
RIO GRANDE DO NORTE
Carná
Pôrto Franco
MARANHÃO
Amarante
Floriano
Oeiras
Caicó
Pombal
Patos
Guarabira
João Pessoa
Teles Pires (São Manuel)
Carolina
Loreto
Urucuí
PIAUÍ
Picos
Crato
Cajàzeiras
Juàzeiro do Norte
Serra Talhada
Campina Grande
PARAIBA
Goiana
Olinda
Araguacema
Pedro Afonso
Sta. Filomena
Parnaíba
Gurguéia
São João do Piauí
Piauí
Salgueiro
Pesqueira
Caruaru
PERNAMBUCO
Recife
A
Z
I
L
Arinos
Fresco
Araguaia
Chapada
TOCANTINS
Pto. Nacional
Balsas
das
Mangabeiras
884
Parnaguá
Remanso
Petrolina
Juàzeiro
Garanhuns
Palmeira dos Indios
Viçosa
Palmares
Barreiros
Xingu
Sta. Isabel do Morro
Peixe
Paranã
Campos Belos
Barra
Xique Xique
Jacobina
Queimadas
Itapicuru
Pedrinhas
Paulo Afonso
Arapiraca
Penedo
Maceió
SERGIPE
Serra Formosa
Manso (Mortes)
Tocantins
Paranã
Barreiras
Ibotirama
BAHIA
Brazilian
Highlands
Feira de Santana
Alagoinhas
Santo Amaro
Cachoeira
Serrinha
Aracaju
Estância
MATO GROSSO
Planalto do
Araguaia
Paranã
Posse
Serra Geral do Paranã
Serra Geral de Goiás
Nazaré
Salvador
Valença
Mato Grosso
Diamantino
915
Aruanã
Uruaçu
1006
MINAS GERAIS
Brumado
Vitória da Conquista
1500
Monte Azul
Jequié
Tpiau
Ilhéus
Itabuna
GOIÁS
Cáceres
Cuiabá
Aragarças
Goiás
DIST. FED.
Brasília
Formosa
Januária
Ibicaraí
Itapetinga
Canavieiras
Rondonópolis
Anápolis
Luziânia
Salto da Divisa
Cuiabá
Alto Araguaia
Goiânia
MATO GROSSO

18

4402

4235

1060

Equator

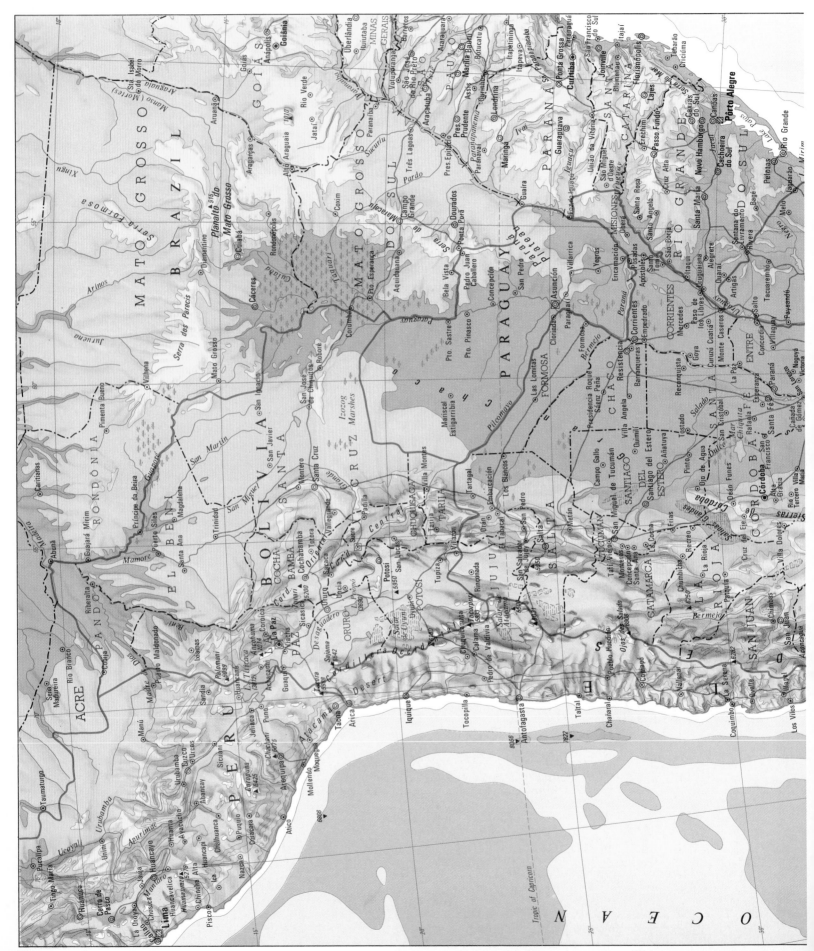

Southern South America

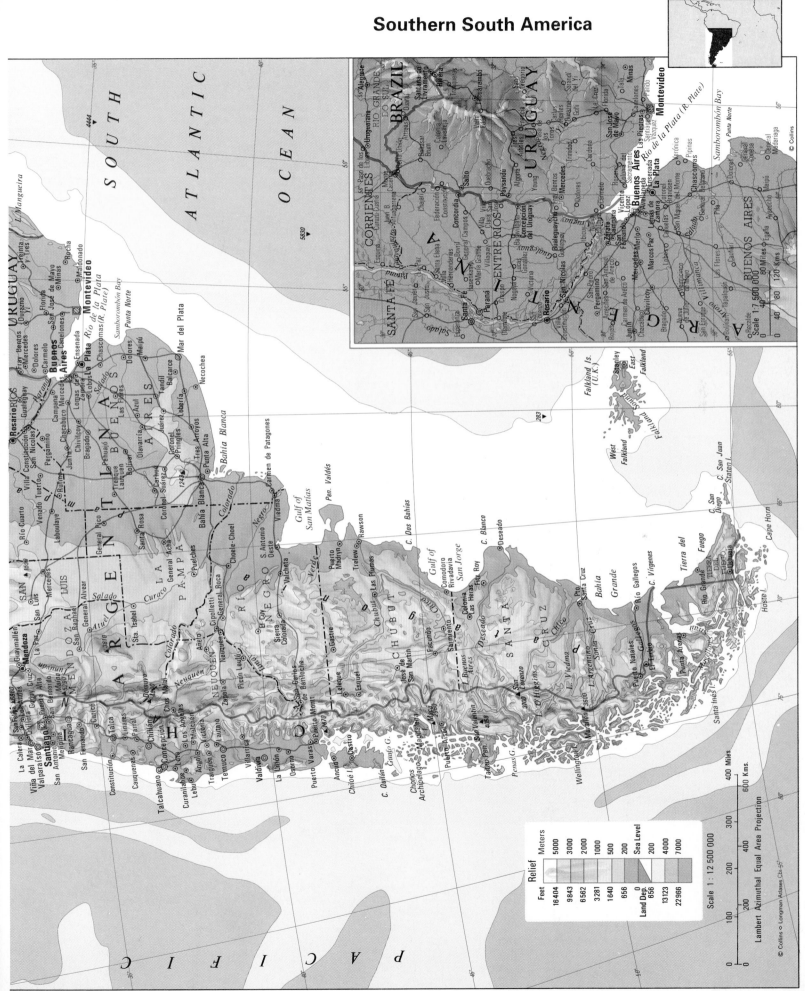

Regions (South America)

Eastern South America

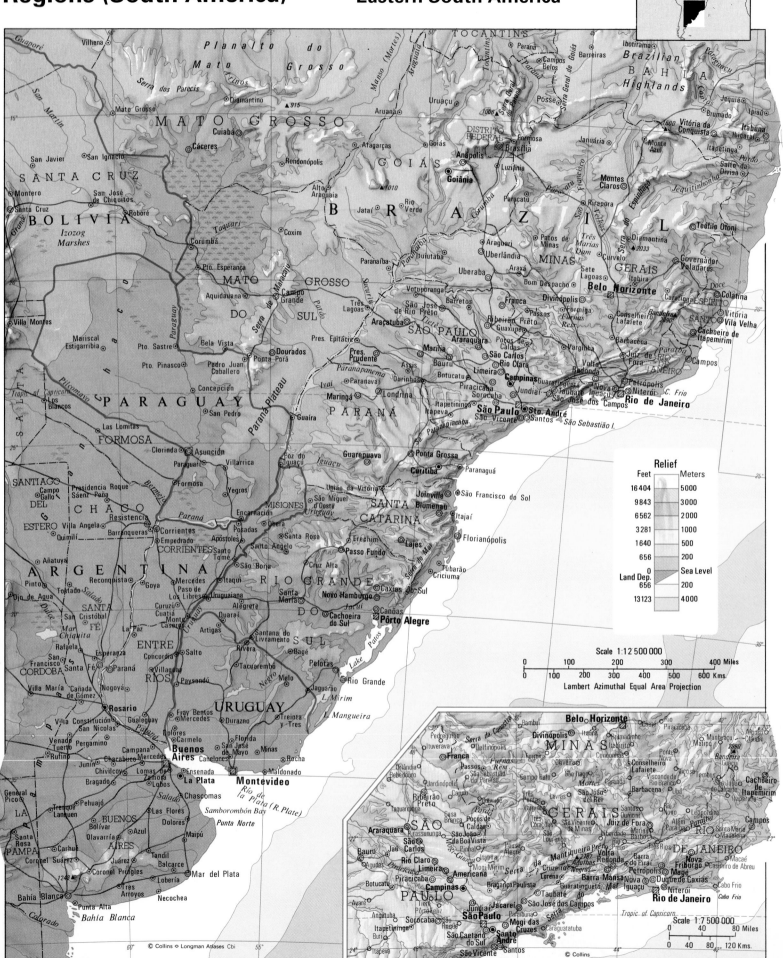

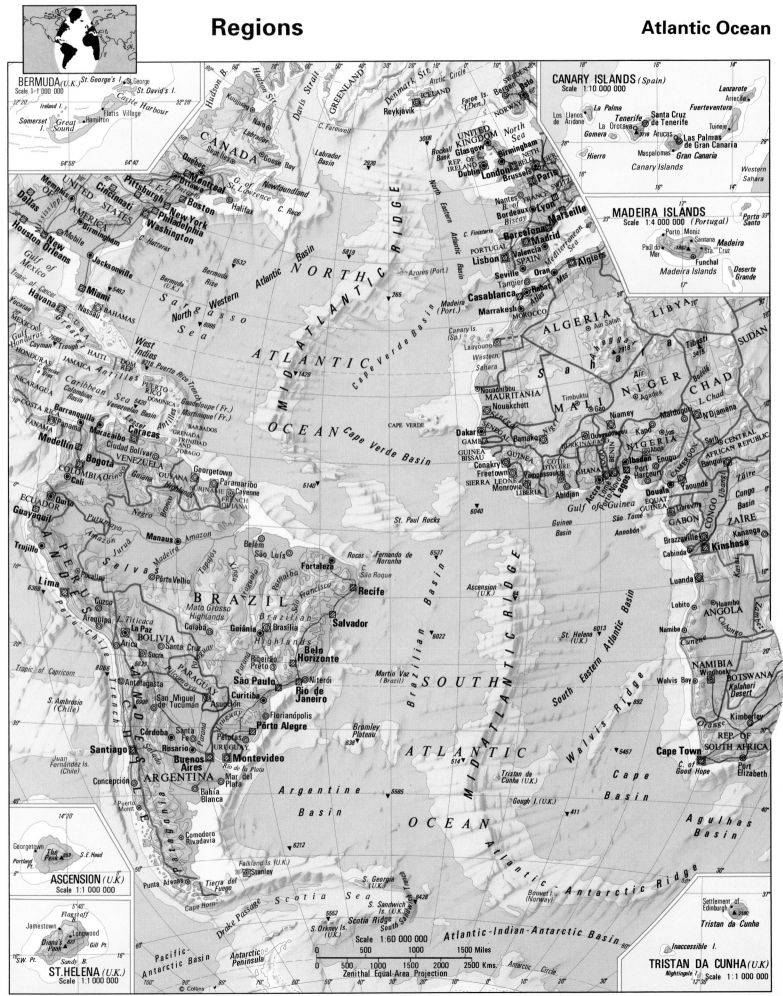

BERMUDA (U.K.)
Scale 1:1 000 000

CANARY ISLANDS (Spain)
Scale 1:10 000 000

MADEIRA ISLANDS
Scale 1:4 000 000 (Portugal)

ASCENSION (U.K.)
Scale 1:1 000 000

St.HELENA (U.K.)
Scale 1:1 000 000

Scale 1:60 000 000
0   500   1000   1500 Miles
0 500 1000 1500 2000 2500 Kms.
Zenithal Equal-Area Projection

TRISTAN DA CUNHA (U.K.)
Scale 1:1 000 000

© Collins

Regions (Europe)

Relief

Feet	Meters
16 404	5000
9843	3000
6562	2000
3281	1000
1640	500
656	200
0	Sea Level

Land Dep.

Feet	Meters
656	200
13 123	4000
22 966	7000

Scale 1:16 000 000

0 100 200 300 400 500 Miles

0 100 200 300 400 500 600 700 800 Kms.

Conic Projection

ARCTIC

North Cape
Varanger fjord
Vesterålen
Lofoten
Vestfjorden
Inari
Lappland
Kebnekaise 2123
Torne
Lule
Kemi
Storavan
Skellefte
Ume
Oulujärvi
Frohavet
Indals
Gulf of Bothnia
Näsijärvi
Saimaa
Storsjön
Ljusnan
Kallavesi
Dovrefjell
Glittertind 2470
Jotunheimen
Sognefjorden
Glåma
Klar
Dal
Åland Is.
Gulf of Finland
Hardangerfjorden
Orra
Oslofjorden
Mjøsa
Vänern
Mälaren
L. Peipus
Pskov
Lindesnes
Skagerrak
Vättern
Gotland
Öland
Sääremaa
Gulf of Riga
Limfjorden
Jutland
Kattegat
Lagan
Bornholm
Neman
Funen
Zealand
Kiel Canal
BALTIC SEA
Neman
Frisian Is.
Elbe
Oder
Vistula
Bug
IJsselmeer
Warta
NORTH EUR

NORWEGIAN SEA
Arctic Circle

Faroe Is.
Shetland Is.
NORTH SEA

Hebrides
Orkney Is.
Moray Firth
Ben Nevis 1343
Grampian Mountains
Firth of Forth
Malin Head
Southern Uplands
Galway Bay
The Pennines
Irish Sea
Shannon
Wicklow Mts.
Snowdon 1085
Cambrian Mts.
Cape Clear
Celtic Sea
St. George's Channel
Trent
The Wash
The Fens
Land's End
Severn
Thames
Isles of Scilly
English Channel
Channel Is.
Str. of Dover

ATLANTIC OCEAN

Stregennes
Vatnajökull
Snaefell
Surtsey
Mt. Hekla 1491

Brittany
Bay of Biscay
C. Finisterre
Loire
Seine
Marne
Seine
Vienne
Loire
Ardennes
Maas
Rhine
Harz Mts.
Weser
Spree
Ore Mts.
Sudeten Mts.
Silesian Plateau
Vistula
Mosel
Taunus
Bohemian Forest
Moselle
Morava
Gerlachovka 2663
Carpathian Mts.
Dnestr
Vosges
Black Forest
Danube
Inn
Tisza
Hungarian Plain

Cantabrian Mts.
Iberian Mts.
Douro
Ebro
Pyrénées
Pico de Aneto 3404
Gulf of Gascony
Garonne
Dordogne
Mont Dore 1886
Massif Central
Rhône
Cévennes
Durance
Jura Mts.
L. Geneva
Rhône
Mt. Blanc 4807
Mt. Rosa 4634
Gross Glockner 3798
Brenner Pass
ALPS
Dolomites
Adige
Po
Drava
Sava
Danube
Mures
Transylvanian Alps
Negoiu 2546
Iron Gate
Morava
Danube
Balkan

C. Roca
Douro
Tagus
Guadiana
C. St. Vincent
Iberian Peninsula
Sierra Morena
Guadalquivir
Gulf of Cadiz
Mulhacén 3482
Sierra Nevada
Str. of Gibraltar
C. Palos
Ebro Delta
Balearic Is.
C. Creus
Gulf of Lions
Minorca
Ibiza
Majorca
C. de la Nao
Corsica
Str. of Bonifacio
Sardinia
Ligurian Sea
G. of Genoa
Arno
Apennines
Mt. Corno 2914
ADRIATIC SEA
Dinaric Alps
Durmitor 2522
L. Shkoder
Rhodope Mts.
Strimon
Mesala 2925
Axios
Tyrrhenian Sea
Vesuvius 1277
G. of Taranto
Str. of Otranto
Corfu
Ionian Islands
Mt. Olympus 2911
Pindus Mts.
Mt. Athos 2033
Euboea
Aegean

Rif Mts.
Oum er Rbia
Toubkal 4165
High Atlas
Tell Atlas
Cheliff
Sebou
Chott ech Chergui
Saharan Atlas
Mejerda
C. Bon
MEDITERRANEAN
Stromboli 926
Sicily
Mt. Etna 3340
C. Spartivento
C. Passero
Ionian Sea
Killini 2376
Cyclades
C. Matapan
Crete

© Collins & Longman Atlases

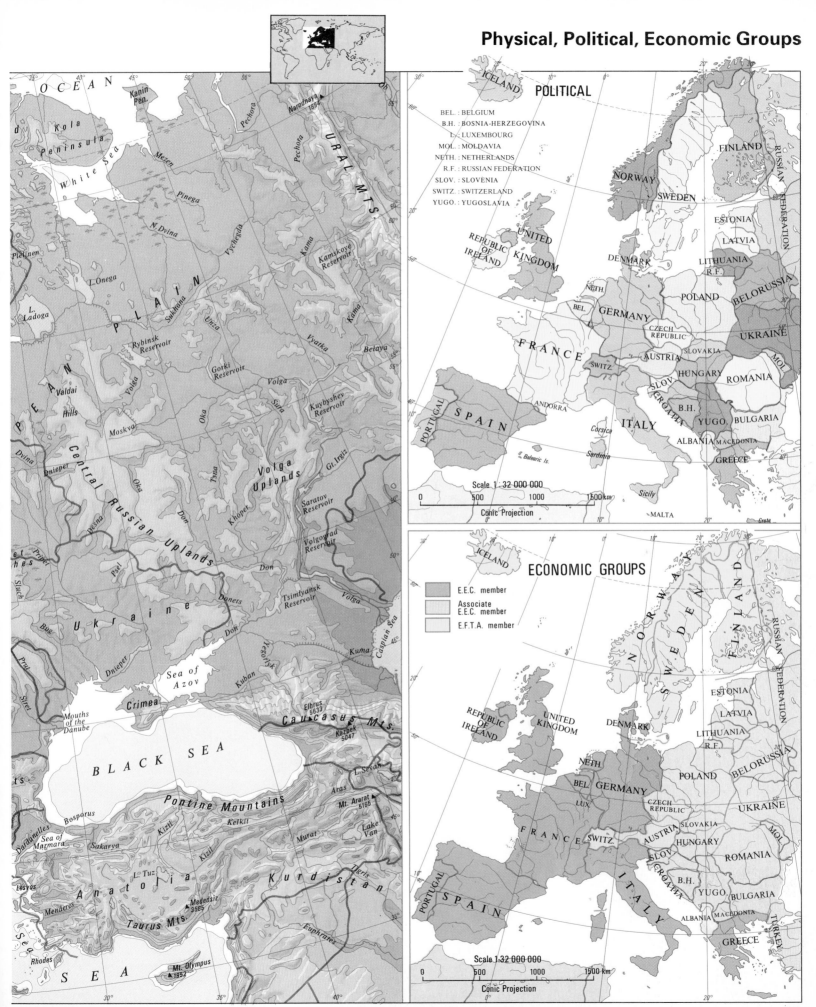

Physical, Political, Economic Groups

POLITICAL

BEL. : BELGIUM
B.H. : BOSNIA-HERZEGOVINA
L. : LUXEMBOURG
MOL. : MOLDAVIA
NETH. : NETHERLANDS
R.F. : RUSSIAN FEDERATION
SLOV. : SLOVENIA
SWITZ. : SWITZERLAND
YUGO. : YUGOSLAVIA

ICELAND

FINLAND

NORWAY
SWEDEN

RUSSIAN FEDERATION

REPUBLIC OF IRELAND
UNITED KINGDOM

ESTONIA
LATVIA
DENMARK
LITHUANIA
R.F.

NETH.
POLAND
BELORUSSIA
BEL.
GERMANY
L.
CZECH REPUBLIC
UKRAINE

FRANCE
SWITZ.
AUSTRIA
SLOVAKIA
HUNGARY
MOL.
SLOV.
ROMANIA
CROATIA

PORTUGAL
SPAIN
ANDORRA
B.H.
YUGO.
BULGARIA

Corsica
ITALY
ALBANIA
MACEDONIA
GREECE

Balearic Is.
Sardinia

Sicily
MALTA
Crete

Scale 1 : 32 000 000

0   500   1000   1500 km

Conic Projection

ECONOMIC GROUPS

ICELAND

[legend:]
E.E.C. member
Associate E.E.C. member
E.F.T.A. member

NORWAY
SWEDEN
FINLAND
RUSSIAN FEDERATION

REPUBLIC OF IRELAND
UNITED KINGDOM

DENMARK

ESTONIA
LATVIA
LITHUANIA
R.F.

NETH.
BEL.
GERMANY
LUX.
POLAND
BELORUSSIA
CZECH REPUBLIC
UKRAINE

FRANCE
SWITZ.
AUSTRIA
SLOVAKIA
HUNGARY
MOL.
SLOV.
ROMANIA
CROATIA

PORTUGAL
SPAIN
B.H.
YUGO.
BULGARIA
ITALY
ALBANIA
MACEDONIA
TURKEY
GREECE

Scale 1:32 000 000

0   500   1000   1500 km

Conic Projection

OCEAN

Kanin Pen.
Kola Peninsula
White Sea
Narodnaya 1894
Pechora
Mezen
Pinega
N. Dvina
Pechora
URAL MTS.

Pielinen
L. Onega
Vychegda
Kama
Kamskoye Reservoir

L. Ladoga
Sukhona
Uftza
Kama

PEAN PLAIN

Rybinsk Reservoir
Gorki Reservoir
Vyatka
Belaya

Valdai Hills
Volga
Oka
Volga
Kuybyshev Reservoir

Moskva
Moskva
Sura
Gt. Irgiz

Dvina
Vesna
Don
Khoper
Saratov Reservoir

Dnieper
Central Russian Uplands
Tsna
Volga Uplands

Pripet
Psel
Don
Volgograd Reservoir

Slach
Ukraine
Donets
Tsimlyansk Reservoir
Volga

Bug
Don
Volga

Prut
Siret
Dnieper
Kuban
Yegorlyk
Kuma
Caspian Sea

Mouths of the Danube
Crimea
Sea of Azov
Elbrus 5633
Kazbek 5047
Caucasus Mts.
Kuma

BLACK SEA
L. Sevan
Aras
Mt. Ararat 5165

Bosporus
Pontine Mountains
Kizil
Kelkit
Murat
Lake Van

Dardanelles
Sea of Marmara
Sakarya
Kizil
Tigris
Kurdistan

Lesvos
Menderes
Anatolia
L. Tuz
Medediz 3585

Taurus Mts.
Euphrates

Rhodes
Mt. Olympus 1952

SEA

Sea

CLIMATIC REGIONS

- Tropical / mid-latitude semi-arid
- Mediterranean
- Humid subtropical
- Maritime
- Continental warm summer
- Continental cool summer
- Mountain
- Subarctic
- Tundra

Scale 1:32 000 000

0   200   400   600 miles

0   400   800 km

NATURAL VEGETATION

- Grassland-short varieties
- Grassland-long varieties
- Mediterranean scrub & xerophytic woodland
- Mixed coniferous & deciduous forest
- Temperate deciduous forest
- Coniferous forest
- Mountain regions -little vegetation
- Tundra
- Ice cap

LAND USE

- Fishing
- Forestry
- Nomadic herding
- Commercial farming-grain dominant
- Commercial farming-crops and livestock
- Extensive livestock rearing
- Intensive livestock rearing
- Specialised - plantation and market gardening
- Major urban and industrial area
- Little or no economic activity

© Collins

POPULATION

Persons per sq. km	Persons per sq. mile
Over 100	Over 250
50-100	125-250
10-50	25-125
1-10	2-25
0-1	0-2

Cities

- ■ Over 5 000 000 population
- ● 1 000 000 - 5 000 000 population

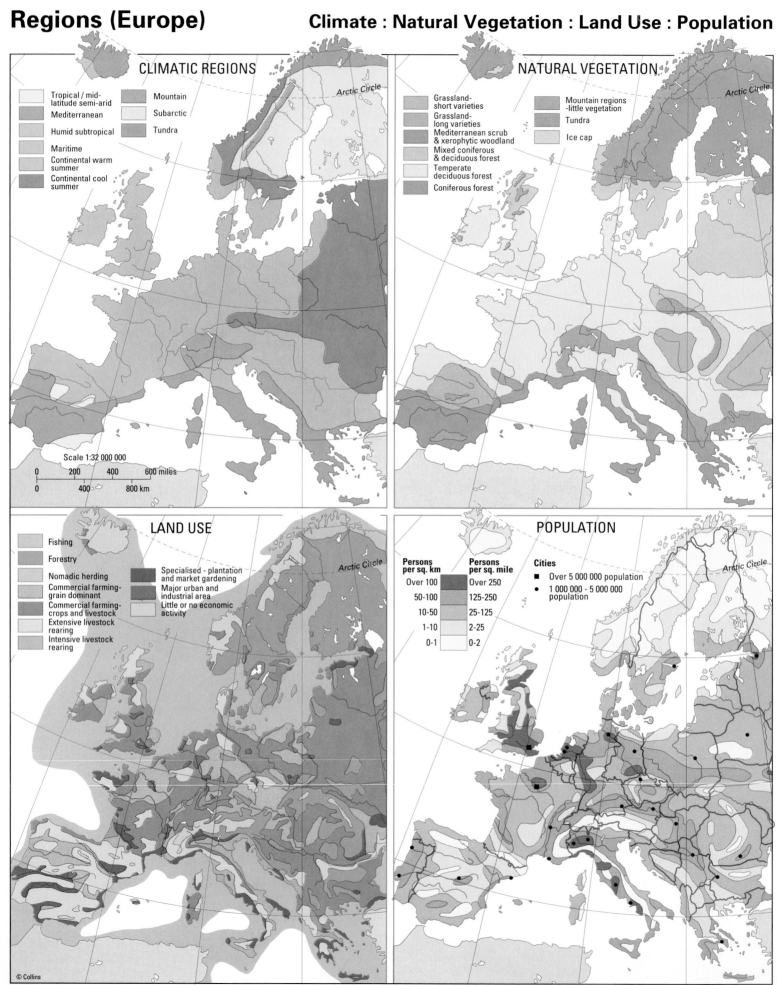

ORKNEY ISLANDS

Westray
Sanday
Stronsay
Stromness
Kirkwall
Hoy
South Ronaldsay
Pentland Firth
Thurso
Wick

SHETLAND ISLANDS

Unst
Yell
Fetlar
Foula
Lerwick
Fair Isle

ATLANTIC OCEAN

NORTH SEA

IRISH SEA

REPUBLIC OF IRELAND

NORTHERN IRELAND

SCOTLAND

UNITED KINGDOM

ENGLAND

WALES

ENGLISH Channel

FRANCE

Scale 1:4 000 000

0   20   40   60   80   100 Miles
0   40   80   120   160 km

Conic Projection

© Collins ○ Longman Atlases

Netherlands, Belgium and Luxembourg

Scale 1:2 000 000

0 10 20 30 40 50 60 Miles
0 20 40 60 80 Kms.
Conic Projection

Relief

Feet	Meters
16 404	5000
9843	3000
6562	2000
3281	1000
1640	500
656	200
0	Sea Level
Land Dep. 656	200
13123	4000
22966	7000

© Collins ♦ Longman Atlases

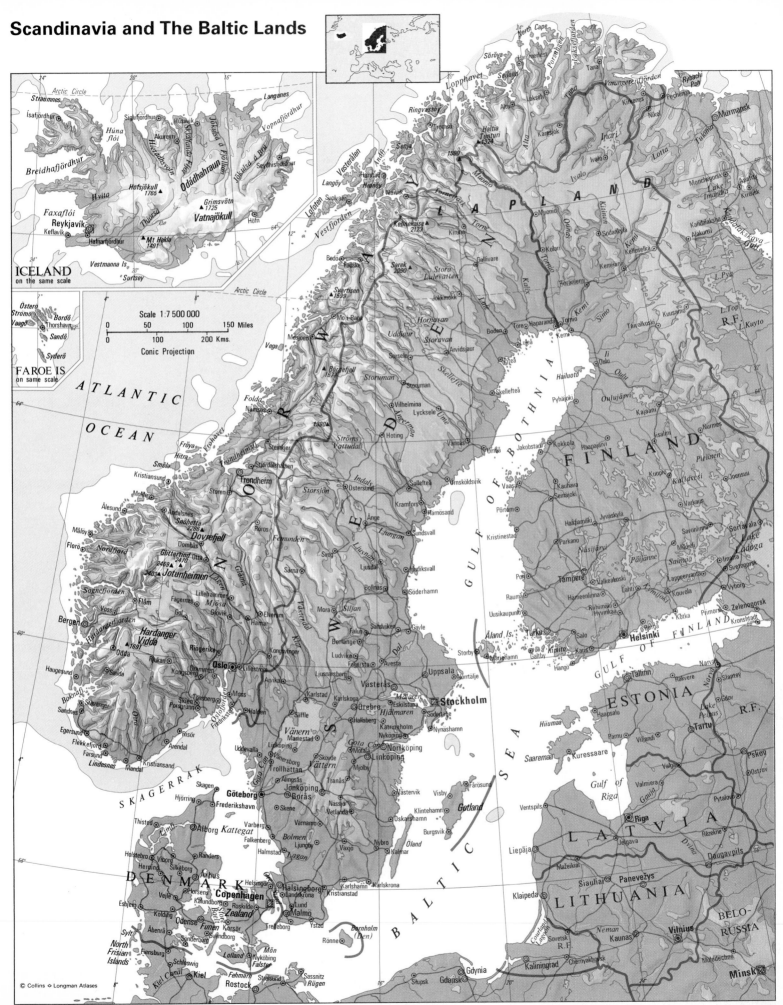

Scandinavia and The Baltic Lands

ICELAND on the same scale

FAROE IS on same scale

Scale 1:7 500 000
0 50 100 150 Miles
0 100 200 Kms.
Conic Projection

ATLANTIC OCEAN

N O R W A Y

S W E D E N

L A P L A N D

FINLAND

GULF OF BOTHNIA

GULF OF FINLAND

ESTONIA

LATVIA

LITHUANIA

BALTIC SEA

DENMARK

SKAGERRAK

Kattegat

BELO-RUSSIA

© Collins ⬦ Longman Atlases

81

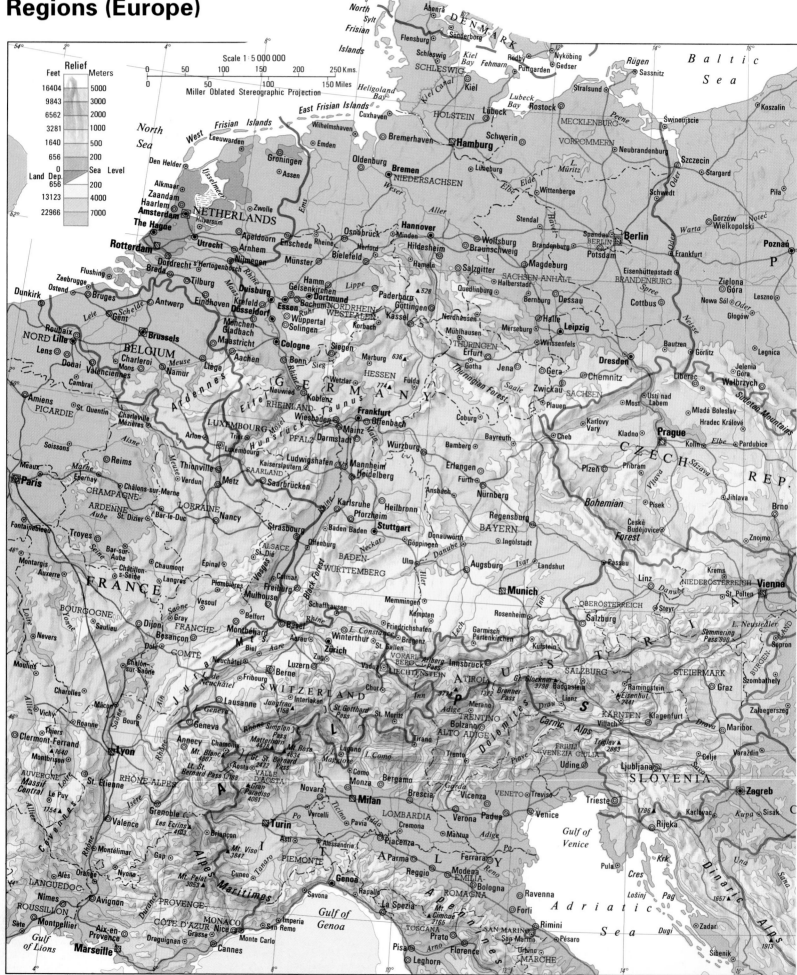

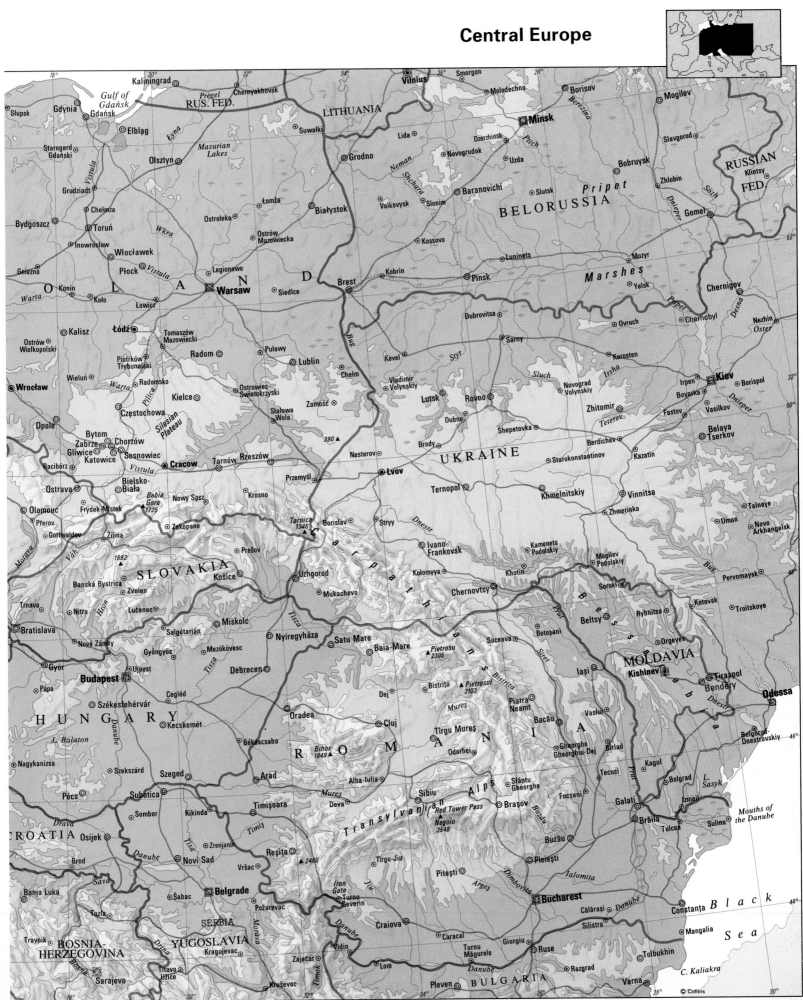

Regions (Europe)

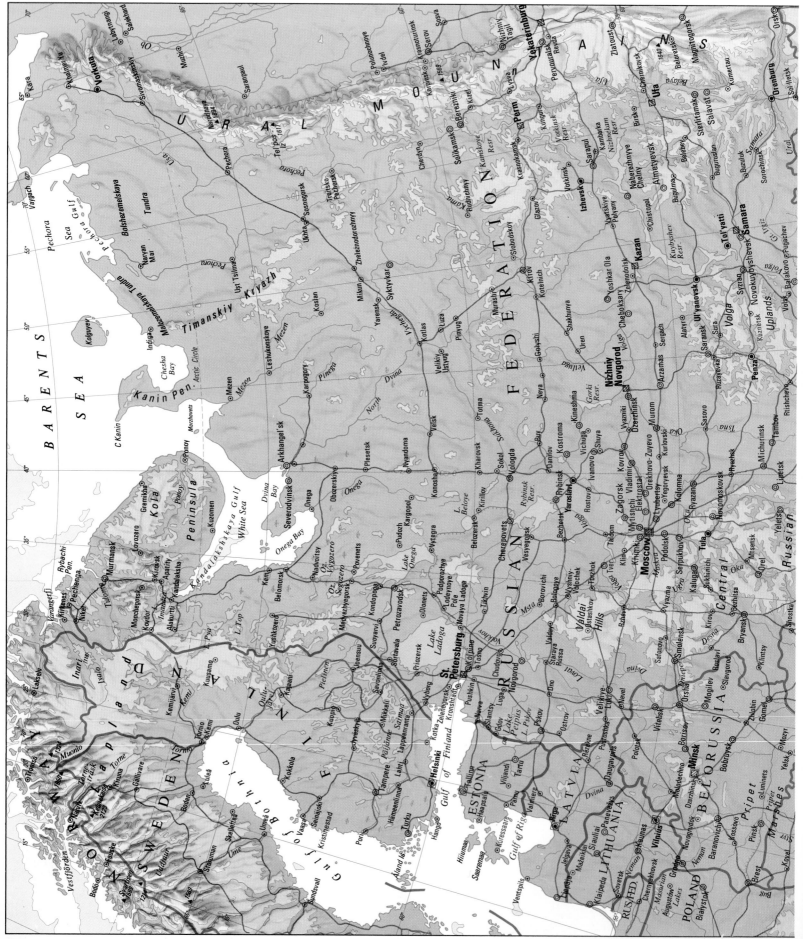

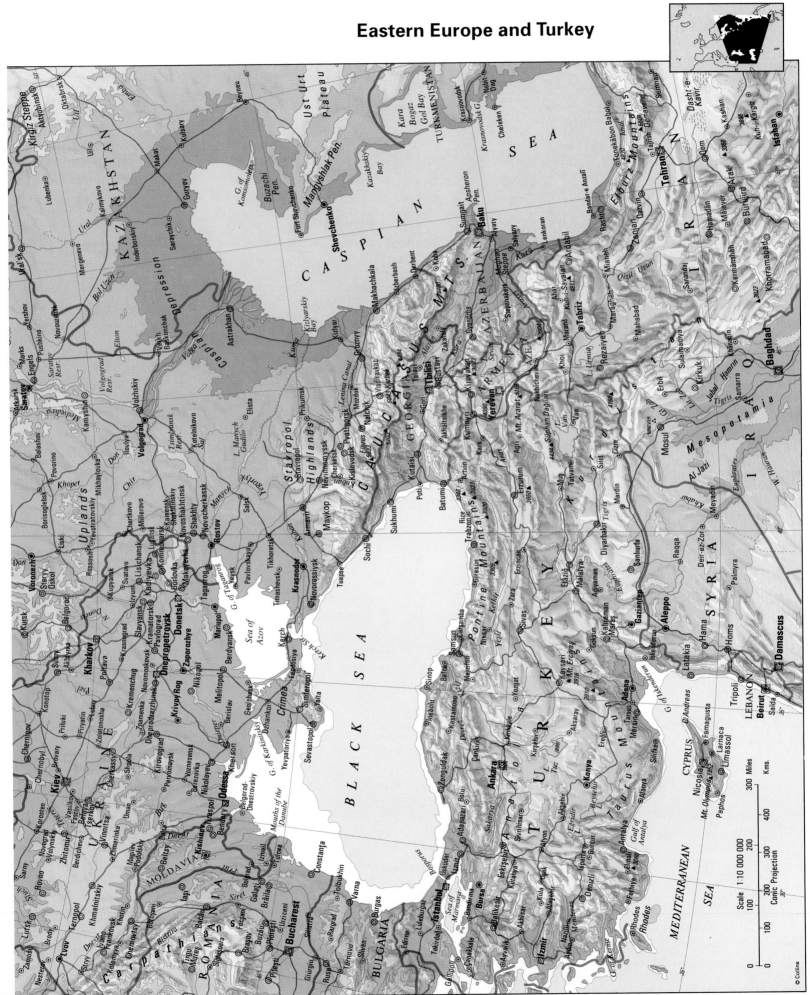

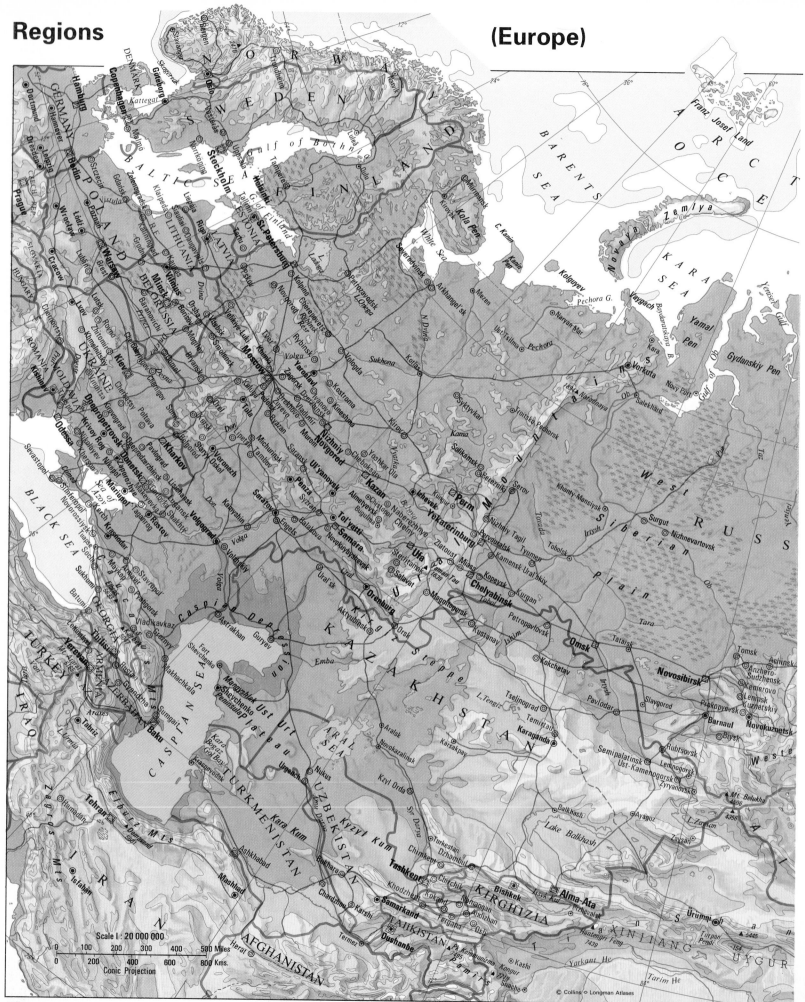

Scale 1 : 20 000 000

| 0 | 100 | 200 | 300 | 400 | 500 Miles |

| 0 | 200 | 400 | 600 | 800 Kms. |

Conic Projection

© Collins ○ Longman Atlases

Northern Eurasia
(Former Soviet Union)

Relief

Feet	Meters
16404	5000
9843	3000
6562	2000
3281	1000
1640	500
656	200
0	Sea Level

Land Dep

656	200
13123	4000
22966	7000

ARCTIC OCEAN

Komsomolets
October Revolution
Bolshevik
Severnaya Zemlya
C. Chelyuskin

New Siberian Is
Novaya Siberia
Kotelnyy
Bolshoi Lyakhovskiy
EAST SIBERIAN SEA
Wrangel I.
De Long Str.
Bering Str.
Chuckchee Pen.
Gulf of Anadyr

LAPTEV SEA
Taymyr Peninsula
Byrranga Mts.
Pyasina
Upper Taymyr
L.Taymyr
Nordvik
Khatangskiy G.
Olenekskiy Gulf
G. of Tona
Tiksi
Kazachye
Yana
Srednekolymskaya
Kolyma
Omolon
Anadyr
Koryak Range
Kamchatka Peninsula
Ust Kamchatsk
Kyluchevskaya 4950

Dudinka
Norilsk
Kamen 2037
Putoran Mts
Khatanga
Anabar
Bulun
Lena
Verkhoyansk
Indigirka
Verkhoyansk Range
Mt Chen 2882
Mt Pobeda 3147
Cherskogo Range
Oymyakon
Magadan
Okhotsk
Gizhiga
G. of Penzina
Palana
Petropavlovsk Kamchatskiy

Yenisey
Yattsevo
Central Siberian Plateau
Tura
Markha
Vilyuy
Vilyuysk
Yakutsk
Aldan
Angu
Amga
Ust Maya
Dzhugdzhur Range
Topko 1906
Ayan
SEA OF OKHOTSK

Stony Tunguska
Lower Tunguska
Yeniseysk
Angara
Chuna
Olekminsk
Lena
Aldan
Olekma
Skalingy 2482
Stanovoy Range
Shantar Is
Okha
Aleksandrovsk
Sakhalin

RUSSIAN FEDERATION

Krasnoyarsk
Kansk
Taysht
Bratsk
Bratsk Resr
Nizhneudinsk
Tulun
Abakan
Kirensk
Ust Kut
Vitim
Shilke
Yablonovoy Range
Skovorodina
Zeya
Svobodnyy
Amur
Komsomolsk-na-Amur
Sovetskaya Gavan
Uglegorsk
Yuzhno Sakhalinsk
Gulf of Tartary
La Perouse Str.
Kuril Islands

Cheremkhovo
Usolye Sibirskoye
Angarsk
Irkutsk
L. Baikal
Ulan Ude
Chita
Petrovsk Zabaykal'skiy
Da Hinggan Ling
Blagoveshchensk
Birobidzhan
Khabarovsk
Sikhote-Alin Range
Wakkanai
HOKKAIDO
Sapporo
Hakodate

Eastern Sayan
Kyzyl
Tannu Ola Ra.
Munku Sardyk 3492
Khöbsögöl Dalai
Ubsa Nur

MONGOLIA
Ulan Bator
Undur Khan
Ulan Bator

Altai
Gobi
Baotou
Hohhot
Zhangjiakou
Beijing
INNER MONGOLIA (NEI MONGGOL)

CHINA
Harbin
Songhua Jiang
Mudanjiang
Ussuriysk
Vladivostok
Nakhodka
Changchun
Jilin
Fushun
Shenyang
Anshan
NORTH KOREA
Pyongyang
SOUTH KOREA
Seoul
Korea Bay
Liaodong Bay

SEA OF JAPAN

JAPAN
HONSHU
Niigata
Tokyo
Yokohama
Fujiyama 3776
Nagoya
Kyoto
Kobe
Osaka
Hachinohe

BERING SEA

Regions (Asia)

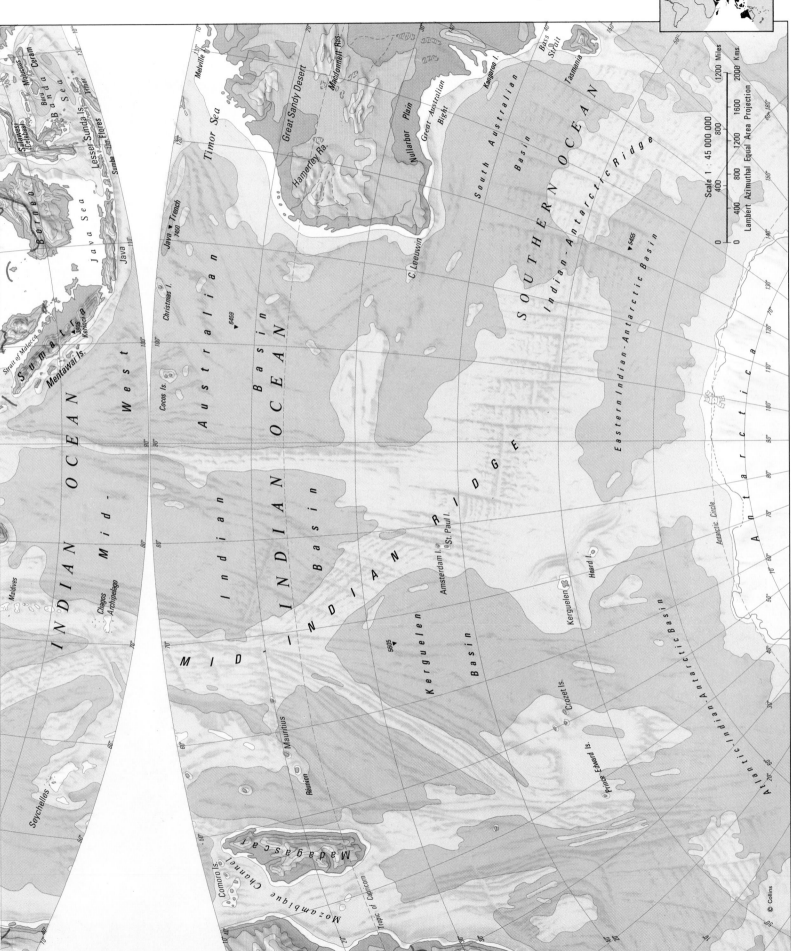

Java Trench 7450

6459

Scale 1 : 45 000 000

0 400 800 1200 Miles

0 400 800 1200 1600 2000 Kms.

Lambert Azimuthal Equal Area Projection

SOUTHERN OCEAN

Indian-Antarctic Ridge

5455

Eastern Indian-Antarctic Basin

Great Sandy Desert

Macdonnell Ras.

Hamersley Ra.

Nullarbor Plain

Great Australian Bight

South Australian Basin

Kangaroo I.

Bass Strait

Tasmania

C. Leeuwin

Timor Sea

Melville I.

INDIAN OCEAN Mid - West

Borneo

Sulawesi (Celebes)

Moluccas

Ceram

Buru

Banda Sea

Timor

Lesser Sunda Is.

Flores

Sumba

Java Sea

Java

Sumatra

3806 Kerinci

Strait of Malacca

Mentawai Is.

Christmas I.

Cocos Is.

Australian Basin

I N D I A N   O C E A N   Basin

Indian Basin

MID - INDIAN Basin

MID - INDIAN RIDGE

Amsterdam I.

St. Paul I.

Maldives

Chagos Archipelago

Seychelles

Mauritius

Réunion

Comoro Is.

Mozambique Channel

Madagascar

Tropic of Capricorn

Kerguelen Basin

5605

Kerguelen

Heard I.

Crozet Is.

Prince Edward Is.

Atlantic-Indian-Antarctic Basin

Antarctic Circle

A n t a r c t i c a

© Collins

Regions (Asia)

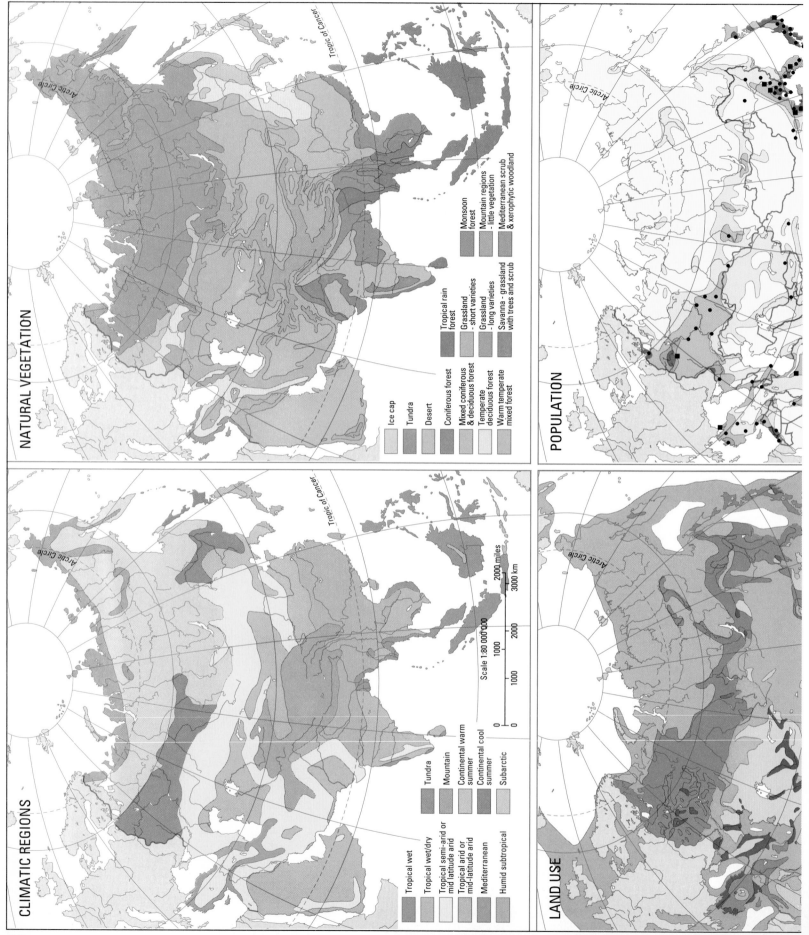

NATURAL VEGETATION

Ice cap
Tundra
Desert
Coniferous forest
Mixed coniferous & deciduous forest
Temperate deciduous forest
Warm temperate mixed forest

Tropical rain forest
Grassland - short varieties
Grassland - long varieties
Savanna - grassland with trees and scrub

Monsoon forest
Mountain regions - little vegetation
Mediterranean scrub & xerophytic woodland

POPULATION

CLIMATIC REGIONS

Tropical wet
Tropical wet/dry
Tropical semi-arid or mid latitude arid
Tropical arid or mid-latitude arid
Mediterranean
Humid subtropical

Tundra
Mountain
Continental warm summer
Continental cool summer
Subarctic

Scale 1:80 000 000

0   1000   2000 miles

0   1000   2000   3000 km

LAND USE

92

© Collins

POLITICAL

JAPAN
N. KOREA
S. KOREA
TAIWAN
Tropic of Cancer
HONG KONG
PHILIPPINES
VIETNAM
LAOS
MYANMAR (BURMA)
THAILAND
CAMBODIA
BRUNEI
MALAYSIA
SINGAPORE
I N D O N E S I A

Arctic Circle

R U S S I A N   F E D E R A T I O N

MONGOLIA

C H I N A

BHUTAN
NEPAL
BANGLADESH
KAZAKHSTAN
UZBEKISTAN
KYRGHIZIA
TAJIKISTAN
TURKMENISTAN
AFGHANISTAN
JAMMU AND KASHMIR
PAKISTAN
I N D I A
SRI LANKA

IRAN
GEORGIA
AR.
AZ.
OMAN
KUWAIT
IRAQ
SYRIA
JORDAN
TURKEY
CYPRUS
L.
ISRAEL
B.
Q.
U.A.E.
SAUDI ARABIA
YEMEN

AR. : ARMENIA
AZ. : AZERBAIJAN
B. : BAHRAIN
L. : LEBANON
Q. : QATAR
U.A.E. : UNITED ARAB EMIRATES

Persons per sq. km
	Persons per sq. mile
Over 100	Over 250
50-100	125-250
10-50	25-125
1-10	2-25
0-1	0-2

Cities
■ Over 5 000 000 population
● 1 000 000 - 5 000 000 population

Tropic of Cancer

Fishing

Forestry

Shifting and marginal cultivation

Subsistence farming - crops and livestock

Nomadic herding

Commercial farming - grain dominant

Commercial farming - crops and livestock

Specialised - plantation and market gardening

Extensive livestock rearing

Intensive livestock rearing

Major urban and industrial area

Subsistence - crops dominant

Little or no economic activity

SOUTHEAST ASIA MONSOON - WINTER AND SUMMER

WINTER MONSOON

Pressure

HIGH			LOW	
in	mb		in	mb
30.2	1026		29.8	1011
30.1	1020		29.7	1008
29.9	1014			

Equator
Tropic of Cancer

30.2
30.1
29.9
29.9
29.8
29.7

SUMMER MONSOON

Pressure

HIGH			LOW		
in	mb		in	mb	
29.9	1014		29.8	1011	
29.8	1011		29.7	1008	
			29.5	1002	
			29.4	998	

Isobars in inches reduced to sea level
Wind direction

Equator
Tropic of Cancer

29.7
29.5
29.4

93

Regions (Asia)

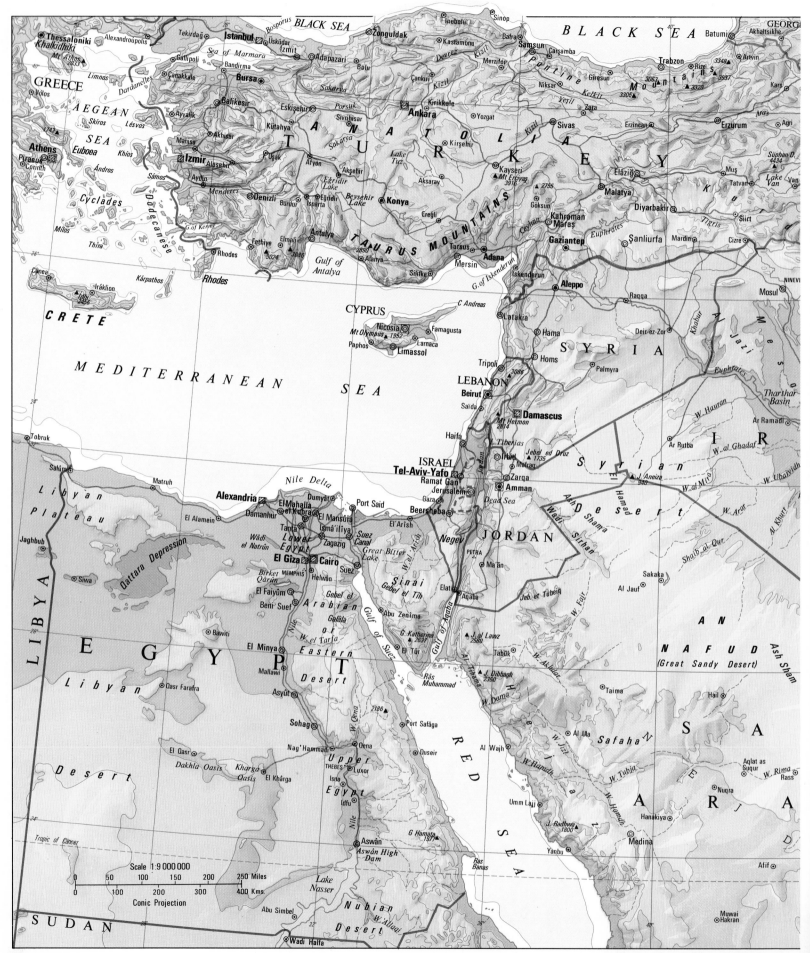

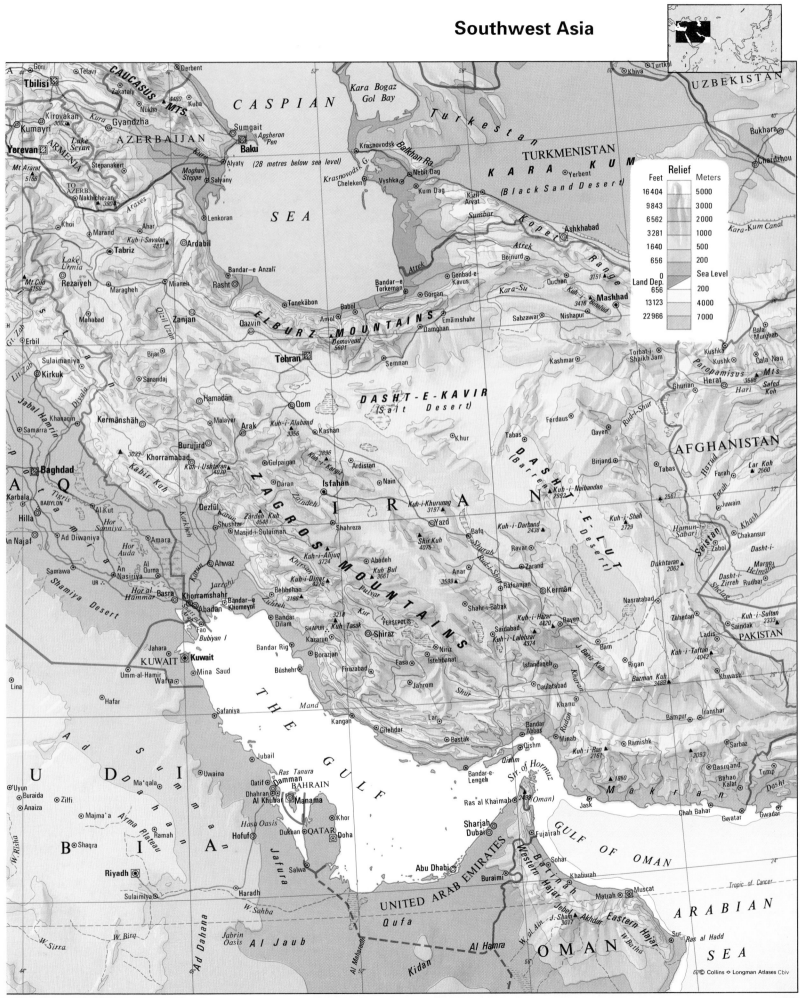

Regions (Asia)

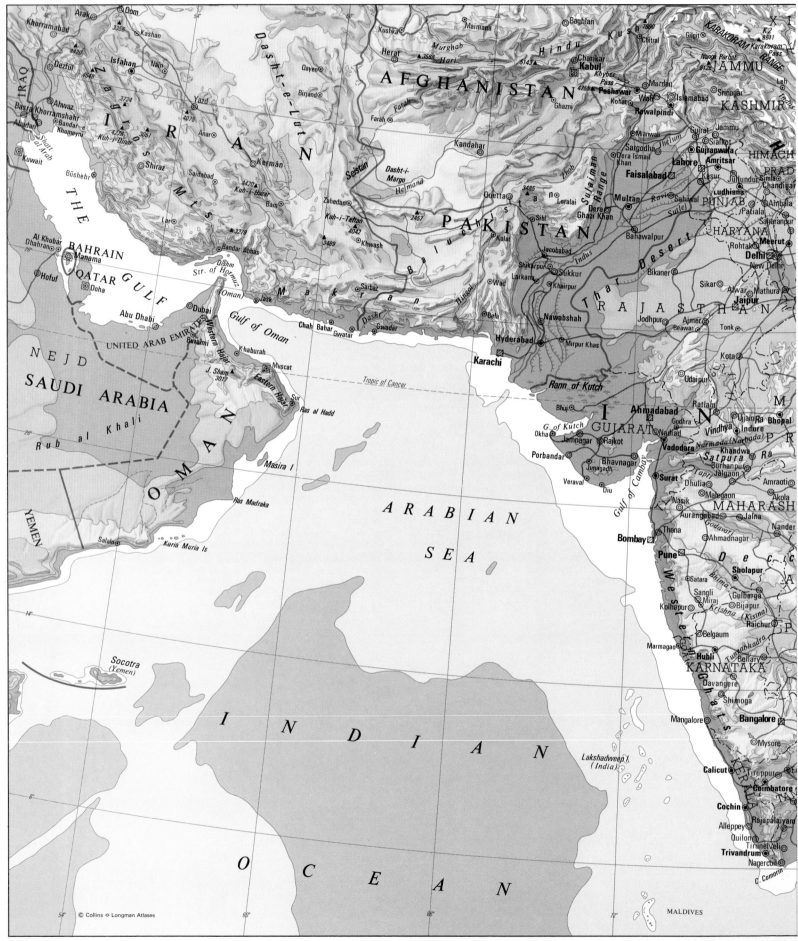

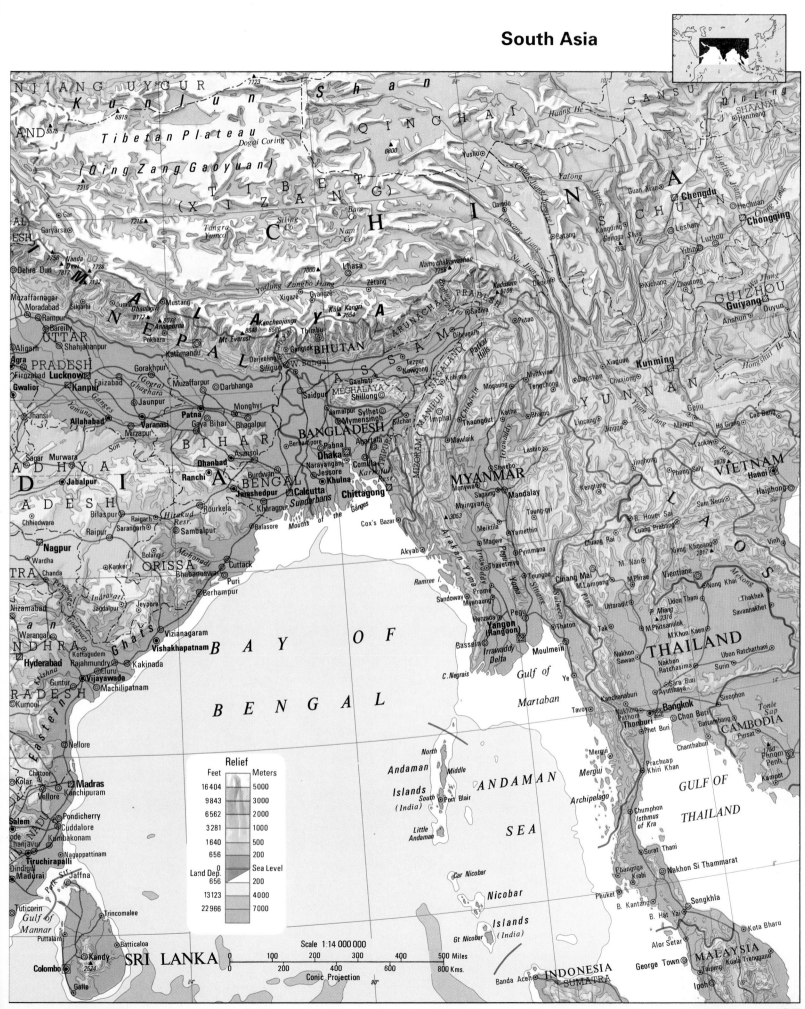

Relief

Feet		Meters
16 404		5000
9843		3000
6562		2000
3281		1000
1640		500
656		200
0		Sea Level
Land Dep.		200
656		4000
13 123		7000
22 966		7000

Scale 1:14 000 000

0   100   200   300   400   500 Miles

0   200   400   600   800 Kms.

Conic Projection

Regions (Asia)

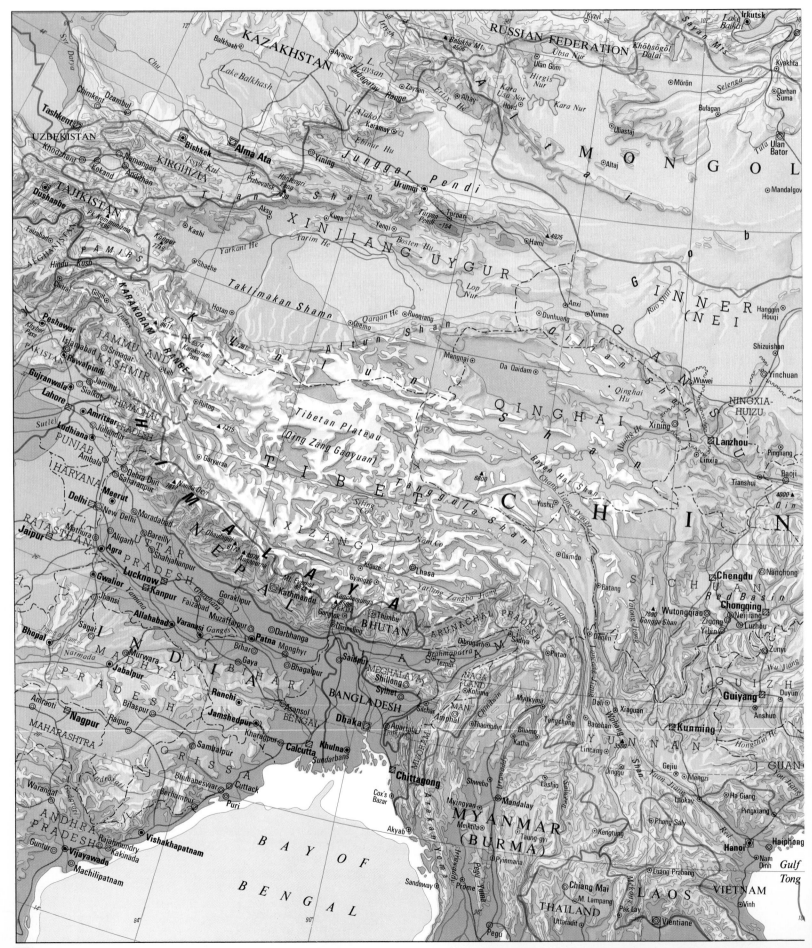

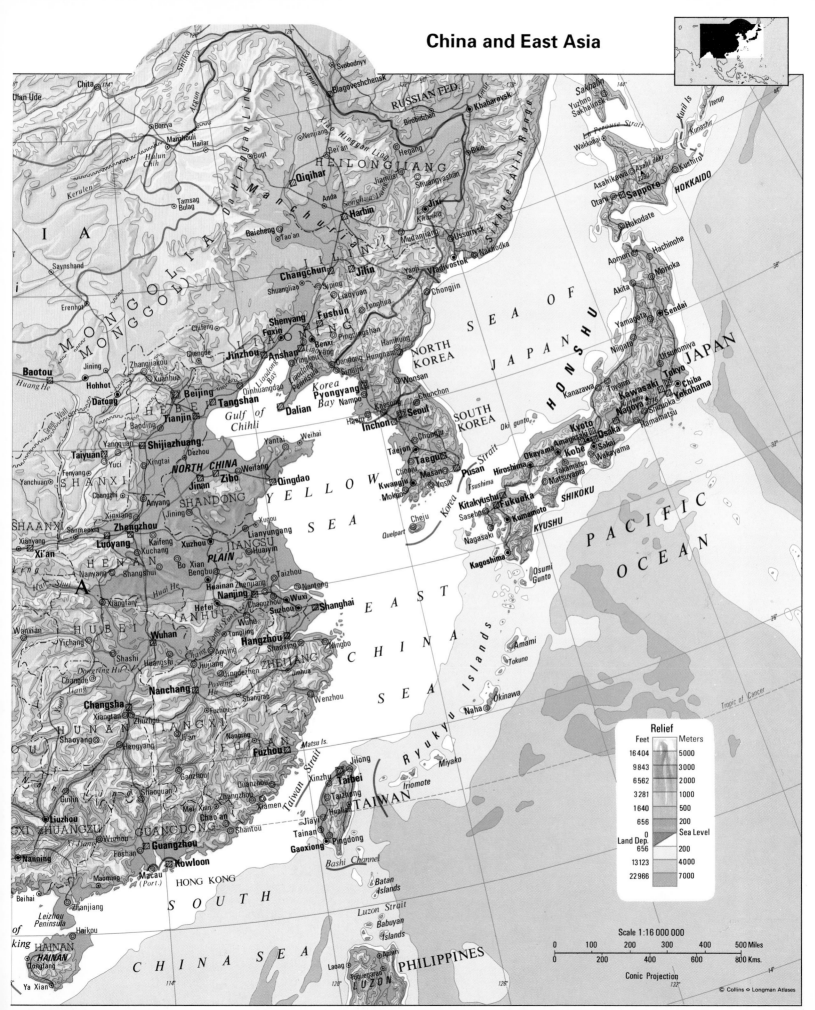

China and East Asia

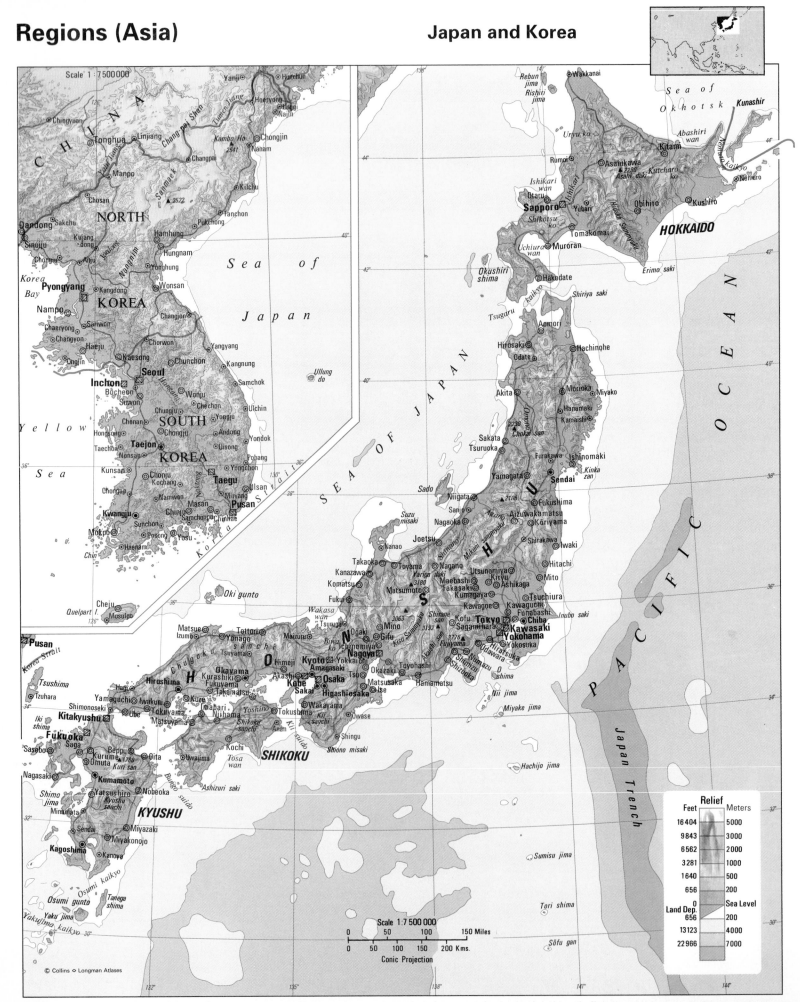

Scale 1 : 7 500 000

Relief

Feet		Meters
16 404		5000
9843		3000
6562		2000
3281		1000
1640		500
656		200
0		Sea Level
Land Dep.		
656		200
13 123		4000
22 966		7000

Scale 1:7 500 000

0   50   100   150 Miles

0   50   100   150   200 Kms.

Conic Projection

© Collins ◇ Longman Atlases

PHILIPPINE

SEA

SOUTH

CHINA

SEA

LUZON

C. Bojeador
Laoag
San Nicolas
Vigan
Mt. Sicapoo 2352
Tuguegarao
Bontoc
Baguio
San Fernando
Lingayen Gulf
C. Bolinao
Lingayen
Dagupan
San Carlos
Iba
Zambales Mts.
Tarlac
Cabanatuan
Angeles
Olongapo
Balanga
Caloocan
Manila
Cavite
Pasay
Laguna de Bay
Nasugbu
Tagaytay City
Balayan
Lemery
Batangas
Lubang I.
Lubang Islands
C. Calavite
Mamburao
Mt. Halcon 2582
Calapan
Mindoro 2498
Pinamalayan
Bongabong
Aparri
Escarpada Pt.
San Vicente
Palanan Pt.
2216
Ilagan
Solano
Bayombong
San Jose
Casiguran
C. San Ildefonso
Dingalan Bay
Polillo I.
Polillo Islands
Quezon City
Lamon Bay
Paete
Lucban
San Pablo
Lipa
Lucena
Tayabas Bay
Marinduque I.
Calagua Is.
Labo
Daet
Naga
Iriga
Lagonoy Gulf
Vitac
Tabaco 2462
Legaspi
Donsol
Burias I.
Sorsogon
Bulan
Catanduanes I.

Cordillera Central
Cagayan
Sierra Madre
Polillo Str.
Mompog Pass
Bondoc Pen.
Ragay Gulf
Ticao I.
Bernardino Str.

Mindoro Strait
Tablas Str.
San Jose
Looc
Tablas I.
Romblon I.
Sibuyan I.
Masbate
Masbate
Irosin
Laoang
Catarman
Samar
Samar Sea
Calbayong
Oras
Catbalogan
Borongan

PHILIPPINES

Busuanga I.
Calamian Group
Culion I.
Coron I.
Linapacan Str.
Linapacan I.
Semirara Islands
Cuyo Islands
Kalibo
Roxas
Visayan Sea
Bulalaqui Pt.
Bantayan I.
Bogo
Carigara
Tacloban
Palo
Leyte
Ormoc
Leyte Gulf
Baybay
Guiuan
Homonhon I.

C. Ross
Taytay Bay
Taytay
Panay
Pototan
Alimodian
Iloilo
San Jose de Buenavista
Guimaras I.
Bayo Pt.
Panay Gulf
Cadiz
Silay
Guimaras Str.
Toboso
Bacolod
2460
Calamba
Binalbagan
Negros
Tanjay
Bayawan
Dumaguete
Carcar
Cebu
Cebu
Camotes Is.
Camotes Sea
Bohol
Tagbilaran
Tañon Str.
Maasin
Canigao Channel
Surigao
Siargao I.
Bucas Grande I.
Dinagat I.
Cape Johnson Depth 10497
Siquijor I.
Camiguin I.
Mambajao
Tandag

Honda Bay
Puerto Princesa
Palawan
Eran Bay
Island Bay
Mt. Mantalingajan 2085
Brooke's Point
Cagayan Dondonay I. Islands
Mindanao Sea
Diuata Mts.
Butuan
Bakulin Pt.

SULU
SEA

C. Buliluyan
Bugsuk I.
Balabac I.
C. Melville
Balabac Strait
Bancoran I.
San Miguel Is.
P. Banggi
Keenapusan I.
Cagayan Sulu I.
P. Jambongan
MALAYSIA
SABAH
Sandakan

Sulu Archipelago
Pangutaran Group
Pangutaran I.
Jolo
Jolo I.
Zamboanga
Pilas Group
Basilan Str.
Basilan
Basilan I.

Dapitan
Dipolog
Iligan Bay
Cagayan de Oro
2566
2425
Iligan
Malaybalay
Ozamiz
2895
Sindangan
Marawi
Lake Lanao
Liloy
Pagadian
Zamboanga Pen.
Sibuguey Bay
MINDANAO
Pulangi
Agusan
2815
Mt. Piapayungan
Cotabato
Datu Piang
Midsayap
Agusan
Tagum
Davao
2954
Mt. Apo
Samal I.
Digos
Davao Gulf
Lais
Lebak
Moro Gulf
Illana Bay
Olutanga I.
Cateel Bay
Baganga
Mati
Tugubun Pt.
Cape San Augustin
General Santos
Tuna Pt.

CELEBES SEA

Philippine Trench

Scale 1 : 6 000 000
0   50   100   150 Miles
0   50   100   150   200 Kms.
Stereographic Projection

Relief
Feet | Meters
16 404 | 5000
9843 | 3000
6562 | 2000
3281 | 1000
1640 | 500
656 | 200
0 | Sea Level
Land Dep.
656 | 200
13 123 | 4000
22 966 | 7000

© Collins ◇ Longman Atlases

Regions (Asia)

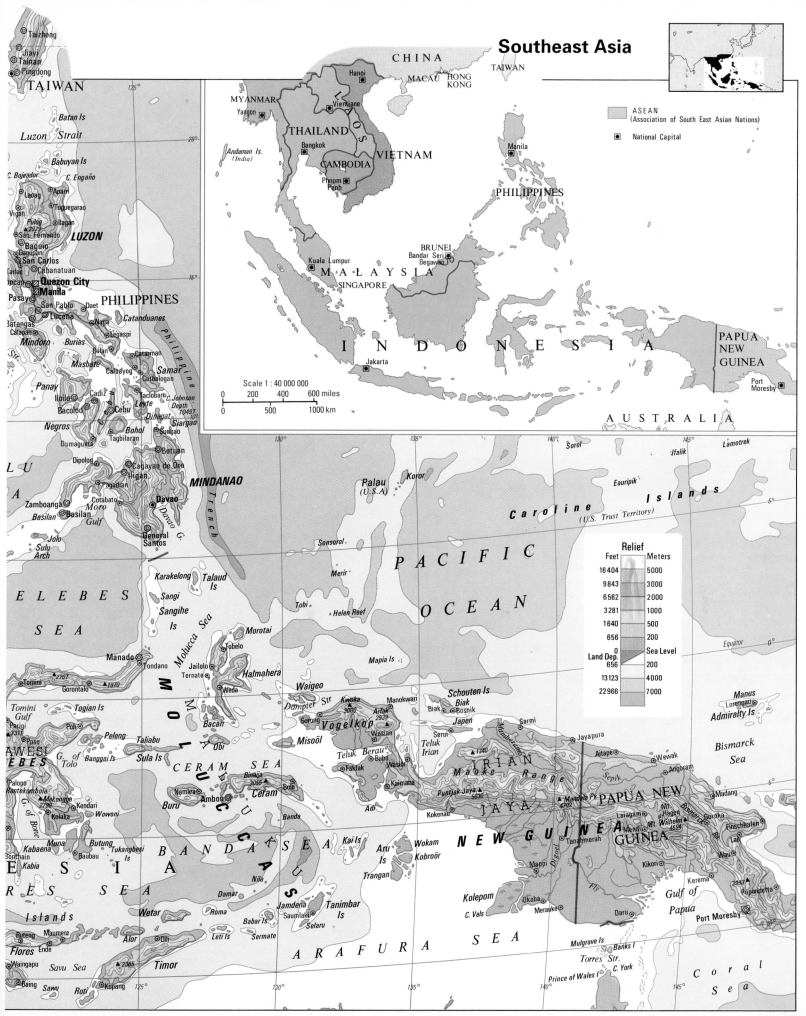

Southeast Asia

ASEAN
(Association of South East Asian Nations)

☐ National Capital

Scale 1 : 40 000 000

0   200   400   600 miles

0   500   1000 km

Relief

Feet	Meters
16 404	5000
9843	3000
6562	2000
3281	1000
1640	500
656	200
0	Sea Level
Land Dep.	
656	200
13 123	4000
22 966	7000

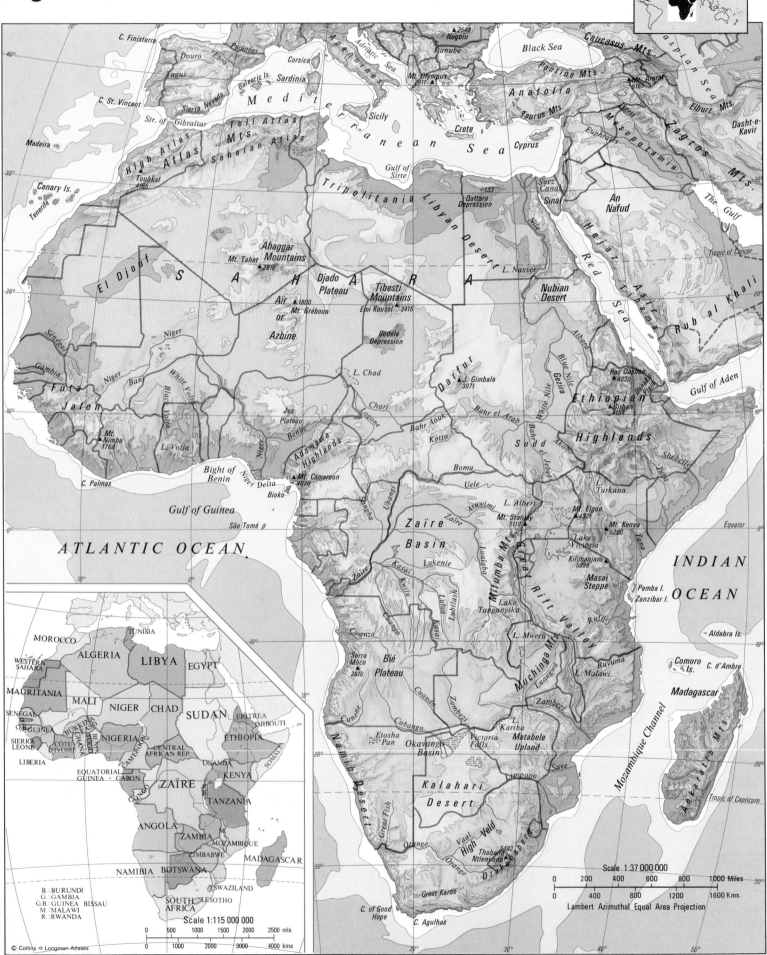

Regions (Africa) — Physical and Political

C. Finisterre · Pyrenees · Negoiu 2548 · Danube · Black Sea · Caucasus Mts. · Caspian Sea
Douro · Ebro · Apennines · Adriatic Sea · Pontine Mts. · Elburz Mts.
Tagus · Corsica · Mt. Olympus 2917 · Anatolia · Mt. Ararat 5165 · Dasht-e-Kavir
C. St. Vincent · Sierra Nevada · Balearic Is. · Sardinia · Taurus Mts. · Mesopotamia · Zagros Mts.
Madeira · Str. of Gibraltar · Toll Atlas Mts. · Sicily · Crete · Cyprus · Herss · Euphrates · The Gulf
Canary Is. · High Atlas · Atlas Mts. · Saharan Atlas · Mediterranean Sea · Gulf of Sirte · Tripolitania · Qattara Depression -133 · Suez Canal · Sinai · An Nafud
Tenerife · Toubkal 4165

S A H A R A
El Djouf · Mt. Tahat 2918 · Ahaggar Mountains · Djado Plateau · Tibesti Mountains · Emi Koussi 3415 · Nubian Desert · Red Sea · Rub al Khali
Aïr or Azbine · Mt. Gréboun 1800 · Bodélé Depression · L. Nasser
Senegal · Niger · White Volta · L. Chad · Darfur · J. Gimbala 3071 · Blue Nile · Gezira · Ras Dashan 4620 · Danakil Plain · Gulf of Aden
Gambia · Niger · Bani · Black Volta · Chari · Logone · Bahr Aouk · Kotto · Bahr el Arab · White Nile · Bahr el Jebel · Sudd · Akobo · Ethiopian Highlands · Birhan 4154 · Shebelle
Futa Jalon · Jos Plateau · Benue · Bomu · Uele · Sobat
Mt. Nimba 1768 · L. Volta · Niger · Adamawa Highlands · Mt. Cameroon 4070 · Ubangi · Aruwimi · L. Albert · Mt. Elgon 4321 · L. Turkana · Juba
C. Palmas · Bight of Benin · Niger Delta · Bioko · Sangha · Zaïre · Mt. Stanley 5119 · Lake Victoria · Mt. Kenya 5200
Gulf of Guinea · São Tomé · Zaïre Basin · Lukenie · Kilimanjaro 5895 · Masai Steppe · Tana
ATLANTIC OCEAN · Zaïre · Kasai · Mitumba Mts · Great Rift Valley · Pemba I. · Zanzibar I. · **INDIAN OCEAN**
Kwilu · Lubilash · Lake Tanganyika · Rufiji · Aldabra Is.
Kwango · Lulua · L. Mweru · Muchinga Mts · Luangwa · Ruvuma · L. Malawi · Comoro Is. · C. d'Ambre
Cuanza · Serra Môco 2610 · Bié Plateau · Luangwa · Zambezi · Madagascar
Cuando · Victoria Falls · L. Kariba · Matabele Upland · Mozambique Channel
Cunene · Cubango · Etosha Pan · Okavango Basin · Zambezi · Save · Ankaratra Mts.
Namib Desert · Limpopo · Tropic of Capricorn
Kalahari Desert · Vaal · High Veld · Thaban Ntlenyana 3482 · Drakensberg
Great Fish · Orange · Orange · Great Karoo
C. of Good Hope · C. Agulhas

Scale 1:37 000 000
0 200 400 600 800 1000 Miles
0 400 800 1200 1600 Kms.
Lambert Azimuthal Equal Area Projection

Inset map (political):
MOROCCO · TUNISIA · ALGERIA · LIBYA · EGYPT
WESTERN SAHARA · MAURITANIA · MALI · NIGER · CHAD · SUDAN · ERITREA · DJIBOUTI
SENEGAL · G.-B. · GUINEA · BURKINA FASO · NIGERIA · CENTRAL AFRICAN REP. · ETHIOPIA · SOMALIA
SIERRA LEONE · CÔTE D'IVOIRE · GHANA · TOGO · BENIN · CAMEROON · UGANDA · KENYA
LIBERIA · EQUATORIAL GUINEA · GABON · CONGO · ZAÏRE · R · B · TANZANIA
ANGOLA · ZAMBIA · MALAWI · MOZAMBIQUE · MADAGASCAR
ZIMBABWE
NAMIBIA · BOTSWANA · SWAZILAND
SOUTH AFRICA · LESOTHO

B.: BURUNDI
G.: GAMBIA
G.B.: GUINEA BISSAU
M.: MALAWI
R.: RWANDA

Scale 1:115 000 000
0 500 1000 1500 2000 2500 mls
0 1000 2000 3000 4000 kms

© Collins ◊ Longman Atlases

Climate : Natural Vegetation : Land Use : Population

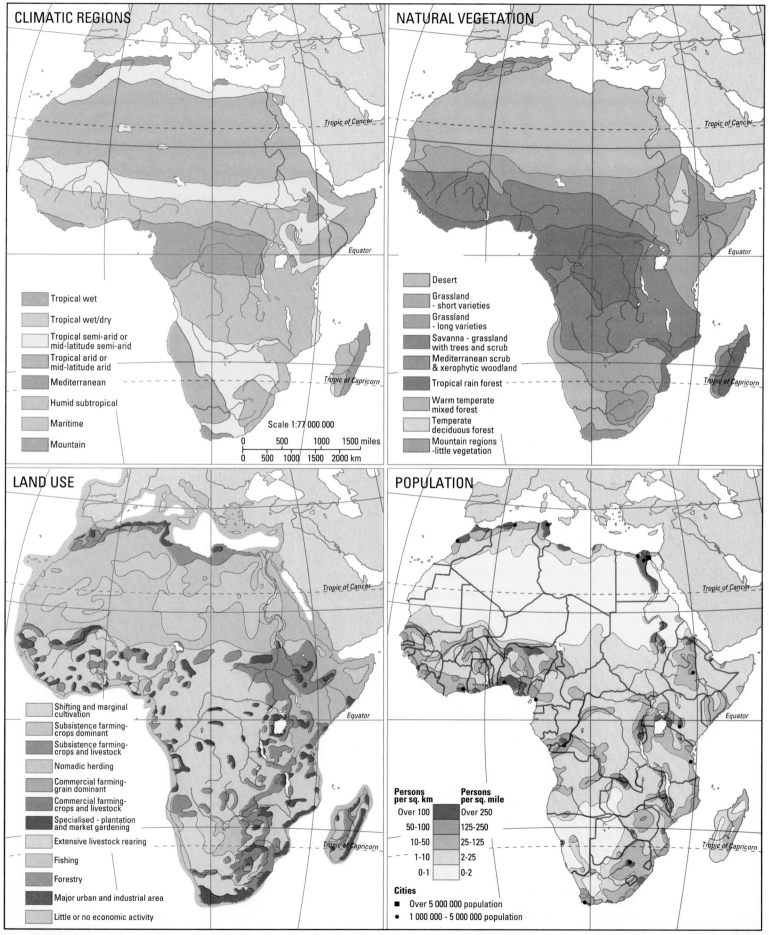

CLIMATIC REGIONS

- Tropical wet
- Tropical wet/dry
- Tropical semi-arid or mid-latitude semi-arid
- Tropical arid or mid-latitude arid
- Mediterranean
- Humid subtropical
- Maritime
- Mountain

Scale 1:77 000 000

| 0 | 500 | 1000 | 1500 miles |
| 0 | 500 1000 | 1500 | 2000 km |

NATURAL VEGETATION

- Desert
- Grassland - short varieties
- Grassland - long varieties
- Savanna - grassland with trees and scrub
- Mediterranean scrub & xerophytic woodland
- Tropical rain forest
- Warm temperate mixed forest
- Temperate deciduous forest
- Mountain regions - little vegetation

LAND USE

- Shifting and marginal cultivation
- Subsistence farming - crops dominant
- Subsistence farming - crops and livestock
- Nomadic herding
- Commercial farming - grain dominant
- Commercial farming - crops and livestock
- Specialised - plantation and market gardening
- Extensive livestock rearing
- Fishing
- Forestry
- Major urban and industrial area
- Little or no economic activity

POPULATION

Persons per sq. km	Persons per sq. mile
Over 100	Over 250
50-100	125-250
10-50	25-125
1-10	2-25
0-1	0-2

Cities
- ■ Over 5 000 000 population
- ● 1 000 000 - 5 000 000 population

Tropic of Cancer
Equator
Tropic of Capricorn

105

Regions (Africa)

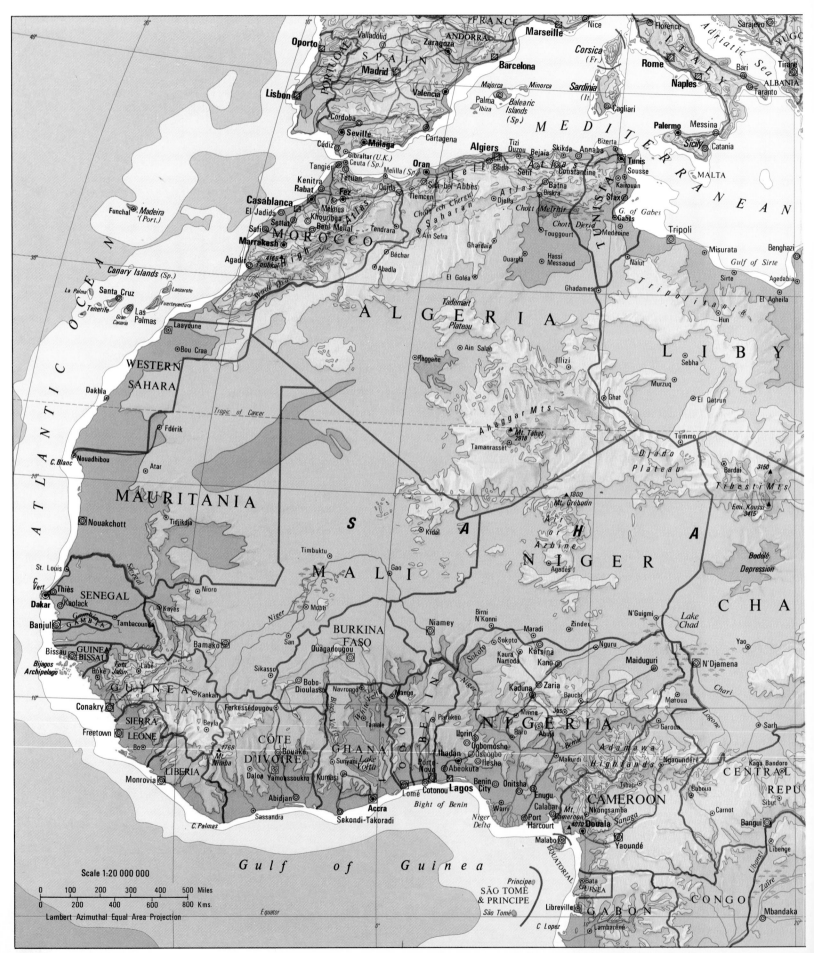

Scale 1:20 000 000

Lambert Azimuthal Equal Area Projection

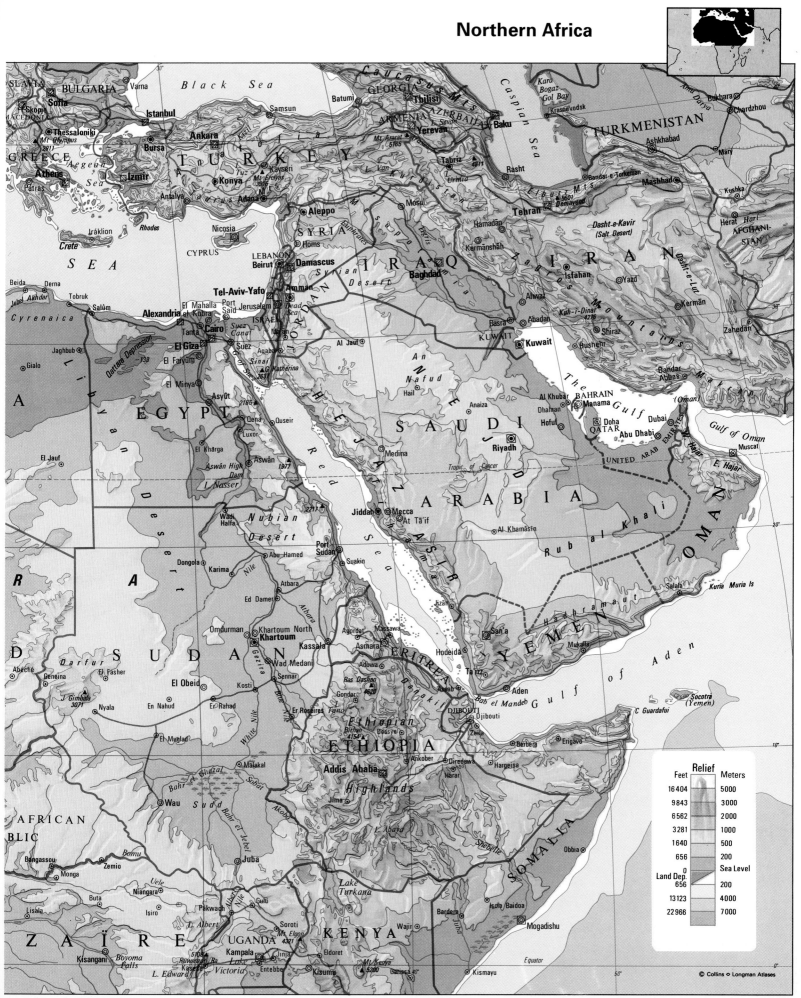

SLAVIA BULGARIA · Varna
□ Sofia
Skopje □
MACEDONIA · Thessaloniki □ Istanbul
· Mt. Olympus
2911 Bursa
GREECE Ankara □
Aegean Konya
· Athens Izmir □
Pátras Sea
Iráklion
Crete
SEA

Black Sea
Samsun
T U R K E Y
Kayseri
Mt. Erciyas
3916 Adana
Antalya Taurus Mountains
Nicosia
CYPRUS

Caucasus Mts.
Batumi GEORGIA □ Tbilisi
ARMENIA AZERBAIJAN
Yerevan □ Baku
Mt. Ararat 4811
5165 Tabriz
L. Van Kurdistan Urmia Rasht
Mosul
Aleppo
SYRIA Euphrates Tigris Mosul
Homs
LEBANON Syrian Baghdad
Beirut □ Damascus I R A Q
Tel-Aviv-Yafo Desert
Amman
El Mahalla Port Jerusalem □ Dead Al Jauf
el Kubra Said ISRAEL Sea
Alexandria Suez Maan KUWAIT Kuwait □
Tanta Cairo Canal Aqaba
El Giza Suez Sinai
El Faiyûm St. Katharina An
Gialo El Minya 2637 Nafud
Libyan Asyût Hail
EGYPT 2186 Qena Quseir Medina
El Khârga Luxor
Aswân High Aswân 1977 Tropic of Cancer
Dam
L. Nasser
2217
Jiddah Mecca
Wadi Nubian At Tâ'if
Halfa Desert
Port Al Khamâsîn
Sudan
Abu Hamed Rub al Khali
Dongola Suakin Jizân
Karima Atbara
Ed Damer
Omdurman Khartoum North Agordat Massawa
Khartoum Kassala Asmara San'a
Gezira ERITREA Hodeidâ
SUDAN Wad Medani Adowa
Darfur El Obeid Kosti Ras Dashan Ta'izz
Geneina El Fasher Sennar 4620 Aden
J.Gimbala Nyala En Nahud Er Rahad Gondar Assab
3071 Er Roseires Tana Zeila
El Muglad Blue Bichan Dessye
White Nile 4154 DJIBOUTI
AFRICAN Malakal ETHIOPIA Djibouti
BLIC Bahr el Ghazal Highlands Ankober Diredawa Hargeisa
Wau Sobat Jima Hârar
Bahr el Jebel Berbera
Akobo
Bonu L. Abayd
Bangassou Juba Shebelle
Zemio
Monga Lake SOMALIA
Buta Turkana Obbia
Niangara Uele
Lisala Isiro Albert Nile Wajir
ZAÏRE Pakwach Gulu Soroti KENYA
Boyoma Mt. Elgon Eldoret
Falls 4321 Mt. Kenya Mogadishu
Kisangani Kampala Jinja 5200
Ruwenzori Ra. Lake UGANDA Kisumu Garissa
L. Edward 5109 Victoria Entebbe Equator

Relief

Feet		Meters
16 404		5000
9843		3000
6562		2000
3281		1000
1640		500
656		200
0	Sea Level	
Land Dep.		200
656		4000
13 123		7000
22 966		

© Collins · Longman Atlases

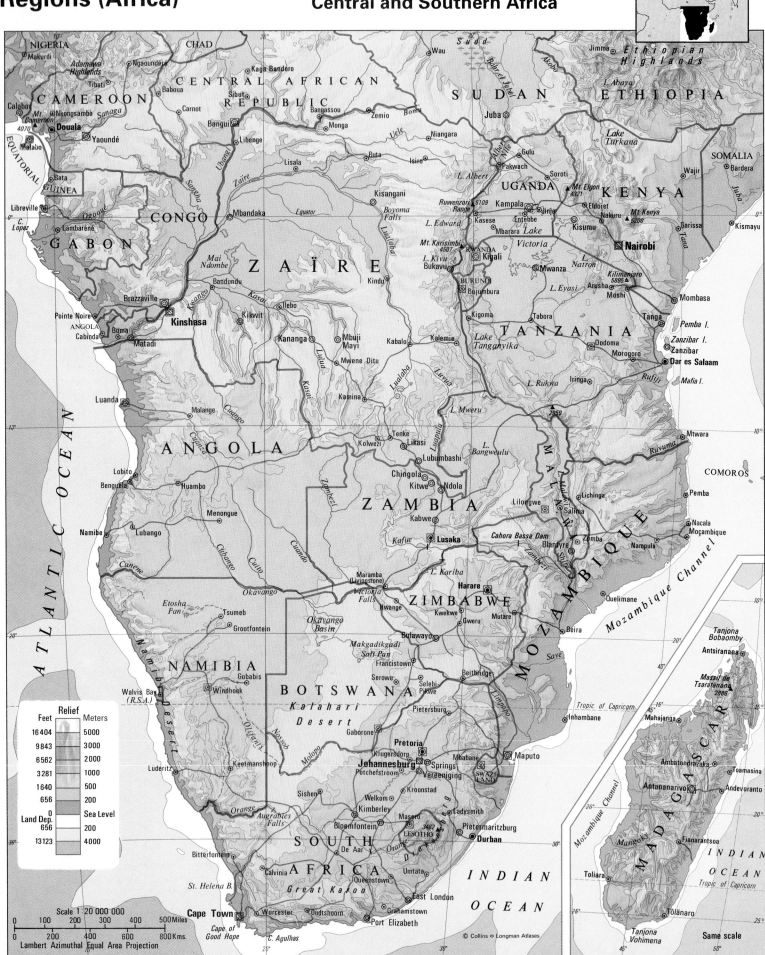

NIGERIA
Makurdi
CHAD
Wau
Sudd
Bahr el Jebel
Jimma
Ethiopian Highlands

CAMEROON
Ngaoundéré
Kaga Bandoro
CENTRAL AFRICAN REPUBLIC
Sibut
Bangassou
Zemio
Bomu
Juba
Akobo
L. Abaya
ETHIOPIA

Calabar
Nkongsamba
Tibati
Adamawa Highlands
Baboua
Carnot
Bangui
Monga
Uele
Niangara
Gulu
Pakwach
Albert Nile
Soroti
Mt. Elgon 4321
Eldoret
Wajir
SOMALIA
Bardera

Mt. Cameroon 4070
Douala
Yaoundé
Sanaga
Libenge
Buta
Isiro
L. Albert
UGANDA
Kampala
Jinja
Mt. Kenya 5200
KENYA
Garissa
Juba

Malabo
Bata
Ogooué
Ubangi
Zaïre
Kisangani
Ruwenzori Range 5109
Kasese
Entebbe
Nakuru
Kismayu

EQUATORIAL GUINEA
Libreville
C. Lopez
Lambaréné
CONGO
Mbandaka
Equator
Boyoma Falls
L. Edward
Mbarara
Lake Victoria
Kisumu
Nairobi

GABON
Mai Ndombe
ZAÏRE
Kindu
Mt. Karisimbi 4507
RWANDA
Kigali
Bukavu
L. Kivu
BURUNDI
Bujumbura
Mwanza
L. Natron
Kilimanjaro 5895
Arusha
Moshi
Mombasa

Bandundu
Kasai
Ilebo
Kikwit
Kigoma
Tabora
TANZANIA
Dodoma
Morogoro
Pemba I.
Zanzibar I.
Zanzibar
Tanga
Dar es Salaam

Brazzaville
Kinshasa
Kikwit
Kananga
Mbuji Mayi
Kabalo
Kalemie
Lake Tanganyika
Mafia I.

Pointe Noire
ANGOLA
Boma
Matadi
Mwene Ditu
Kamina
Kamina
Luvua
L. Rukwa
Iringa
Rufiji

Luanda
Malange
Cuango
Kasai
Lualaba
L. Mweru
2959
Mtwara
Ruvuma

Lobito
Benguela
Cubango
ANGOLA
Huambo
Tenke
Kolwezi
Likasi
MALAWI
Lichinga
COMOROS
Pemba

Namibe
Lubango
Menongue
Zambezi
Chingola
Kitwe
Ndola
Lubumbashi
L. Bangweulu
Lilongwe
Salima
Nacala
Moçambique

Cunene
Cubango
Cuito
Cuando
ZAMBIA
Kabwe
Kafue
Lusaka
Cahora Bassa Dam
Blantyre
Zomba
Nampula

Okavango
Okavango Basin
Maramba (Livingstone)
Victoria Falls
L. Kariba
Harare
Zambezi
Shire
Quelimane

Etosha Pan
Tsumeb
Grootfontein
Hwange
ZIMBABWE
Kwekwe
Gweru
Mutare
Beira
Save

Windhoek
Gobabis
Makgadikgadi Salt Pan
Francistown
Bulawayo
MOZAMBIQUE
Mozambique Channel

Walvis Bay (R.S.A.)
NAMIBIA
Namib Desert
BOTSWANA
Kalahari Desert
Serowe
Selebi Pikwe
Beitbridge
Inhambane
Tropic of Capricorn

Luderitz
Keetmanshoop
Olifants
Nossob
Gaborone
Pietersburg
Pretoria
Krugersdorp
Mbabane
SWAZILAND
Maputo

Sishen
Molopo
Limpopo
Johannesburg
Springs
Vereeniging
Potchefstroom

Bitterfontein
Calvinia
Orange
Augrabies Falls
Kimberley
Welkom
Kroonstad
Maseru
LESOTHO 3482
Ladysmith
Pietermaritzburg

SOUTH AFRICA
De Aar
Bloemfontein
Drakensberg
Umtata
Durban

St. Helena B.
Great Karoo
Queenstown
INDIAN OCEAN

Cape Town
Worcester
Oudtshoorn
Grahamstown
East London
Cape of Good Hope
C. Agulhas
Port Elizabeth

ATLANTIC OCEAN

MADAGASCAR
Tanjona Bobaomby
Antsiranana
Massif de Tsaratanana 2886
Mahajanga
Ambatondrazaka
Toamasina
Antananarivo
Andevoranto
Fianarantsoa
Mangoky
Toliara
Tôlanaro
Tanjona Vohimena
INDIAN OCEAN
Mozambique Channel
Tropic of Capricorn

Same scale

Relief
Feet		Meters
16 404		5000
9843		3000
6562		2000
3281		1000
1640		500
656		200
0		Sea Level
Land Dep.		200
656		4000
13 123		

Scale 1: 20 000 000
0 100 200 300 400 500 Miles
0 200 400 600 800 Kms.
Lambert Azimuthal Equal Area Projection

© Collins ● Longman Atlases

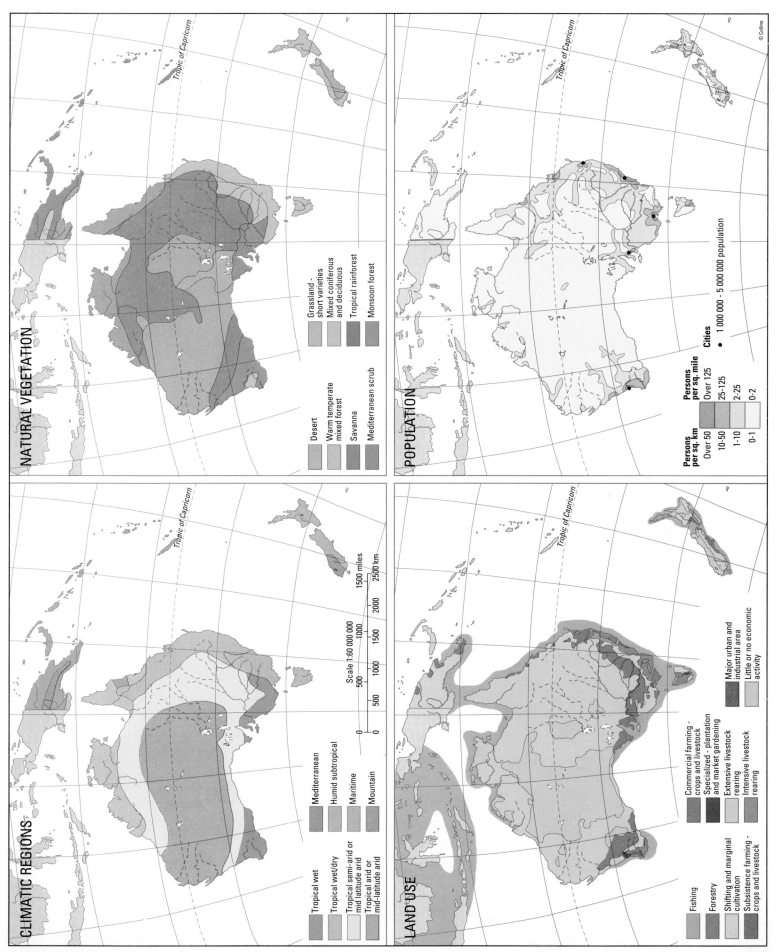

NATURAL VEGETATION

Desert

Warm temperate
mixed forest

Savanna

Mediterranean scrub

Grassland -
short varieties

Mixed coniferous
and deciduous

Tropical rainforest

Monsoon forest

POPULATION

Persons
per sq. km

Over 50

10-50

1-10

0-1

Persons
per sq. mile

Over 125

25-125

2-25

0-2

Cities

● 1 000 000 - 5 000 000 population

CLIMATIC REGIONS

Tropical wet

Tropical wet/dry

Tropical semi-arid or
mid latitude arid

Tropical arid or
mid-latitude arid

Mediterranean

Humid subtropical

Maritime

Mountain

Scale 1:60 000 000

0   500   1000   1500   2000   2500 km

0   500   1000   1500 miles

LAND USE

Fishing

Forestry

Shifting and marginal
cultivation

Subsistence farming -
crops and livestock

Commercial farming -
crops and livestock

Specialized - plantation
and market gardening

Extensive livestock
rearing

Intensive livestock
rearing

Major urban and
industrial area

Little or no economic
activity

© Collins

Tropic of Capricorn

109

Scale 1:20 000 000

| 0 | 100 | 200 | 300 | 400 | 500 Miles |

| 0 | 200 | 400 | 600 | 800 Kms. |

Lambert Azimuthal Equal Area Projection

© Collins ○ Longman Atlases

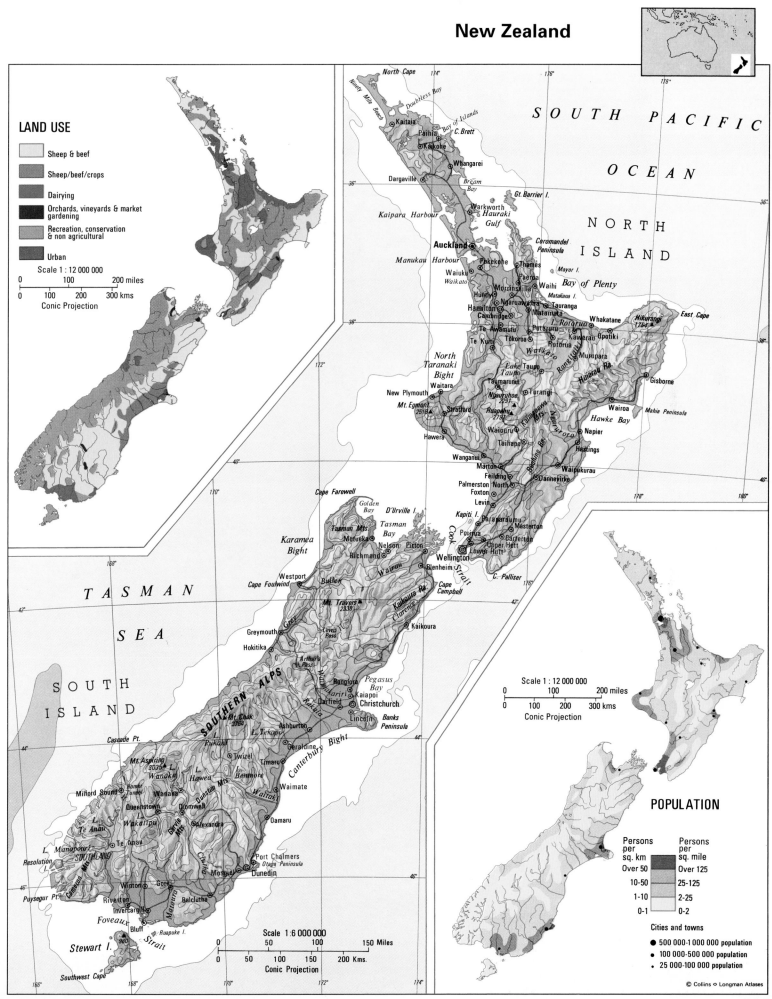

New Zealand

LAND USE

- Sheep & beef
- Sheep/beef/crops
- Dairying
- Orchards, vineyards & market gardening
- Recreation, conservation & non agricultural
- Urban

Scale 1 : 12 000 000

0   100   200 miles
0   100   200   300 kms
Conic Projection

North Island

SOUTH PACIFIC OCEAN

North Cape
Ninety Mile Beach
Doubtless Bay
Kaitaia
Paihia   C. Brett
Bay of Islands
Kaikohe
Whangarei
Dargaville   Bream Bay
Gt. Barrier I.
Kaipara Harbour
Warkworth
Hauraki Gulf
Coromandel Peninsula
Auckland
Pukekohe   Thames
Manukau Harbour
Waiuku   Paeroa
Waikato   Morrinsville   Waihi
Huntly   Ngaruawahia   Mayor I.
Hamilton   Matakana I.
Cambridge   Matamata   Tauranga   Bay of Plenty
Te Awamutu   Putaruru   Whakatane   Hikurangi   East Cape
Te Kuiti   Tokoroa   L. Rotorua   1754
Rotorua   Kawerau   Opotiki
North Taranaki Bight   Taumarunui   Murupara
Waitara   Lake Taupo   Huiarau Ra.
New Plymouth   Ngauruhoe   Turangi
Mt. Egmont   2291   Gisborne
2518   Stratford   Ruapehu   Wairoa
2797   Waiouru   Hawke Bay   Mahia Peninsula
Hawera   Taihape   Napier
Wanganui   Hastings
Marton   Waipukurau
Feilding   Dannevirke
Palmerston North
Foxton   Levin
Kapiti I.   Paraparaumu   Masterton
Porirua   Carterton
Upper Hutt
Wellington   Lower Hutt   C. Palliser

South Island

Cape Farewell
Golden Bay   D'Urville I.
Tasman Mts.   Tasman Bay
Karamea Bight   Motueka   Cook Strait
Nelson   Picton
Richmond   Wairau
Westport   Blenheim
Cape Foulwind   Buller   Cape Campbell
Mt. Travers   Kaikoura Ra.
2338   Clarence
Greymouth   Grey   Kaikoura
Hokitika   Lewis Pass
Arthur's Pass
SOUTHERN ALPS   Rangiora
Waimakariri   Pegasus Bay
Mt. Cook   Kaiapoi
3764   Darfield   Christchurch
Cascade Pt.   L. Tekapo   Lincoln   Banks Peninsula
Ashburton
Pukaki   Geraldine
Mt. Aspiring   Twizel   Timaru
3035   L. Wanaka   L. Hawea   L. Benmore   Waitaki
Milford Sound   Waimate
Homer Tunnel   Wanaka   Canterbury Bight
Queenstown   Cromwell   Oamaru
L. Wakatipu   Dunstan Mts.
Garvie Mts.   Alexandra
L. Te Anau   Te Anau   Port Chalmers
L. Manapouri   SOUTHLAND   Mosgiel   Otago Peninsula
Resolution I.   Clutha   Dunedin
Winton   Gore
Puysegur Pt.   Riverton
Invercargill   Balclutha
Foveaux   Bluff   Ruapuke I.
Stewart I.   980   Strait
Southwest Cape

TASMAN SEA

Scale 1:6 000 000

0   50   100   150 Miles
0   50   100   150   200 Kms.
Conic Projection

Scale 1 : 12 000 000

0   100   200 miles
0   100   200   300 kms
Conic Projection

POPULATION

Persons per sq. km	Persons per sq. mile
Over 50	Over 125
10-50	25-125
1-10	2-25
0-1	0-2

Cities and towns

● 500 000-1 000 000 population
• 100 000-500 000 population
· 25 000-100 000 population

© Collins ◇ Longman Atlases

111

Regions

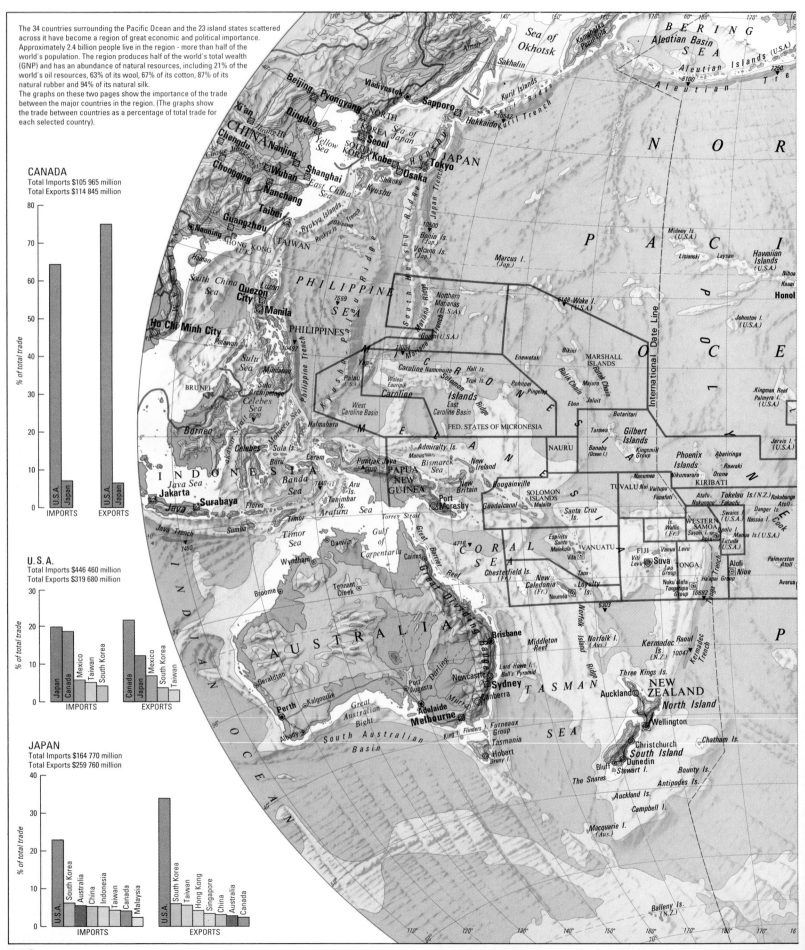

The 34 countries surrounding the Pacific Ocean and the 23 island states scattered across it have become a region of great economic and political importance. Approximately 2.4 billion people live in the region - more than half of the world's population. The region produces half of the world's total wealth (GNP) and has an abundance of natural resources, including 21% of the world's oil resources, 63% of its wool, 67% of its cotton, 87% of its natural rubber and 94% of its natural silk.

The graphs on these two pages show the importance of the trade between the major countries in the region. (The graphs show the trade between countries as a percentage of total trade for each selected country).

CANADA
Total Imports $105 965 million
Total Exports $114 845 million

% of total trade

IMPORTS — U.S.A., Japan
EXPORTS — U.S.A., Japan

U.S.A.
Total Imports $446 460 million
Total Exports $319 680 million

% of total trade

IMPORTS — Japan, Canada, Mexico, Taiwan, South Korea
EXPORTS — Canada, Japan, Mexico, South Korea, Taiwan

JAPAN
Total Imports $164 770 million
Total Exports $259 760 million

% of total trade

IMPORTS — U.S.A., South Korea, Australia, China, Indonesia, Taiwan, Canada, Malaysia
EXPORTS — U.S.A., South Korea, Taiwan, Hong Kong, Singapore, China, Australia, Canada

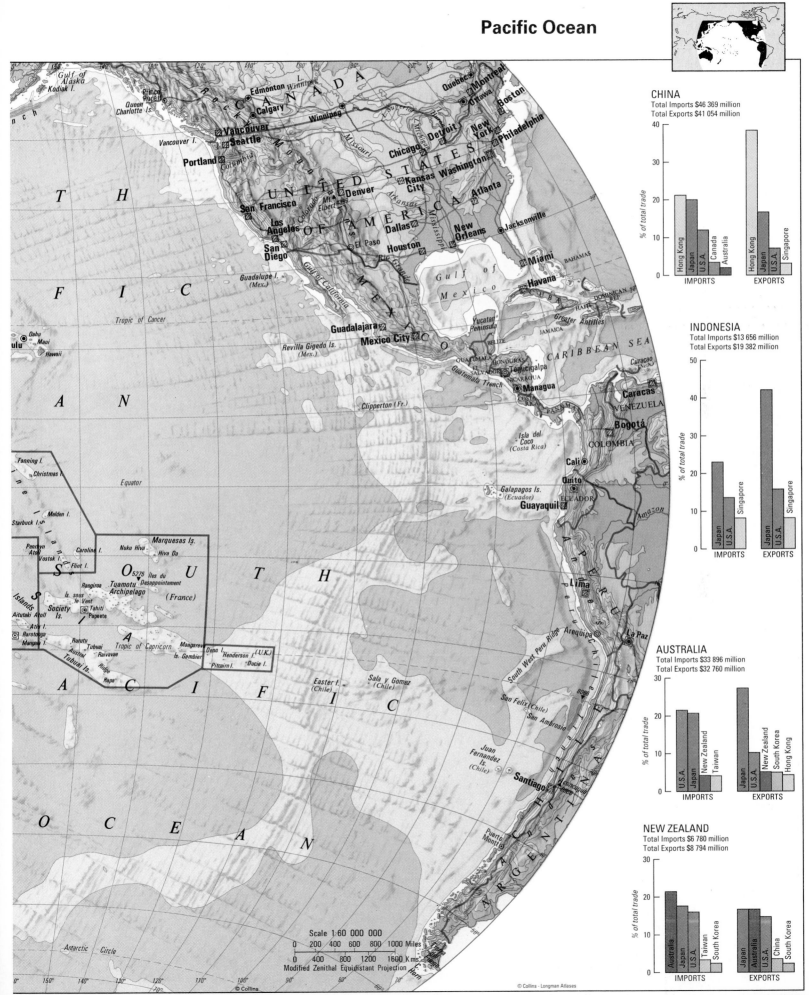

CHINA
Total Imports $46 369 million
Total Exports $41 054 million

IMPORTS: Hong Kong, Japan, U.S.A., Canada, Australia
EXPORTS: Hong Kong, Japan, U.S.A., Singapore

% of total trade

INDONESIA
Total Imports $13 656 million
Total Exports $19 382 million

IMPORTS: Japan, U.S.A., Singapore
EXPORTS: Japan, U.S.A., Singapore

% of total trade

AUSTRALIA
Total Imports $33 896 million
Total Exports $32 760 million

IMPORTS: U.S.A., Japan, New Zealand, Taiwan
EXPORTS: Japan, U.S.A., New Zealand, South Korea, Hong Kong

% of total trade

NEW ZEALAND
Total Imports $6 780 million
Total Exports $8 794 million

IMPORTS: Australia, Japan, U.S.A., Taiwan, South Korea
EXPORTS: Japan, Australia, U.S.A., China, South Korea

% of total trade

Scale 1:60 000 000

0 200 400 600 800 1000 Miles

0 400 800 1200 1600 Kms.

Modified Zenithal Equidistant Projection

© Collins - Longman Atlases

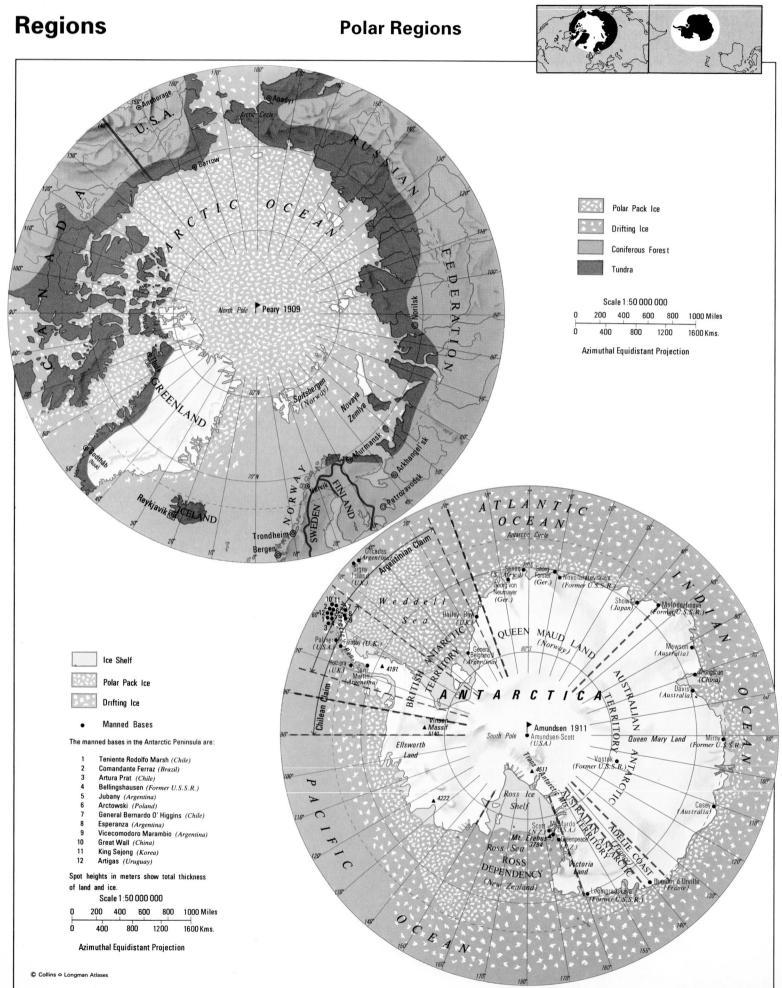

Polar Regions

Polar Pack Ice

Drifting Ice

Coniferous Forest

Tundra

Scale 1:50 000 000

| 0 | 200 | 400 | 600 | 800 | 1000 Miles |

| 0 | 400 | 800 | 1200 | 1600 Kms. |

Azimuthal Equidistant Projection

Ice Shelf

Polar Pack Ice

Drifting Ice

• Manned Bases

The manned bases in the Antarctic Peninsula are:

1. Teniente Rodolfo Marsh (Chile)
2. Comandante Ferraz (Brazil)
3. Artura Prat (Chile)
4. Bellingshausen (Former U.S.S.R.)
5. Jubany (Argentina)
6. Arctowski (Poland)
7. General Bernardo O' Higgins (Chile)
8. Esperanza (Argentina)
9. Vicecomodoro Marambio (Argentina)
10. Great Wall (China)
11. King Sejong (Korea)
12. Artigas (Uruguay)

Spot heights in meters show total thickness of land and ice.

Scale 1:50 000 000

| 0 | 200 | 400 | 600 | 800 | 1000 Miles |

| 0 | 400 | 800 | 1200 | 1600 Kms. |

Azimuthal Equidistant Projection

© Collins ◇ Longman Atlases

ARCTIC OCEAN

North Pole ▷ Peary 1909

U.S.A.

CANADA

GREENLAND

ICELAND

NORWAY SWEDEN FINLAND

RUSSIAN FEDERATION

Anchorage

Anadyr

Barrow

Norilsk

Godthåb (Nuuk)

Reykjavik

Trondheim

Bergen

Narvik

Murmansk

Arkhangel'sk

Petrozavodsk

Spitsbergen (Norway)

Novaya Zemlya

Thule (Qaanaaq)

ANTARCTICA

ATLANTIC OCEAN

INDIAN OCEAN

PACIFIC OCEAN

Antarctic Circle

South Pole

▷ Amundsen 1911
• Amundsen-Scott (U.S.A.)

Weddell Sea

QUEEN MAUD LAND (Norway)

BRITISH ANTARCTIC TERRITORY

AUSTRALIAN ANTARCTIC TERRITORY

Queen Mary Land

Ellsworth Land

Ross Ice Shelf

Ross Sea

Victoria Land

ROSS DEPENDENCY (New Zealand)

Argentinian Claim

Chilean Claim

Vinson Massif 5140 ▲

Trans Antarctic Mts

4511 ▲

4222 ▲

4191 ▲

Mt Erebus 3794 ▲

Orcadas (Argentina)

Signy Island (U.K.)

Palmer (U.S.A.)

Faraday (U.K.)

Rothera (U.K.)

San Martin (Argentina)

Halley Bay (U.K.)

Sanae (S. Africa)

Georg von Neumayer (Ger.)

Georg Forster (Ger.)

Novolazarevskaya (Former U.S.S.R.)

General Belgrano II (Argentina)

Showa (Japan)

Molodezhnaya (Former U.S.S.R.)

Mawson (Australia)

Zhongshan (China)

Davis (Australia)

Mirny (Former U.S.S.R.)

Vostok (Former U.S.S.R.)

Casey (Australia)

McMurdo (U.S.A.)

Scott (N.Z.)

Greenpeace (N.Z.)

Dumont d'Urville (France)

Leningradskaya (Former U.S.S.R.)

ADÉLIE COAST

Countries of the World[1]

Flag	Country	Capital[2]	Area[2] (sq. mi) (sq. km)	Population[3]	Major or[2] Official Languages	Important[3] Products
	Afghanistan	Kabul	260,000 647,497	16,560,000	Pushtu, Dari	karakul skins, cotton, fruit, natural gas
	Albania	Tirana (Tiranë)	11,097 28,489	3,200,000	Albanian, Greek	minerals, sugar beets, livestock, electricity, wheat
	Algeria	Algiers	918,497 2,400,000	25,360,000	Arabic, Berber dialects, French	wheat, barley, petroleum, fruit, natural gas
	Andorra	Andorra	185 466	53,000	Catalan, French, Spanish	livestock, tobacco
	Angola	Luanda	481,351 1,246,700	10,020,000	Portuguese, Bantu languages	petroleum, diamonds, coffee, sugar, bananas
	Antigua and Barbuda	St. John's	108 281	85,000	English	cotton, clothing, rum, livestock, bananas
	Argentina	Buenos Aires	1,100,000 2,766,890	32,690,000	Spanish, Italian	meat, wool, sugar cane, iron ore, sunflower seeds
	Armenia	Yerevan	11,490 29,800	3,290,000	Armenian, Russian	almonds, cotton, grain, minerals, machinery
	Australia	Canberra	3,000,000 7,700,000	17,200,000	English	wheat, wool, livestock, metal ores, coal, bauxite
	Austria	Vienna	32,377 83,857	7,800,000	German	lumber, metal products, paper, wheat, barley
	Azerbaijan	Baku	33,430 86,600	7,130,000	Azerbaijani, Russian	cotton, fruit, grain, oil, steel, iron ore, rice
	Bahamas	Nassau	5,380 13,934	255,000	English, Creole	pharmaceuticals, chemicals, lobsters, rum, livestock
	Bahrain	Manama	268 693	486,000	Arabic, English, Farsi	petroleum products, aluminum processing
	Bangladesh	Dhaka	55,813 143,998	108,000,000	Bengali, English	jute goods, tea, fish, newsprint, hides and skins
	Barbados	Bridgetown	166 430	257,000	English	clothing, rum, sugar, fish, electronic components
	Belarus (Belorussia)	Minsk	80,134 207,600	10,260,000	Byelorussian, Russian	flax, grain, livestock, potatoes, peat, machinery
	Belgium	Brussels	11,799 30,519	9,980,000	Dutch, French, German	precious stones, metals, chemical products
	Belize	Belmopan	8,866 22,963	193,000	English, Spanish, Mayan	lumber, sugar, livestock, fish, fruit, clothing, molases
	Benin	Porto-Novo	43,483 112,622	4,760,000	French, Fon	palm oil, cotton, cocoa, sugar
	Bhutan	Thimphu (Thimbu)	18,000 46,620	600,000	Dzongkha, Sharchop, Nepali, English	lumber, fruit, vegetables, cement
	Bolivia	La Paz, Sucre	425,000 1,100,000	6,410,000	Spanish, Quechua, Aymara	petroleum, tin, gold, silver, zinc, coffee
	Bosnia and Herzegovina	Sarajevo	19,736 51,129	4,355,000	Serbo Croatian	wheat, corn, plums, potatoes, textiles
	Botswana	Gaborone	224,710 600,372	1,350,000	English, Setswana	livestock, diamonds, copper, nickel, salt

[1]Includes Independent Countries; flags are based on most recent information available at time of publication.

[2]Source: *Background Notes*, United States Department of State

[3]Source: *Statesman's Year-Book 1991-1992*

Countries of the World[1]

Flag	Country	Capital[2]	Area[2] (sq. mi) (sq. km)	Population[3]	Major or[2] Official Languages	Important[3] Products
	Brazil	Brasilia	3,290,000 8,511,965	155,600,000	Portuguese	iron ore, steel, coffee, soybeans, shoes
	Brunei	Bandar Seri Begawan	2,227 5,769	256,500	Malay, Chinese, English	petroleum, rubber, lumber, rice, pepper
	Bulgaria	Sofia	44,365 110,987	8,900,000	Bulgarian	farm products, minerals, machinery, equipment
	Burkina Faso	Ouaga-dougou	106,000 274,200	8,760,000	French, others	livestock, cotton, rice, peanuts, sesame, grains
	Burundi	Bujumbura	10,747 27,834	5,460,000	Kirundi, French, Swahili	cotton, tea, coffee, bananas, grain, cattle
	Cambodia	Phnom Penh	69,900 181,040	8,300,000	Khmer, French	fish, rubber, maize, beans
	Cameroon	Yaoundé	183,568 475,439	11,540,000	English, French, African languages	cotton, coffee, cocoa, sugar, rubber, palm oil
	Canada	Ottawa	3,800,000 9,970,000	27,000,000	English, French	food products, machinery, lumber, metal ores
	Cape Verde	Praia	1,557 4,033	369,000	Portuguese, Crioulo	tuna, shellfish, salt, bananas, coffee, sugar
	Central African Republic	Bangui	242,000 623,000	3,040,000	French, Sangho	coffee, diamonds, peanuts, lumber, cotton
	Chad	N'Djaména	496,000 1,284,634	5,540,000	French, Arabic, Chadian languages	livestock, cotton, millet, fish, sugar
	Chile	Santiago	302,778 756,945	13,700,000	Spanish	paper, lumber, copper, nitrates, fish meal, gold
	China	Beijing	3,700,000 9,600,000	1,114,000,000	Mandarin Chinese	petroleum, minerals, grain, tea, raw silk
	Colombia	Bogotá	440,000 1,140,000	33,000,000	Spanish	petroleum, coffee, bananas, textiles
	Comoros	Moroni	838 2,171	503,000	Comoran, French	vanilla, copra, cloves, perfume essences, coffee
	Congo	Brazzaville	132,000 342,000	2,260,000	French, Lingala, Monokutuba	lumber, petroleum, cassava, bananas, plantains
	Costa Rica	San José	19,652 51,032	2,910,000	Spanish	livestock, sugar, cocoa, coffee, palm oil, bananas
	Côte d'Ivoire (Ivory Coast)	Yamoussoukro	124,500 322,500	12,100,000	French, tribal dialects	lumber, coffee, cocoa, sugar, petroleum products
	Croatia	Zagreb	21,829 56,538	4,690,000	Croato-Serbian	grain, livestock, timber, coal, petroleum, cement
	Cuba	Havana	44,200 110,860	10,580,000	Spanish	sugar, citrus fruit, tobacco, minerals, fish
	Cyprus	Nicosia	3,572 9,251	702,100	Greek, Turkish, English	citrus fruits, grapes, potatoes, copper, cement
	Czech Republic	Prague	30,442 78,864	10,000,000	Czech	iron and steel, machinery, timber, wheat, potatoes
	Denmark	Copenhagen	16,632 43,076	5,150,000	Danish, English	machinery, meat, fish, dairy products, metals
	Djibouti	Djibouti	9,000 23,310	510,000	French, Arabic, Afar, Somali	livestock, hides, fish
	Dominica	Roseau	290 754	108,812	English, French patois	fruit juices, bananas, soap, coconuts, fruit
	Dominican Republic	Santo Domingo	18,704 48,442	7,200,000	Spanish	coffee, bananas, bauxite, nickel, sugar, rice

Countries of the World[1]

Flag	Country	Capital[2]	Area[2] (sq. mi) (sq. km)	Population[3]	Major or[2] Official Languages	Important[3] Products
	Ecuador	Quito	109,000 271,000	9,620,000	Spanish, Quechua	bananas, coffee, cocoa beans, shrimp, petroleum
	Egypt	Cairo	386,650 1,001,450	56,000,000	Arabic, English, French	cotton, textiles, aluminum, oranges, crude oil
	El Salvador	San Salvador	8,260 21,476	5,380,000	Spanish	cotton, coffee, sugar, livestock, lumber, maize
	Equatorial Guinea	Malabo	10,820 28,023	417,000	Spanish, Fang, Bubi, English	lumber, coffee, cocoa beans, bananas, fish
	Estonia	Tallinn	17,413 45,100	1,580,000	Estonian, Russian	peat, grain, livestock, vegetables, paper, potatoes
	Eritrea	Asmara	45,405 117,600	2,614,700	Semitic languages	salt, sesame seeds, lentils
	Ethiopia	Addis Ababa	426,400 1,104,300	45,000,000	Amharic, Tiqrinya, Arabic	hides, coffee, sugar, maize
	Fiji	Suva	7,055 18,376	747,000	Fijian, Hindustani, English	copra, sugar, gold, ginger, canned fish
	Finland	Helsinki	130,160 337,113	4,970,000	Finnish, Swedish, Lappish	lumber, paper, manufactured goods, wood pulp
	France	Paris	220,668 551,670	56,610,000	French	machinery, sugar, grapes, livestock, wheat, clothing
	Gabon	Libreville	102,317 266,024	1,220,000	French, Bantu languages	coffee, petroleum, lumber, manganese, metals
	Gambia	Banjul	4,361 11,300	875,000	English, Mandinka, Wolof, Fula	fish, peanuts, cotton, livestock
	Georgia	Tbilisi	26,900 69,700	5,460,000	Georgian, Russian	grain, tea, coal, manganese, steel, fruit
	Germany	Berlin	137,838 357,000	79,110,000	German	precision instruments, chemicals, cars
	Ghana	Accra	92,100 238,538	14,900,000	English, Akan, Mole-Dagbani	lumber, gold, tobacco, cocoa beans, coffee
	Greece	Athens	51,146 131,957	10,260,000	Greek	textiles, olive oil, fruit, tobacco
	Grenada	St. George's	133 344	91,000	English, French-African Patois	cocoa beans, mace, fish, nutmeg, bananas, sugar
	Guatemala	Guatemala City	42,000 108,700	9,000,000	Spanish, Mayan languages	cotton, chicle gum, bananas, coffee, lumber
	Guinea	Conakry	95,000 246,048	6,710,000	French, Fulani, others	bauxite, sugar, cassava, rice, bananas, alumina
	Guinea-Bissau	Bissau	13,948 36,125	966,000	Portuguese, Crioulo	peanuts, palm oil, fish, coconuts, rice
	Guyana	Georgetown	83,000 215,000	990,000	English, Creole	bauxite, aluminum, sugar, rice, shrimp, rum
	Haiti	Port-au-Prince	10,714 27,750	5,690,000	French, Creole	coffee, sugar, rice, cotton, sisal
	Honduras	Tegucigalpa	43,277 112,088	4,440,000	Spanish, Indian languages	bananas, coffee, sugar, lumber, shrimp, lobster
	Hungary	Budapest	35,919 93,030	10,450,000	Hungarian (Magyar)	consumer goods, tools, machinery, wheat, wine
	Iceland	Reykjavik	39,709 102,845	255,000	Icelandic	fish, marine products, metals
	India	New Delhi	1,268,884 3,287,263	844,320,000	Hindi, English others	clothing, textiles, leather, jems, chemicals, tea

Countries of the World[1]

Flag	Country	Capital[2]	Area[2] (sq. mi) (sq. km)	Population[3]	Major or[2] Official Languages	Important[3] Products
	Indonesia	Jakarta	736,000 2,000,000	179,100,000	Bahasa Indonesia, Dutch	petroleum, lumber, coffee, manufactured goods
	Iran	Tehran	636,294 1,648,000	53,920,000	Farsi, Kurdish, Azerbaijani	wheat, petroleum, rice, sugar, tobacco
	Iraq	Baghdad	167,924 434,934	17,800,000	Arabic, Kurdish	petroleum, dates, wheat, rice
	Ireland	Dublin	27,136 70,282	3,520,000	Irish, English	chemicals, dairy products, machinery, peat, barley
	Israel	Jerusalem	7,850 20,325	4,980,000	Hebrew, Arabic, English	citrus, chemicals, textiles, machinery, diamonds
	Italy	Rome	116,303 301,225	57,700,000	Italian	clothing, shoes, textiles, machinery, cars, fruit
	Jamaica	Kingston	4,244 10,991	2,400,000	English, Creole	bauxite, bananas, sugar, citrus, molasses, cocoa
	Japan	Tokyo	145,856 377,765	123,610,000	Japanese	cars, metal products, textiles, electronics
	Jordan	Amman	35,000 91,000	3,170,000	Arabic	phosphates, citrus fruits, olives, chemicals, grapes
	Kazakhstan	Alma-Ata	1,049,155 2,717,300	16,690,000	Kazakh, Russian	cotton, grain, livestock, metal ores, oil, coal
	Kenya	Nairobi	244,960 582,646	24,030,000	Kiswahili, Bantu languages, English	coffee, tea, textiles, sugar, chemicals, leather
	Kiribati	Tarawa	276 717	72,298	English, Gilbertese	copra, tuna, coconuts, poultry
	Korea, North	Pyongyang	47,000 121,730	22,420,000	Korean	chemicals, fertilizers, minerals, rice, maize
	Korea, South	Seoul	38,000 98,500	42,790,000	Korean	machinery, steel, rice, fish, electronics
	Kuwait	Kuwait	6,880 17,818	2,040,000	Arabic, Kurdish, English	petroleum, shrimp, fertilizer
	Kyrgyzstan (Kirghizia)	Bishkek	76,640 198,500	4,370,000	Kirghiz, Russian	livestock, sugar beets, wheat, hemp, fruit, tobacco
	Laos	Vientiane	91,430 236,804	4,050,000	Lao, French, English	lumber, coffee, maize, textiles, rice, sugar
	Latvia	Riga	24,595 63,700	2,690,000	Latvian, Russian	barley, oats, livestock, electric railway cars
	Lebanon	Beirut	4,015 10,452	3,000,000	Arabic, French, English	citrus fruits, grapes, wheat, olives
	Lesotho	Maseru	11,718 30,350	1,720,000	English	diamonds, mohair, wool, wheat
	Liberia	Monrovia	43,000 111,370	2,440,000	English, Mande, Kwa, West Atlantic	lumber, iron ore, gold, cocoa, coffee, rubber
	Libya	Tripoli	679,536 1,758,610	4,000,000	Arabic	petroleum, olives, dates, barley, wheat
	Liechtenstein	Vaduz	62 160	28,877	German	textiles, steel screws, precision instruments
	Lithuania	Vilnius	25,170 65,200	3,720,000	Lithuanian, Russian	grain, potatoes, sugar beets, timber, machinery
	Luxembourg	Luxembourg	1,034 2,586	378,400	Luxembourgish, German, French	steel, maize, barley, potatoes, wheat, wine
	Macedonia[4]	Skopje	9,925 25,713	1,909,136	Macedonian, Albanian	wheat, cotton, corn, livestock, steel

[4]Macedonia declared independence from Yugoslavia in November 1991. It has not been widely recognized as an independent state by the international community.

Countries of the World[1]

Flag	Country	Capital[2]	Area[2] (sq. mi) (sq. km)	Population[3]	Major or[2] Official Languages	Important[3] Products
	Madagascar	Antananarivo	228,880 592,800	11,440,000	Malagasy, French	chromium, graphite, cloves, vanilla, coffee
	Malawi	Lilongwe	45,747 118,484	7,980,000	Chichewa, English	tobacco, peanuts, maize, tea
	Malaysia	Kuala Lumpur	127,316 329,749	17,810,000	Bahasa Malaysia, Chinese, Tamil	petroleum, lumber, tin, rubber, palm oil, fruit
	Maldives	Malé	115 298	213,215	Divehi, English	coconuts, fish, millet, tropical fruits
	Mali	Bamako	474,764 1,240,278	9,090,000	Bambara, French	fish, livestock, cotton, peanuts, rice, millet
	Malta	Valletta	121 316	355,910	Maltese, English	manufactured goods, chemicals, fish
	Marshall Islands	Majuro	70 181	45,563	English, Marshallese	coconuts, fruit, phosphates
	Mauritania	Nouakchott	419,212 1,085,760	1,970,000	Arabic, Pulaar, Wolot, Soninke	iron ore, dates, cereals, vegetables, fish
	Mauritius	Port Louis	720 1,865	1,091,682	English, Creole, French, Hindi	molasses, sugar, tea, fish, clothing, plastics
	Mexico	Mexico City	764,000 2,000,000	81,400,000	Spanish, Indian languages	cotton, petroleum, maize, livestock, coffee, minerals
	Micronesia	Palikir	271 701	107,900	English, others	copra, fish
	Moldova (Moldovia)	Kishinev	13,000 33,700	4,360,000	Moldavian (Romanian), Russian	grain, sugar beets, steel, clothing, fish
	Monaco	Monaco	0.8 1.95	26,000	French, English, Italian	plastics, electronics, chemicals, perfume
	Mongolia	Ulan Baatar	604,103 1,566,500	2,150,000	Mongolian	livestock, wheat, oats, footwear, minerals
	Morocco	Rabat	172,413 446,550	24,370,000	Arabic, Berber, French, Spanish	phosphates, citrus, cereals, sugar
	Mozambique	Maputo	303,769 789,800	16,110,000	Portuguese, Bantu languages	cashews, shrimp, sugar, copra, petroleum products
	Myanmar (Burma)	Yangon (Rangoon)	261,228 676,577	40,780,000	Burmese	teak, rice, sugar, cement, rubber
	Namibia	Windhoek	320,827 823,145	1,290,000	English, Afrikaans, German	livestock, diamonds, uranium, fertilizers
	Nauru	Yaren	8 21	8,100	Nauruan, English	phosphates
	Nepal	Kathmandu	56,136 147,181	18,900,000	Nepali, Bihari	lumber, grain, cattle, jute, potatoes, oil seeds
	Netherlands	Amsterdam, The Hague	16,464 41,473	15,010,000	Dutch	manufactured goods, wheat, flower bulbs
	New Zealand	Wellington	103,886 269,063	3,420,000	English, Maori	meat, dairy products, wool, manufactured goods
	Nicaragua	Managua	57,000 148,000	3,870,000	Spanish, Indian languages	coffee, cotton, sugar, chemicals, meat
	Niger	Niamey	490,000 1,267,000	8,040,000	French, Hausa, Djerma	coal, phosphates, uranium, peanuts, livestock
	Nigeria	Abuja	356,700 923,768	88,500,000	English, Hausa, Ibo, Yoruba	petroleum, lumber, tin, cocoa, palm oil
	Norway	Oslo	150,000 386,000	4,240,000	Norwegian, Lapp	petroleum, lumber, fish, ships, chemicals

Countries of the World[1]

Flag	Country	Capital[2]	Area[2] (sq. mi) (sq. km)	Population[3]	Major or[2] Official Languages	Important[3] Products
	Oman	Muscat	82,030 212,457	1,500,000	Arabic, English	petroleum, fish, dates, cement
	Pakistan	Islamabad	310,527 803,943	114,000,000	Urdu, English, Punjabi	cotton, rice, garments, sugar, leather
	Panama	Panama City	29,762 77,381	2,300,000	Spanish, English	bananas, sugar, rice, coffee, lumber, fruit
	Papua New Guinea	Port Moresby	178,260 461,693	3,700,000	Melanesian languages, English	coffee, copra, lumber, copper, rubber
	Paraguay	Asunción	157,047 406,750	4,160,000	Guarani, Spanish	meat, tobacco, cotton, soybeans, lumber
	Peru	Lima	496,222 1,280,000	21,550,000	Spanish, Quechua	coffee, cotton, sugar, fish, copper, petroleum
	Philippines	Manila	117,187 300,000	60,900,000	Pilipino, English	copper, sugar, garments, coconuts, electronics
	Poland	Warsaw	120,725 312,680	37,930,000	Polish	grains, textiles, coal, copper, ships
	Portugal	Lisbon	36,390 94,276	10,390,000	Portuguese	cork, fish, wine, chemicals, textiles, manufactured goods
	Qatar	Doha	4,427 11,437	371,863	Arabic, English	petroleum, fish, steel
	Romania	Bucharest	91,699 237,499	23,000,000	Romanian, Hungarian, German	petroleum, grains, machinery, minerals, cement
	Russia	Moscow	6,592,800 17,075,000	148,040,000	Russian	petroleum, coal, iron ore, grain, machinery, metals
	Rwanda	Kigali	10,169 26,338	6,710,000	Kinyarwanda, French	coffee, tea, pyrethrom, potatoes, tin
	St. Kitts and Nevis	Basseterre	68 168	44,380	English	sugar, cotton, fish, coconuts
	St. Lucia	Castries	238 619	146,600	English, French patois	bananas, coconuts, citrus fruit, cocoa beans, spices
	St. Vincent and the Grenadines	Kingstown	150 388	113,950	English	bananas, eddoes, copra, coconuts
	San Marino	San Marino	24 62	23,200	Italian	tiles, chemicals, wheat, textiles, wine
	São Tomé and Príncipe	São Tomé	387 1,001	124,000	Portuguese, Fang	copra, palm oil, cocoa beans, coffee, bananas
	Saudi Arabia	Riyadh	830,000 2,331,000	12,000,000	Arabic	petroleum, dates, chemicals, livestock, wheat
	Senegal	Dakar	76,000 196,840	7,330,000	French, Wolof, others	phosphates, fertilizer, petroleum products
	Seychelles	Victoria	171 444	67,378	Creole, English, French	copra, fish, coconuts, cinnamon bark
	Sierra Leone	Freetown	27,925 72,325	4,140,000	English, Mende, Krio	coffee, cocoa beans, fish, ginger, peanuts
	Singapore	Singapore	239 620	2,690,000	Malay, English, Chinese, Tamil	machinery, textiles, fish, optical instruments
	Slovakia	Bratislava	18,928 49,035	5,000,000	Slovak	iron ore, livestock, timber, wheat, potatoes

Countries of the World[1]

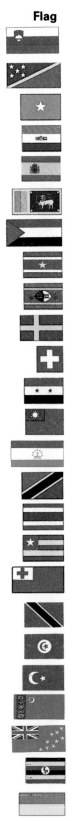

Flag	Country	Capital[2]	Area[2] (sq. mi) (sq. km)	Population[3]	Major or[2] Official Languages	Important[3] Products
	Slovenia	Ljubljana	7,819 20,251	1,950,000	Slovenian	wheat, maize, potatoes, timber, lignite, machinery
	Solomon Islands	Honiara	11,599 27,556	325,600	Melanesian languages, English	fish, copra, rice, palm oil, rattan furniture
	Somalia	Mogadishu	246,000 686,803	7,560,000	Somali, Arabic, English, Italian	livestock, bananas, fruit, hides and skins
	South Africa	Capetown, Pretoria	472,359 1,233,404	33,000,000	Afrikaans, English, Bantu languages	gold, diamonds, coal, fruits, textiles, cotton
	Spain	Madrid	194,884 504,750	38,420,000	Spanish, Catalan, Galician, Basque	fruit, grain, wine, cars, clothing, cotton
	Sri Lanka	Colombo	25,332 65,610	16,900,000	Sinhala, Tamil, English	rubber, tea, gems, fish, copra, textiles
	Sudan	Khartoum	967,500 2,500,000	25,560,000	Arabic, English, tribal languages	peanuts, sugar, cotton, sesame seeds, gum arabic
	Suriname	Paramaribo	63,037 163,265	416,839	Dutch, English, Surinamese	aluminum, bauxite, lumber, shrimp, bananas
	Swaziland	Mbabane	6,704 17,363	681,059	Siswati, English	citrus, canned fruit, sugar, asbestos, wood pulp
	Sweden	Stockholm	173,731 449,964	8,600,000	Swedish	lumber, cars, chemicals, machinery, paper
	Switzerland	Bern	15,941 41,288	6,750,000	German, French, Italian, Romansch	precision instruments, dairy products, chemicals
	Syria	Damascus	71,500 185,170	11,300,000	Arabic, English, French, Kurdish	textiles, grains, olives, cotton, petroleum
	Taiwan[5]	Taipei (Taibei)	14,000 35,981	20,400,000	Mandarin Chinese	electrical machinery, footwear, textiles, toys
	Tajikistan	Dushanbe	55,240 143,100	5,250,000	Tajik, Russian	grain, livestock, textiles, coal, lead, oil, zinc
	Tanzania	Dodoma	363,950 942,623	25,090,000	Kiswahill, English	diamonds, cashews, sisal, cloves, coffee, tea, cotton
	Thailand	Bangkok	198,114 513,115	55,900,000	Thai	rubber, tapioca, jewelry, rice, textiles, lumber
	Togo	Lomé	21,853 56,600	3,400,000	Ewe, French, Kabre	coffee, cocoa beans, phosphates, cotton
	Tonga	Nuku'alofa	288 747	103,000	Tongan, English	coconuts, bananas, vanilla, tapa cloth, footwear, fish
	Trinidad and Tobago	Port-of-Spain	1,980 5,128	1,240,000	English	ammonia, fertilizer, petroleum, sugar, cement
	Tunisia	Tunis	63,378 164,149	8,180,000	Arabic, French	textiles, phosphates, olive oil, cereals
	Turkey	Ankara	296,000 766,640	56,470,000	Turkish, Kurdich, Arabic	textiles, iron and steel, chemicals, cotton, nuts
	Turkmenistan	Ashkhabad	186,400 488,100	3,620,000	Turkmen, Russian	minerals, cotton, livestock, clothing, carpets
	Tuvalu	Funafuti	10 26	8,229	Tuvaluan, English	coconuts, handicrafts, copra, postage stamps
	Uganda	Kampala	94,354 235,885	18,440,000	English, Swahili, Bantu languages	cotton, coffee, tea, tobacco, sugar, cement
	Ukraine	Kiev	171,770 445,000	51,840,000	Ukrainian, Russian	grain, sugar beets, coal, steel, chemicals

[5]Both Taiwan and China claim to be the sole legitimate government of all of China. In 1971 Taiwan lost its UN seat to mainland China, and in 1979 the United States changed its diplomatic recognition from Taipei to Beijing. Taiwan has diplomatic relations with about two dozen countries.

Countries of the World[1]

Flag	Country	Capital[2]	Area[2] (sq. mi) (sq. km)	Population[3]	Major or[2] Official Languages	Important[3] Products
	United Arab Emirates	Abu Dhabi	30,000 82,880	1,840,000	Arabic, English, Hindi, Urdu	petroleum, fish, chemicals, dates, fertilizers
	United Kingdom	London	94,251 244,111	57,410,000	English, Welsh, Gaelic	chemicals, foods, iron and steel, machinery
	United States of America	Washington, D.C.	3,615,105 9,363,123	253,600,000	English, Spanish	aircraft, chemicals, machinery, grain, fruits
	Uruguay	Montevideo	68,037 176,215	3,110,000	Spanish	livestock, wool, leather, textiles, wheat, rice
	Uzbekistan	Tashkent	172,741 447,400	20,320,000	Uzbek, Russian	cotton, livestock, rice, coal, cement, clothing, oil
	Vanuatu	Port-Vila	4,706 12,189	142,630	Bislama, English, French	fish, copra, cocoa beans, livestock, timber
	Vatican City	Vatican City	109 acres 0.439	1,000	Italian, Latin, French	coins, postage stamps
	Venezuela	Caracas	352,143 912,050	19,250,000	Spanish	petroleum, iron ore, coffee, cocoa beans
	Vietnam	Hanoi	127,330 329,707	65,000,000	Vietnamese, French, Chinese, Khmer	coal, minerals, fish, vegetables, rice, rubber
	Western Samoa	Apia	1,133 2,934	157,158	Samoan, English	coconuts, cocoa beans, lumber, bananas, fruit
	Yemen	Sanaa (Sana'a)	203,796 527,970	12,000,000	Arabic	cotton, fish, salt, fruit, grains
	Yugoslavia[6]	Belgrade	39,438 102,173	9,900,000	Serbo-Croatian, Slovenian	wheat, lumber, sheep, sugar, fabrics
	Zaire	Kinshasa	905,063 2,350,000	38,550,000	French, Bantu languages	copper, diamonds, cobalt, petroleum, coffee
	Zambia	Lusaka	290,585 752,614	8,500,000	English, Bantu languages	cobalt, copper, emeralds, cotton, sugar
	Zimbabwe	Harare	151,000 391,090	9,600,000	English, Shona, Sindebele	cotton, fruits, tobacco, coal, chrome, nickel

[6]Yugoslavia, formerly comprised of six replublics, now consists of the two republics of Serbia and Montenegro.

Outlying Territories of the United States

Flag	Country	Capital[2]	Area[2] (sq. mi) (sq. km)	Population[3]	Major or[2] Official Languages	Important[3] Products
	American Samoa (US)	Pago Pago	76 198	39,500	Samoan, English	tuna, pet food, fish meal, handicrafts
	Guam (US)	Agaña	209 541	133,000	Chamorro, English	fruits, vegetables, fish, shrimp, livestock
	Northern Marianas (US)	Saipan	185 480	21,200	Chamorro, English	copra, livestock, fish, fruits, vegetables, sugar
	Palau (US)	Koror	188 488	14,208	English, Palauan	bauxite, yams, copra, fruits, fish, handicrafts
	Puerto Rico (US)	San Juan	3,435 8,897	3,291,000	Spanish, English	chemicals, clothing, fish, electronic goods, sugar
	Virgin Islands (US)	Charlotte Amalie	133 344	103,200	English	manufacturing, petroleum refining, fruits, sugar

Index

How to Use the Index

The number in dark type which precedes each name in the index refers to the number of the page where that feature or place will be found.

The geographical coordinates which follow the place name are sometimes only approximate but are close enough for the place name to be located.

The alphabetical order of names composed of two or more words is governed primarily by the first word and then by the second. This is an example of the rule:

White Nile   Whitehorse
White Sea   Whitney, Mt,

Latitude and Longitude

In the index each place name is followed by its geographical coordinates which allow the reader to find the place on the map. These coordinates give the latitude and longitude of a particular place.

The latitude (or parallel) is the distance of a point north or south of the Equator measured as an angle with the center of the earth. The Equator is latitude 0°, the North Pole is 90°N and the South Pole 90°S. On a globe the lines could be drawn as concentric circles parallel to the Equator, decreasing in diameter from the Equator until they become a point at the Poles. On the maps these lines of latitude are usually represented as lines running across the map from East to West in smooth curves. They are numbered on the sides of the map; north of the Equator the numbers increase southwards. The degree interval between them depends on the scale of the map. On a large scale map (for example, 1:2 000 000) the interval is one degree, but on a small scale (for example, 1:50 000 000) it will be ten degrees.

Lines of longitude (or meridians) cut the latitude lines at right angles on the globe and intersect with one another at the Poles. Longitude is measured by the angle at the center of the earth between it and the meridian of origin which runs through Greenwich, London, U.K. (0°). It may be a measurement East or West of this line and from 0° to 180° in each direction. The longitude line of 180° runs North-South through the Pacific Ocean. On a particular map the interval between the lines of longitude is always the same as that between the lines of latitude and normally they are drawn vertically. They are numbered in the top and bottom margins and a note states East or West from Greenwich.

The unit of measurement for latitude and longitude is the degree. It is subdivided into 60 minutes. An index entry states the position of a place in degrees and minutes, a space being left between the degrees and minutes. The latitude is followed by N(orth) or S(outh) and the longitude by E(ast) or W(est).

The following is a list of the principal abbreviations used in the index:

Afghan.	Afghanistan	est.	estuary	Miss.	Mississippi	Resr.	Reservoir
Ala.	Alabama	f.	physical feature eg. valley,	Mo.	Missouri	Russian Fed.	Russian Federation
Ark.	Arkansas		plain	Mt.	Mount	S.C.	South Carolina
b., B.	bay, Bay	Fla.	Florida	mtn., Mtn.	mountain, Mountain	Sd.	Sound
Bangla.	Bangladesh	g., G.	gulf, Gulf	mts., Mts.	mountains, Mountains	S.Korea	South Korea
Bosnia.	Bosnia-Herzegovina	Ga.	Georgia	N.C.	North Carolina	str., Str.	strait, Strait
c., C.	cape, Cape	i., I., is., Is.	island, Island, islands,	Neth.	Netherlands	Switz.	Switzerland
C.A.R.	Central African		Islands	N.Korea	North Korea	Tenn.	Tennessee
	Republic	Ill.	Illinois	N.Mex	New Mexico	Tex.	Texas
Calif.	California	Ind.	Indiana	N.Y	New York State	U.A.E.	United Arab Emirates
Colo.	Colorado	l., L.	lake, Lake	Oreg.	Oregon	U.K.	United Kingdom
d.	internal division eg.	La.	Louisiana	pen., Pen.	peninsula, Peninsula	U.S.A.	United States of America
	county, state	Liech.	Liechtenstein	Phil.	Philippines	Vt.	Vermont
Del.	Delaware	Lux.	Luxembourg	P.N.G.	Papua New Guinea	Wash.	Washington
des.	desert	Mass.	Massachusetts	Pt.	Point	W. Sahara	Western Sahara
Dom. Rep.	Dominican Republic	Mich.	Michigan	r., R.	river, River	W. Va.	West Virginia
Equat. Guinea	Equatorial Guinea	Minn.	Minnesota	Rep. of Ire.	Republic of Ireland	Yugo.	Yugoslavia

PAGE	PLACENAME	LATITUDE	LONGITUDE
60	Bloomington, *U.S.A.*	40 29N	89 0W
62	Blue Mts., *U.S.A.*	45 30N	118 15W
107	Blue Nile, *r., Sudan*	15 45N	32 25E
74	Blumenau, *Brazil*	26 55S	49 7W
106	Bobo-Dioulasso, *Burkina Faso*	11 11N	4 18W
80	Bochum, *Germany*	51 28N	7 11E
102	Bogor, *Indonesia*	6 34S	106 45E
70	Bogotá, *Colombia*	4 38N	74 5W
82	Bohemian Forest, *mts., Germany/Czech Rep.*	49 20N	13 10E
101	Bohol, *i., Phil.*	9 55N	124 13E
62	Boise, *U.S.A.*	43 37N	116 13W
61	Boise City, *U.S.A.*	36 44N	102 31W
72	Bolivia, *S. America*	17 0S	65 0W
82	Bologna, *Italy*	44 30N	11 20E
89	Bolshevik, *i., Russian Fed.*	78 30N	102 0E
79	Bolton, *U.K.*	53 35N	2 26W
82	Bolzano, *Italy*	46 30N	11 20E
96	Bombay, *India*	18 56N	72 51E
84	Bonifacio, Str. of, *Med. Sea*	41 18N	9 10E
80	Bonn, *Germany*	50 44N	7 6E
53	Boothia, G. of, *Canada*	70 0N	90 0W
81	Borås, *Sweden*	57 44N	12 55E
84	Bordeaux, *France*	44 50N	0 34W
102	Borneo, *i., Asia*	1 0N	114 0E
81	Bornholm, *i., Denmark*	55 2N	15 0E
85	Bosnia-Herzegovina, *Europe*	44 20N	18 0E
94	Bosporus, *str., Turkey*	41 7N	29 4E
58	Boston, *U.S.A.*	42 15N	71 5W
81	Bothnia, G. of, *Europe*	63 30N	20 30E
108	Botswana, *Africa*	22 0S	24 0E
80	Bottrop, *Germany*	51 31N	6 55E
112	Bougainville, *i., Pacific Oc.*	6 0S	155 0E
60	Boulder, *U.S.A.*	40 1N	105 17W
84	Boulogne, *France*	50 43N	1 37E
79	Bournemouth, *U.K.*	50 43N	1 53W
75	Bouvet I., *Atlantic Oc.*	54 26S	3 24E
59	Bradenton, *U.S.A.*	27 29N	82 33W
79	Bradford, *U.K.*	53 47N	1 45W
97	Brahmaputra, *r., Asia*	23 50N	89 45E
83	Brăila, *Romania*	45 18N	27 58E
70	Branco, *r., Brazil*	1 0S	62 0W
71	Brasília, *Brazil*	15 45S	47 57W
83	Braşov, *Romania*	45 40N	25 35E
83	Bratislava, *Slovakia*	48 10N	17 10E
89	Bratsk, *Russian Fed.*	56 20N	101 15E
82	Braunschweig, *Germany*	52 15N	10 30E
71	Brazil, *S. America*	10 0S	50 0W
71	Brazilian Highlands, *Brazil*	12 50S	42 30W
61	Brazos, *r., U.S.A.*	28 53N	95 23W
108	Brazzaville, *Congo*	4 14S	15 14E
80	Breda, *Neth.*	51 35N	4 46E
81	Breidhafjördhur, *est., Iceland*	65 15N	23 0W
82	Bremen, *Germany*	53 5N	8 48E
82	Bremerhaven, *Germany*	53 33N	8 35E
62	Bremerton, *U.S.A.*	47 34N	122 38W
82	Brenner Pass, *Italy/Austria*	47 0N	11 30E
82	Brescia, *Italy*	45 33N	10 12E
83	Brest, *Belorussia*	52 8N	23 40E
84	Brest, *France*	48 23N	4 30W
58	Bridgeport, *U.S.A.*	41 12N	73 12W
65	Bridgetown, *Barbados*	13 6N	59 37W
79	Brighton, *U.K.*	50 50N	0 9W
110	Brisbane, *Australia*	27 30S	153 0E
79	Bristol, *U.K.*	51 26N	2 35W
79	Bristol Channel, *U.K.*	51 20N	3 30W
52	British Columbia, *d., Canada*	55 0N	125 0W
79	British Isles, *Europe*	54 0N	5 0W
82	Brno, *Czech Rep.*	49 11N	16 39E
57	Brooks Range, *mts., U.S.A.*	68 50N	152 0W
110	Broome, *Australia*	17 58S	122 15E
61	Brownsville, *U.S.A.*	25 54N	97 30W
80	Bruay-en-Artois, *France*	50 29N	2 36E
80	Bruges, *Belgium*	51 13N	3 14E
102	Brunei, *Asia*	4 56N	114 58E
80	Brussels, *Belgium*	50 50N	4 23E
61	Bryan, *U.S.A.*	30 40N	96 22W
86	Bryansk, *Russian Fed.*	53 15N	34 9E
70	Bucaramanga, *Colombia*	7 8N	73 1W
83	Bucharest, *Romania*	44 25N	26 6E
83	Budapest, *Hungary*	47 30N	19 3E
70	Buenaventura, *Colombia*	3 54N	77 2W
73	Buenos Aires, *Argentina*	34 40S	58 25W
58	Buffalo, *U.S.A.*	42 52N	78 55W
83	Bug, *r., Poland*	52 29N	21 11E
87	Bug, *r., Ukraine*	46 55N	31 59E
108	Bujumbura, *Burundi*	3 22S	29 21E
108	Bukavu, *Zaïre*	2 30S	28 49E
95	Bukhara, *Uzbekistan*	39 47N	64 26E
108	Bulawayo, *Zimbabwe*	20 10S	28 43E
85	Bulgaria, *Europe*	42 30N	25 0E
97	Burdwan, *India*	23 15N	87 52E
85	Burgas, *Bulgaria*	42 30N	27 29E
84	Burgos, *Spain*	42 21N	3 41W
106	Burkina Faso, *Africa*	12 15N	1 30W
60	Burlington, *Iowa, U.S.A.*	40 49N	91 14W
59	Burlington, *N.C., U.S.A.*	36 5N	79 27W
58	Burlington, *Vt., U.S.A.*	44 25N	73 14W
94	Bursa, *Turkey*	40 11N	29 4E
95	Burujird, *Iran*	33 54N	48 47E
108	Burundi, *Africa*	3 30S	30 0E
101	Butuan, *Phil.*	8 58N	125 32E
83	Buzău, *Romania*	45 10N	26 49E
83	Bydgoszcz, *Poland*	53 16N	17 33E
89	Byrranga Mts., *Russian Fed.*	74 50N	101 0E
83	Bytom, *Poland*	50 22N	18 54E

C

PAGE	PLACENAME	LATITUDE	LONGITUDE
101	Cabanatuan, *Phil.*	15 30N	120 58E
70	Cabimas, *Venezuela*	10 26N	71 27W
108	Cabinda, *Angola*	5 34S	12 12E
74	Cachoeira do Sul, *Brazil*	30 3S	52 52W
101	Cadiz, *Phil.*	10 57N	123 18E
84	Cádiz, *Spain*	36 32N	6 18W
84	Caen, *France*	49 11N	0 22W
101	Cagayan de Oro, *Phil.*	8 30N	124 40E
84	Cagliari, *Italy*	39 14N	9 7E
67	Caguas, *Puerto Rico*	18 8N	66 0W
110	Cairns, *Australia*	16 51S	145 43E
94	Cairo, *Egypt*	30 3N	31 15E
70	Cajamarca, *Peru*	7 9S	78 32W
106	Calabar, *Nigeria*	4 56N	8 22E
84	Calais, *France*	50 57N	1 52E
101	Calbayog, *Phil.*	12 4N	124 38E
97	Calcutta, *India*	22 35N	88 21E
52	Calgary, *Canada*	51 5N	114 5W
70	Cali, *Colombia*	3 24N	76 30W
96	Calicut, *India*	11 15N	75 45E
62	California, *d., U.S.A.*	37 29N	119 58W
63	California, G. of, *Mexico*	28 0N	112 0W
72	Callao, *Peru*	12 5S	77 8W
66	Camagüey, *Cuba*	21 25N	77 55W
96	Cambay, G. of, *India*	20 30N	72 0E
102	Cambodia, *Asia*	12 0N	105 0E
79	Cambrian Mts., *U.K.*	52 30N	3 35W
52	Cambridge Bay, *town, Canada*	69 9N	105 0W
59	Camden, *U.S.A.*	39 57N	75 7W
106	Cameroon, *Africa*	5 30N	12 15E
101	Camotes Sea, *Phil.*	10 20N	124 25E
64	Campeche, *Mexico*	19 50N	90 30W
64	Campeche B., *Mexico*	19 30N	94 0W
71	Campina Grande, *Brazil*	7 15S	35 50W
74	Campinas, *Brazil*	22 54S	47 6W
72	Campo Grande, *Brazil*	20 24S	54 35W
74	Campos, *Brazil*	21 46S	41 21W
102	Can Tho, *Vietnam*	10 3N	105 46E
52	Canada, *N. America*	60 0N	105 0W
75	Canary Is., *Atlantic Oc.*	28 0N	15 0W
110	Canberra, *Australia*	35 18S	149 8E
82	Cannes, *France*	43 33N	7 0E
84	Cantabrian Mts., *Spain*	42 55N	5 10W
58	Canton, *U.S.A.*	40 48N	81 22W
65	Cap Haïtien, *town, Haiti*	19 47N	72 17W
53	Cape Breton I., *Canada*	46 0N	61 0W
61	Cape Girardeau, *town, U.S.A.*	37 19N	89 32W
108	Cape Town, *South Africa*	33 56S	18 28E
75	Cape Verde, *Atlantic Oc.*	16 0N	24 0W
110	Cape York Pen., *Australia*	12 40S	142 20E
70	Caracas, *Venezuela*	10 35N	66 56W
79	Cardiff, *U.K.*	51 28N	3 11W
79	Cardigan B., *U.K.*	52 30N	4 20W
65	Caribbean Sea, *C. America*	15 0N	75 0W
79	Carlisle, *U.K.*	54 54N	2 55W
110	Carnegie, L., *Australia*	26 15S	123 0E
56	Caroline Is., *Pacific Oc.*	7 50N	145 0E
83	Carpathians, *mts., Europe*	48 45N	23 45E
110	Carpentaria, G. of, *Australia*	14 0S	140 0E
70	Cartagena, *Colombia*	10 24N	75 33W
84	Cartagena, *Spain*	37 36N	0 59W
71	Caruarú, *Brazil*	8 15S	35 55W
84	Casablanca, *Morocco*	33 39N	7 35W
62	Cascade Range, *mts., U.S.A.*	46 15N	121 0W
62	Casper, *U.S.A.*	42 51N	106 19W
87	Caspian Depression, *f., Asia*	47 0N	48 0E
87	Caspian Sea, *Asia*	42 0N	51 0E
84	Castellón de la Plana, *Spain*	39 59N	0 3W
65	Castries, *St. Lucia*	14 1N	60 59W
101	Catanduanes I., *Phil.*	13 50N	124 15E
84	Catania, *Italy*	37 31N	15 5E
87	Caucasus Mts., *Asia*	43 0N	44 0E
74	Caxias do Sul, *Brazil*	29 14S	51 10W
71	Cayenne, *Fr. Guiana*	4 55N	52 18W
65	Cayman Is., *C. America*	19 0N	81 0W
101	Cebu, *Phil.*	10 20N	123 55E
60	Cedar Rapids, *town, U.S.A.*	41 59N	91 40W
64	Celaya, *Mexico*	20 32N	100 48W
103	Celebes, *i., Indonesia*	2 0S	120 30E
103	Celebes Sea, *Indonesia*	3 0N	122 0E
106	Central African Republic, *Africa*	6 30N	20 0E
89	Central Siberian Plateau, *f., Russian Fed.*	66 0N	108 0E
103	Ceram, *i., Indonesia*	3 10S	129 30E
106	Chad, *Africa*	13 0N	19 0E
106	Chad, L., *Africa*	13 30N	14 0E
60	Champaign, *U.S.A.*	40 7N	88 14W
58	Champlain, L., *U.S.A.*	44 45N	73 20W
96	Chandigarh, *India*	30 44N	76 54E
99	Chang Jiang, *r., China*	31 40N	121 15E
99	Changchun, *China*	43 50N	125 20E
99	Changsha, *China*	28 10N	113 0E
63	Channel Is., *U.S.A.*	34 0N	120 0W
95	Chardzhou, *Turkmenistan*	39 9N	63 34E
80	Charleroi, *Belgium*	50 25N	4 27E
59	Charleston, *S.C., U.S.A.*	32 48N	79 58W
58	Charleston, *W.Va., U.S.A.*	38 23N	81 20W
59	Charlotte, *U.S.A.*	35 3N	80 50W
59	Charlottesville, *U.S.A.*	38 2N	78 29W
53	Charlottetown, *Canada*	46 14N	63 9W
59	Chattahoochee, *r., U.S.A.*	30 52N	84 57W
59	Chattanooga, *U.S.A.*	35 2N	85 18W
86	Cheboksary, *Russian Fed.*	56 8N	47 12E
88	Chelyabinsk, *Russian Fed.*	55 10N	61 25E
82	Chemnitz, *Germany*	50 50N	12 55E
98	Chengdu, *China*	30 37N	104 6E
84	Cherbourg, *France*	49 38N	1 37W
86	Cherepovets, *Russian Fed.*	59 5N	37 55E
87	Cherkassy, *Ukraine*	49 27N	32 4E
83	Chernigov, *Ukraine*	51 30N	31 18E
83	Chernovtsy, *Ukraine*	48 19N	25 52E
59	Chesapeake B., *U.S.A.*	38 0N	76 0W
53	Chesterfield Inlet, *town, Canada*	63 0N	91 0W
79	Cheviot Hills, The, *U.K.*	55 22N	2 24W
62	Cheyenne, *U.S.A.*	41 8N	104 49W
60	Cheyenne, *r., U.S.A.*	44 40N	101 15W
102	Chiang Mai, *Thailand*	18 48N	98 59E
100	Chiba, *Japan*	35 38N	140 7E
60	Chicago, *U.S.A.*	41 50N	87 45W
70	Chiclayo, *Peru*	6 47S	79 47W
73	Chico, *r. Santa Cruz, Argentina*	50 3S	68 35W
58	Chicoutimi-Jonquière, *Canada*	48 26N	71 6W
53	Chidley, C., *Canada*	60 30N	65 0W
99	Chihli, G. of, *China*	38 30N	119 30E
63	Chihuahua, *Mexico*	28 38N	106 5W
72	Chile, *S. America*	32 30S	71 0W
73	Chillán, *Chile*	36 36S	72 7W
70	Chimborazo, *mtn., Ecuador*	1 29S	78 52W
98	Chimkent, *Kazakhstan*	42 16N	69 5E
98	China, *Asia*	33 0N	103 0E
108	Chingola, *Zambia*	12 31S	27 53E
99	Chita, *Russian Fed.*	52 3N	113 35E
97	Chittagong, *Bangla.*	22 20N	91 48E
100	Chongjin, *N. Korea*	41 46N	129 55E
98	Chongqing, *China*	29 31N	106 35E
100	Chonju, *S. Korea*	35 50N	127 5E
83	Chorzów, *Poland*	50 19N	18 56E
111	Christchurch, *New Zealand*	43 33S	172 40E
102	Christmas I., *Indian Oc.*	10 30S	105 40E
63	Chula Vista, *U.S.A.*	32 39N	117 5W
53	Churchill, *r., Canada*	58 20N	94 15W
65	Cienfuegos, *Cuba*	22 10N	80 27W
58	Cincinnati, *U.S.A.*	39 10N	84 30W
70	Ciudad Bolívar, *Venezuela*	8 6N	63 36W
70	Ciudad Guayana, *Venezuela*	8 22N	62 40W
63	Ciudad Juárez, *Mexico*	31 44N	106 29W
64	Ciudad Madero, *Mexico*	22 19N	97 50W
63	Ciudad Obregón, *Mexico*	27 29N	109 56W
64	Ciudad Victoria, *Mexico*	23 43N	99 10W
59	Clarksville, *Tenn., U.S.A.*	36 31N	87 21W
59	Clearwater, *U.S.A.*	27 57N	82 48W
82	Clermont-Ferrand, *France*	45 47N	3 5E
58	Cleveland, *U.S.A.*	41 30N	81 41W
60	Clinton, *U.S.A.*	41 51N	90 12W
61	Clovis, *N.Mex., U.S.A.*	34 24N	103 12W
83	Cluj, *Romania*	46 47N	23 37E
52	Coast Mts., *Canada*	55 30N	128 0W
62	Coast Range, *mts., U.S.A.*	42 40N	123 30W
64	Coatzacoalcos, *Mexico*	18 10N	94 25W
72	Cochabamba, *Bolivia*	17 24S	66 9W
96	Cochin, *India*	9 56N	76 15E
91	Cocos Is., *Indian Oc.*	13 0S	96 0E
96	Coimbatore, *India*	11 0N	76 57E
80	Cologne, *Germany*	50 56N	6 57E
70	Colombia, *S. America*	4 0N	72 30W
97	Colombo, *Sri Lanka*	6 55N	79 52E
73	Colorado, *r., Argentina*	39 50S	62 2W
63	Colorado, *r., U.S.A.*	31 45N	114 40W
63	Colorado Plateau, *f., U.S.A.*	36 30N	108 0W
62	Colorado Springs, *town, U.S.A.*	38 50N	104 49W
60	Columbia, *Mo., U.S.A.*	38 57N	92 20W
62	Columbia, *r., U.S.A.*	46 15N	124 5W
59	Columbia, *S.C., U.S.A.*	34 0N	81 0W
59	Columbus, *Ga., U.S.A.*	32 28N	84 59W
61	Columbus, *Miss., U.S.A.*	33 30N	88 25W
58	Columbus, *Ohio, U.S.A.*	39 59N	83 3W
97	Comilla, *Bangla.*	23 28N	91 10E
73	Comodoro Rivadavia, *Argentina*	45 50S	67 30W
96	Comorin, C., *India*	8 4N	77 35E

126

128

PAGE	PLACENAME	LATITUDE	LONGITUDE
101	Pinamalayan, *Phil.*	13 2 N	121 28 E
85	Pindus Mts., *Albania/Greece*	39 40 N	21 0 E
61	Pine Bluff, *town, U.S.A.*	34 13 N	92 1 W
98	Pingxiang, *China*	22 5 N	106 46 E
74	Piracicaba, *Brazil*	22 50 S	47 40 W
85	Piraeus, *Greece*	37 56 N	23 38 E
82	Pisa, *Italy*	43 43 N	10 24 E
113	Pitcairn I., *Pacific Oc.*	25 4 S	130 6 W
83	Piteşti, *Romania*	44 52 N	24 51 E
61	Pittsburg, *U.S.A.*	37 25 N	94 42 W
58	Pittsburgh, *U.S.A.*	40 26 N	79 58 W
70	Piura, *Peru*	5 15 S	80 38 W
60	Platte, *r., U.S.A.*	41 4 N	95 53 W
82	Plauen, *Germany*	50 29 N	12 8 E
83	Pleven, *Bulgaria*	43 25 N	24 39 E
83	Plock, *Poland*	52 33 N	19 43 E
83	Ploieşti, *Romania*	44 57 N	26 2 E
85	Plovdiv, *Bulgaria*	42 9 N	24 45 E
79	Plymouth, *U.K.*	50 23 N	4 9 W
82	Plzeň, *Czech Rep.*	49 45 N	13 22 E
82	Po, *r., Italy*	44 51 N	12 30 E
62	Pocatello, *U.S.A.*	42 52 N	112 27 W
86	Podolsk, *Russian Fed.*	55 23 N	37 32 E
56	Pohnpei, *i., Pacific Oc.*	6 55 N	158 15 E
108	Pointe Noire, *town, Congo*	4 46 S	11 53 E
84	Poitiers, *France*	46 35 N	0 20 E
83	Poland, *Europe*	52 30 N	19 0 E
101	Polillo Is., *Phil.*	14 50 N	122 15 E
87	Poltava, *Ukraine*	49 35 N	34 35 E
112	Polynesia, *is., Pacific Oc.*	4 0 S	165 0 W
61	Ponca City, *U.S.A.*	36 42 N	97 5 W
67	Ponce, *Puerto Rico*	18 0 N	66 40 W
97	Pondicherry, *India*	11 59 N	79 50 E
74	Ponta Grossa, *Brazil*	25 0 S	50 9 W
61	Pontchartrain, L., *U.S.A.*	30 10 N	90 10 W
58	Pontiac, *U.S.A.*	42 37 N	83 18 W
102	Pontianak, *Indonesia*	0 5 S	109 16 E
94	Pontine Mts., *Turkey*	40 32 N	38 0 E
72	Poopó, L., *Bolivia*	18 45 S	67 7 W
61	Poplar Bluff, *town, U.S.A.*	36 45 N	90 24 W
64	Popocatépetl, *mtn., Mexico*	19 2 N	98 38 W
81	Porsangen, *est., Norway*	70 30 N	25 45 E
62	Port Angeles, *U.S.A.*	48 7 N	123 27 W
66	Port Antonio, *Jamaica*	18 10 N	76 27 W
61	Port Arthur, *U.S.A.*	29 55 N	93 55 W
53	Port Cartier, *Canada*	50 3 N	66 46 W
108	Port Elizabeth, *South Africa*	33 58 S	25 36 E
106	Port Harcourt, *Nigeria*	4 43 N	7 5 E
110	Port Hedland, *Australia*	20 24 S	118 36 E
58	Port Huron, *U.S.A.*	42 58 N	82 27 W
103	Port Moresby, *P.N.G.*	9 30 S	147 7 E
67	Port of Spain, *Trinidad*	10 38 N	61 31 W
94	Port Said, *Egypt*	31 17 N	32 18 E
107	Port Sudan, *Sudan*	19 39 N	37 1 E
60	Portage la Prairie, *town, Canada*	49 58 N	98 20 W
66	Port-au-Prince, *Haiti*	18 33 N	72 20 W
58	Portland, *Maine, U.S.A.*	43 39 N	70 17 W
62	Portland, *Oreg., U.S.A.*	45 33 N	122 36 W
74	Pôrto Alegre, *Brazil*	30 3 S	51 10 W
70	Pôrto Velho, *Brazil*	8 45 S	63 54 W
106	Porto-Novo, *Benin*	6 30 N	2 47 E
70	Portoviejo, *Ecuador*	1 7 S	80 28 W
79	Portsmouth, *U.K.*	50 48 N	1 6 W
59	Portsmouth, *U.S.A.*	36 50 N	76 20 W
84	Portugal, *Europe*	39 30 N	8 5 W
72	Posadas, *Argentina*	27 25 S	55 48 W
59	Potomac, *r., U.S.A.*	38 0 N	76 18 W
72	Potosí, *Bolivia*	19 35 S	65 45 W
82	Potsdam, *Germany*	52 24 N	13 4 E
59	Poughkeepsie, *U.S.A.*	41 42 N	73 56 W
62	Powder, *r., U.S.A.*	46 44 N	105 26 W
62	Powell, L., *U.S.A.*	37 25 N	110 45 W
64	Poza Rica, *Mexico*	20 34 N	97 26 W
82	Poznań, *Poland*	52 25 N	16 53 E
82	Prague, *Czech Rep.*	50 5 N	14 25 E
82	Prato, *Italy*	43 52 N	11 6 E
74	Presidente Prudente, *Brazil*	22 9 S	51 24 W
58	Presque Isle, *town, U.S.A.*	46 41 N	68 1 W
79	Preston, *U.K.*	53 46 N	2 42 W
108	Pretoria, *South Africa*	25 45 S	28 12 E
61	Prichard, *U.S.A.*	30 44 N	88 7 W
52	Prince Albert, *Canada*	53 13 N	105 45 W
53	Prince Edward Island, *d., Canada*	46 15 N	63 10 W
52	Prince George, *Canada*	53 55 N	122 49 W
53	Prince of Wales I., *Canada*	73 0 N	99 0 W
52	Prince Rupert, *Canada*	54 9 N	130 20 W
83	Pripet Marshes, *f., Belorussia/Ukraine*	52 15 N	29 0 E
88	Prokopyevsk, *Russian Fed.*	53 55 N	86 45 E
58	Providence, *U.S.A.*	41 50 N	71 30 W
62	Provo, *U.S.A.*	40 14 N	111 39 W
52	Prudhoe Bay, *town, U.S.A.*	70 20 N	148 25 W
83	Prut, *r., Europe*	45 29 N	28 14 E
83	Przemyśl, *Poland*	49 48 N	22 48 E
64	Puebla, *Mexico*	19 3 N	98 10 W
62	Pueblo, *U.S.A.*	38 16 N	104 37 W
70	Puerto La Cruz, *Venezuela*	10 14 N	64 40 W
73	Puerto Montt, *Chile*	41 28 S	73 0 W
101	Puerto Princesa, *Phil.*	9 46 N	118 45 E
67	Puerto Rico, *C. America*	18 20 N	66 30 W
82	Pula, *Croatia*	44 52 N	13 53 E
62	Pullman, *U.S.A.*	46 44 N	117 10 W
96	Pune, *India*	18 34 N	73 58 E
73	Punta Arenas, *town, Chile*	53 10 S	70 56 W
70	Punto Fijo, *town, Venezuela*	11 50 N	70 16 W
70	Purus, *r., Brazil*	3 58 S	61 25 W
100	Pusan, *S. Korea*	35 5 N	129 2 E
100	Pyongyang, *N. Korea*	39 0 N	125 47 E
84	Pyrénées, *mts., France/Spain*	42 40 N	0 30 E

Q

PAGE	PLACENAME	LATITUDE	LONGITUDE
95	Qatar, *Asia*	25 20 N	51 10 E
94	Qattara Depression, *f., Egypt*	29 40 N	27 30 E
95	Qazvin, *Iran*	36 16 N	50 0 E
98	Qilian Shan, *mts., China*	38 30 N	99 20 E
99	Qingdao, *China*	36 4 N	120 22 E
98	Qinghai Hu, *l., China*	36 40 N	100 0 E
99	Qiqihar, *China*	47 23 N	124 0 E
95	Qom, *Iran*	34 40 N	50 57 E
58	Quebec, *Canada*	46 50 N	71 15 W
53	Quebec, *d., Canada*	51 0 N	70 0 W
52	Queen Charlotte Is., *Canada*	53 0 N	132 30 W
53	Queen Elizabeth Is., *Canada*	78 30 N	99 0 W
114	Queen Maud Land, *Antarctica*	74 0 S	10 0 E
110	Queensland, *d., Australia*	23 30 S	144 0 E
108	Queenstown, *South Africa*	31 54 S	26 53 E
64	Querétaro, *Mexico*	20 38 N	100 23 W
96	Quetta, *Pakistan*	30 15 N	67 0 E
101	Quezon City, *Phil.*	14 39 N	121 1 E
102	Qui Nhon, *Vietnam*	13 47 N	109 11 E
60	Quincy, *U.S.A.*	39 56 N	91 23 W
70	Quito, *Ecuador*	0 14 S	78 30 W

R

PAGE	PLACENAME	LATITUDE	LONGITUDE
84	Rabat, *Morocco*	34 2 N	6 51 W
60	Racine, *U.S.A.*	42 42 N	87 50 W
83	Radom, *Poland*	51 26 N	21 10 E
62	Rainier, Mt., *U.S.A.*	46 52 N	121 46 W
97	Raipur, *India*	21 16 N	81 42 E
97	Rajahmundry, *India*	17 1 N	81 52 E
96	Rajkot, *India*	22 18 N	70 53 E
59	Raleigh, *U.S.A.*	35 46 N	78 39 W
97	Rampur, *India*	28 48 N	79 3 E
73	Rancagua, *Chile*	34 10 S	70 45 W
97	Ranchi, *India*	23 22 N	85 20 E
96	Rann of Kutch, *f., India*	23 50 N	69 50 E
60	Rapid City, *U.S.A.*	44 5 N	103 14 W
95	Rasht, *Iran*	37 18 N	49 38 E
97	Raurkela, *India*	22 16 N	85 1 E
82	Ravenna, *Italy*	44 25 N	12 12 E
96	Rawalpindi, *Pakistan*	33 36 N	73 8 E
62	Rawlins, *U.S.A.*	41 47 N	107 14 W
79	Reading, *U.K.*	51 27 N	0 57 W
59	Reading, *U.S.A.*	40 20 N	75 56 W
71	Recife, *Brazil*	8 6 S	34 53 W
80	Recklinghausen, *Germany*	51 36 N	7 11 E
53	Red, *r., Canada*	50 30 N	96 50 W
61	Red, *r., U.S.A.*	31 0 N	91 40 W
102	Red, *r., Vietnam*	20 15 N	106 32 E
52	Red Deer, *Canada*	52 15 N	113 48 W
107	Red Sea, *Africa/Asia*	20 0 N	39 0 E
62	Redding, *U.S.A.*	40 35 N	122 24 W
62	Redwood City, *U.S.A.*	37 29 N	122 13 W
82	Regensburg, *Germany*	49 1 N	12 7 E
85	Reggio, *Calabria, Italy*	38 7 N	15 38 E
82	Reggio, *Emilia-Romagna, Italy*	44 40 N	10 37 E
60	Regina, *Canada*	50 30 N	104 38 W
59	Reidsville, *U.S.A.*	36 21 N	79 40 W
82	Reims, *France*	49 15 N	4 2 E
52	Reindeer L., *Canada*	57 0 N	102 20 W
61	Reinosa, *Mexico*	26 7 N	98 18 W
80	Remscheid, *Germany*	51 10 N	7 11 E
80	Renaix, *Belgium*	50 45 N	3 36 E
84	Rennes, *France*	48 6 N	1 40 W
62	Reno, *U.S.A.*	39 31 N	119 48 W
79	Republic of Ireland, *Europe*	53 0 N	8 0 W
60	Republican, *r., U.S.A.*	39 3 N	96 48 W
72	Resistencia, *Argentina*	27 28 S	59 0 W
91	Réunion, *i., Indian Oc.*	22 0 S	55 0 E
81	Reykjavík, *Iceland*	64 9 N	21 58 W
82	Rheinland-Pfalz, *d., Germany*	50 0 N	7 0 E
80	Rhine, *r., Europe*	51 53 N	6 3 E
58	Rhode Island, *d., U.S.A.*	41 30 N	71 30 W
85	Rhodes, *i., Greece*	36 12 N	28 0 E
85	Rhodope Mts., *Bulgaria*	41 35 N	24 35 E
82	Rhône, *r., France*	43 25 N	4 45 E
74	Ribeirão Prêto, *Brazil*	21 9 S	47 48 W
62	Richland, *U.S.A.*	46 17 N	119 18 W
59	Richmond, *U.S.A.*	37 34 N	77 27 W
81	Riga, *Latvia*	56 53 N	24 8 E
82	Rijeka, *Croatia*	45 20 N	14 25 E
80	Rijswijk, *Neth.*	52 3 N	4 22 E
82	Rimini, *Italy*	44 1 N	12 34 E
58	Rimouski, *Canada*	48 27 N	68 32 W
70	Rio Branco, *Brazil*	9 59 S	67 49 W
73	Río Cuarto, *Argentina*	33 8 S	64 20 W
74	Rio de Janeiro, *Brazil*	22 53 S	43 17 W
73	Río Gallegos, *Argentina*	51 37 S	69 10 W
73	Rio Grande, *town, Argentina*	53 50 S	67 40 W
65	Rio Grande, *r., Nicaragua*	12 48 N	83 30 W
70	Riobamba, *Ecuador*	1 44 S	78 40 W
63	Riverside, *U.S.A.*	33 59 N	117 22 W
95	Riyadh, *Saudi Arabia*	24 39 N	46 44 E
59	Roanoke, *U.S.A.*	37 15 N	79 58 W
60	Rochester, *Minn., U.S.A.*	44 1 N	92 27 W
58	Rochester, *N.Y., U.S.A.*	43 12 N	77 37 W
59	Rock Hill, *town, U.S.A.*	34 55 N	81 1 W
60	Rock Island, *town, U.S.A.*	41 30 N	90 34 W
62	Rock Springs, *U.S.A.*	41 35 N	109 13 W
60	Rockford, *U.S.A.*	42 17 N	89 6 W
110	Rockhampton, *Australia*	23 22 S	150 32 E
59	Rocky Mount, *town, U.S.A.*	35 56 N	77 48 W
50	Rocky Mts., *N. America*	42 30 N	109 30 W
83	Romania, *Europe*	46 30 N	24 0 E
84	Rome, *Italy*	41 54 N	12 29 E
59	Rome, *U.S.A.*	34 1 N	85 2 W
80	Roosendaal, *Neth.*	51 32 N	4 28 E
70	Roraima, Mt., *Guyana*	5 14 N	60 44 W
73	Rosario, *Argentina*	33 0 S	60 40 W
65	Roseau, *Dominica*	15 18 N	61 23 W
60	Roseau, *U.S.A.*	48 51 N	95 46 W
62	Roseburg, *U.S.A.*	43 13 N	123 20 W
81	Roskilde, *Denmark*	55 39 N	12 7 E
114	Ross Sea, *Antarctica*	73 0 S	179 0 E
82	Rostock, *Germany*	54 6 N	12 9 E
87	Rostov, *Russian Fed.*	47 15 N	39 45 E
63	Roswell, *U.S.A.*	33 24 N	104 32 W
111	Rotorua, *New Zealand*	38 7 S	176 17 E
80	Rotterdam, *Neth.*	51 55 N	4 29 E
80	Roubaix, *France*	50 42 N	3 10 E
84	Rouen, *France*	49 26 N	1 5 E
80	Roulers, *Belgium*	50 57 N	3 6 E
96	Rub al Khali, *des., Saudi Arabia*	20 20 N	52 30 E
80	Ruhr, *r., Germany*	51 27 N	6 41 E
83	Ruse, *Bulgaria*	43 50 N	25 59 E
88	Russian Federation, *Europe/Asia*	62 0 N	80 0 E
108	Rwanda, *Africa*	2 0 S	30 0 E
86	Ryazan, *Russian Fed.*	54 37 N	39 43 E
86	Rybinsk, *Russian Fed.*	58 1 N	38 52 E
99	Ryukyu Is., *Japan*	26 0 N	126 0 E
83	Rzeszów, *Poland*	50 4 N	22 0 E

S

PAGE	PLACENAME	LATITUDE	LONGITUDE
82	Saarbrücken, *Germany*	49 15 N	6 58 E
84	Sabadell, *Spain*	41 33 N	2 7 E
102	Sabah, *d., Malaysia*	5 0 N	117 0 E
62	Sacramento, *U.S.A.*	38 35 N	121 30 W
62	Sacramento, *r., U.S.A.*	38 3 N	121 56 W
63	Sacramento Mts., *U.S.A.*	33 10 N	105 50 W
106	Safi, *Morocco*	32 20 N	9 17 W
97	Sagar, *India*	23 50 N	78 44 E
58	Saginaw, *U.S.A.*	43 25 N	83 58 W
106	Sahara, *des., Africa*	18 0 N	12 0 E
84	Saharan Atlas, *mts., Algeria*	34 0 N	2 0 E
96	Saharanpur, *India*	29 58 N	77 33 E
59	St. Augustine, *U.S.A.*	29 54 N	81 19 W
60	St. Boniface, *Canada*	49 54 N	97 7 W
58	St. Catharines, *Canada*	43 10 N	79 15 W
60	St. Cloud, *U.S.A.*	45 33 N	94 10 W
67	St. Croix, *i., Virgin Is.*	17 45 N	64 35 W
52	St. Elias, Mt., *U.S.A.*	60 20 N	141 0 W
82	St. Étienne, *France*	45 26 N	4 26 E
82	St. Gallen, *Switz.*	47 25 N	9 23 E
65	St. George's, *Grenada*	12 4 N	61 44 W
75	St. Helena, *i., Atlantic Oc.*	15 58 S	5 43 W
62	St. Helens, Mt., *U.S.A.*	46 12 N	122 11 W
58	St. Hyacinthe, *Canada*	45 38 N	72 57 W
58	St. John, *Canada*	45 16 N	66 3 W
65	St. John's, *Antigua*	17 7 N	61 51 W
53	St. John's, *Canada*	47 34 N	52 41 W
59	St. Johns, *r., U.S.A.*	30 24 N	81 24 W
60	St. Joseph, *U.S.A.*	39 46 N	94 51 W
65	St. Kitts-Nevis, *Leeward Is.*	17 20 N	62 45 W
58	St. Lawrence, *r., Canada/U.S.A.*	48 45 N	68 30 W
53	St. Lawrence, G. of, *Canada*	48 0 N	62 0 W
52	St. Lawrence I., *U.S.A.*	63 0 N	170 0 W
60	St. Louis, *U.S.A.*	38 38 N	90 11 W
65	St. Lucia, *Windward Is.*	14 5 N	61 0 W
84	St. Malo, *France*	48 39 N	2 0 W
65	St. Martin, *i., Leeward Is.*	18 5 N	63 5 W
84	St. Nazaire, *France*	47 17 N	2 12 W
60	St. Paul, *U.S.A.*	45 0 N	93 10 W
86	St. Petersburg, *Russian Fed.*	59 55 N	30 25 E
59	St. Petersburg, *U.S.A.*	27 45 N	82 40 W
53	St. Pierre and Miquelon, *is., N. America*	47 0 N	56 15 W

PAGE	PLACENAME	LATITUDE	LONGITUDE
67	St. Thomas, *i., U.S.V.Is.*	18 22 N	64 57 W
67	St. Vincent and the Grenadines, *C. America*	13 10 N	61 15 W
56	Saipan, *i., Mariana Is.*	15 12 N	145 43 E
100	Sakai, *Japan*	34 37 N	135 28 E
89	Sakhalin, *i., Russian Fed.*	50 0 N	143 0 E
72	Salado, *r., Argentina*	31 40 S	60 41 W
84	Salamanca, *Spain*	40 58 N	5 40 W
97	Salem, *India*	11 38 N	78 8 E
62	Salem, *U.S.A.*	44 57 N	123 1 W
84	Salerno, *Italy*	40 41 N	14 45 E
60	Salina, *U.S.A.*	38 50 N	97 37 W
62	Salinas, *U.S.A.*	36 40 N	121 38 W
59	Salisbury, *U.S.A.*	35 20 N	80 30 W
62	Salmon, *r., U.S.A.*	45 51 N	116 46 W
62	Salmon River Mts., *U.S.A.*	44 45 N	115 30 W
62	Salt Lake City, *U.S.A.*	40 46 N	111 53 W
72	Salta, *Argentina*	24 47 S	65 24 W
61	Saltillo, *Mexico*	25 25 N	101 0 W
71	Salvador, *Brazil*	12 58 S	38 29 W
97	Salween, *r., Myanmar*	16 30 N	97 33 E
82	Salzburg, *Austria*	47 54 N	13 3 E
86	Samara, *Russian Fed.*	53 10 N	50 15 E
102	Samarinda, *Indonesia*	0 30 S	117 9 E
88	Samarkand, *Uzbekistan*	39 40 N	66 57 E
94	Samsun, *Turkey*	41 17 N	36 22 E
61	San Angelo, *U.S.A.*	31 28 N	100 26 W
61	San Antonio, *U.S.A.*	29 28 N	98 31 W
63	San Bernardino, *U.S.A.*	34 6 N	117 17 W
101	San Carlos, *Phil.*	15 53 N	120 25 E
70	San Cristóbal, *Venezuela*	7 46 N	72 15 W
63	San Diego, *U.S.A.*	32 43 N	117 9 W
61	San Fernando, *r., Mexico*	24 55 N	97 40 W
70	San Fernando, *Trinidad*	10 16 N	61 28 W
62	San Francisco, *U.S.A.*	37 48 N	122 24 W
62	San Joaquin, *r., U.S.A.*	38 3 N	121 50 W
73	San Jorge, G. of, *Argentina*	46 0 S	66 50 W
65	San José, *Costa Rica*	9 59 N	84 4 W
101	San Jose, *Phil.*	15 47 N	121 0 E
62	San Jose, *U.S.A.*	37 20 N	121 53 W
72	San Juan, *Argentina*	31 30 S	68 30 W
67	San Juan, *Puerto Rico*	18 29 N	66 8 W
62	San Juan Mts., *U.S.A.*	37 35 N	107 10 W
63	San Lucas, C., *Mexico*	22 50 N	109 55 W
63	San Luis Obispo, *U.S.A.*	35 17 N	120 40 W
64	San Luis Potosi, *Mexico*	22 10 N	101 0 W
82	San Marino, *Europe*	43 55 N	12 27 E
72	San Miguel de Tucumán, *Argentina*	26 49 S	65 13 W
101	San Pablo, *Phil.*	14 3 N	121 20 E
65	San Pedro, *Dom. Rep.*	18 30 N	69 18 W
65	San Pedro Sula, *Honduras*	15 26 N	88 1 W
62	San Rafael, *U.S.A.*	37 59 N	122 31 W
65	San Salvador, *i., Bahamas*	24 0 N	74 32 W
72	San Salvador de Jujuy, *Argentina*	24 10 S	65 20 W
84	San Sebastián, *Spain*	43 19 N	1 59 W
107	San'a, *Yemen*	15 23 N	44 14 E
58	Sandusky, *U.S.A.*	41 27 N	82 42 W
59	Sanford, *Fla., U.S.A.*	28 49 N	81 17 W
59	Sanford, *N.C., U.S.A.*	35 29 N	79 10 W
62	Sangre de Cristo Mts., *U.S.A.*	37 30 N	105 15 W
63	Santa Ana, *Mexico*	30 33 N	111 7 W
63	Santa Ana, *U.S.A.*	33 44 N	117 54 W
63	Santa Barbara, *U.S.A.*	34 25 N	119 42 W
66	Santa Clara, *Cuba*	22 25 N	79 58 W
62	Santa Cruz, *U.S.A.*	36 58 N	122 8 W
63	Santa Cruz, *i., U.S.A.*	34 1 N	119 45 W
72	Santa Fé, *Argentina*	31 38 S	60 43 W
63	Santa Lucia Range, *mts., U.S.A.*	36 0 N	121 20 W
74	Santa Maria, *Brazil*	29 40 S	53 47 W
63	Santa Maria, *U.S.A.*	34 57 N	120 26 W
70	Santa Marta, *Colombia*	11 18 N	74 10 W
62	Santa Rosa, *U.S.A.*	38 26 N	122 34 W
84	Santander, *Spain*	43 28 N	3 48 W
71	Santarém, *Brazil*	2 26 S	54 41 W
73	Santiago, *Chile*	33 27 S	70 40 W
66	Santiago, *Dom. Rep.*	19 30 N	70 42 W
84	Santiago de Compostela, *Spain*	42 52 N	8 33 W
66	Santiago de Cuba, *Cuba*	20 0 N	75 49 W
74	Santo André, *Brazil*	23 39 S	46 29 W
65	Santo Domingo, *Dom. Rep.*	18 30 N	69 57 W
74	Santos, *Brazil*	23 56 S	46 22 W
71	São Francisco, *r., Brazil*	10 20 S	36 20 W
74	São José do Rio Prêto, *Brazil*	20 50 S	49 20 W
71	São Luís, *Brazil*	2 34 S	44 16 W
74	São Paulo, *Brazil*	23 33 S	46 39 W
106	São Tomé & Príncipe, *Africa*	1 0 N	7 0 E
82	Saône, *r., France*	45 46 N	4 52 E
100	Sapporo, *Japan*	43 5 N	141 21 E
61	Sapulpa, *U.S.A.*	36 0 N	96 6 W
83	Sarajevo, *Bosnia.*	43 52 N	18 26 E
86	Saransk, *Russian Fed.*	54 12 N	45 10 E
59	Sarasota, *U.S.A.*	27 20 N	82 32 W
87	Saratov, *Russian Fed.*	51 30 N	45 55 E

PAGE	PLACENAME	LATITUDE	LONGITUDE
102	Sarawak, *d., Malaysia*	3 0 N	114 0 E
84	Sardinia, *i., Italy*	40 0 N	9 0 E
75	Sargasso Sea, *Atlantic Oc.*	28 0 N	60 0 W
96	Sargodha, *Pakistan*	32 1 N	72 40 E
58	Sarnia, *Canada*	42 58 N	82 23 W
100	Sasebo, *Japan*	33 10 N	129 42 E
52	Saskatchewan, *d., Canada*	55 0 N	105 0 W
53	Saskatchewan, *r., Canada*	53 25 N	100 15 W
52	Saskatoon, *Canada*	52 10 N	106 40 W
84	Sassari, *Italy*	40 43 N	8 33 E
96	Satpura Range, *mts., India*	21 50 N	76 0 E
83	Satu Mare, *Romania*	47 48 N	22 52 E
107	Saudi Arabia, *Asia*	26 0 N	44 0 E
58	Sault Sainte Marie, *Canada*	46 32 N	84 20 W
83	Sava, *r., Europe*	44 50 N	20 26 E
59	Savannah, *U.S.A.*	32 4 N	81 5 W
59	Savannah, *r., U.S.A.*	32 2 N	80 53 W
60	Sawatch Range, *mts., U.S.A.*	39 10 N	106 25 W
81	Scandinavia, *f., Europe*	65 0 N	18 0 E
53	Schefferville, *Canada*	54 50 N	67 0 W
58	Schenectady, *U.S.A.*	42 47 N	73 53 W
80	Schiedam, *Neth.*	51 55 N	4 25 E
82	Schwerin, *Germany*	53 38 N	11 25 E
79	Scotland, *d., U.K.*	56 30 N	4 0 W
62	Scottsbluff, *U.S.A.*	41 52 N	103 40 W
58	Scranton, *U.S.A.*	41 25 N	75 40 W
62	Seattle, *U.S.A.*	47 36 N	122 20 W
60	Sedalia, *U.S.A.*	38 42 N	93 14 W
84	Seine, *r., France*	49 28 N	0 25 E
106	Sekondi-Takoradi, *Ghana*	4 59 N	1 43 W
68	Selvas, *f., S. America*	7 0 S	66 0 W
52	Selwyn Mts., *Canada*	63 0 N	130 0 W
102	Semarang, *Indonesia*	6 58 S	110 29 E
88	Semipalatinsk, *Kazakhstan*	50 26 N	80 16 E
100	Sendai, *Japan*	38 20 N	140 50 E
106	Senegal, *Africa*	14 15 N	14 15 W
106	Sénégal, *r., Senegal/ Mauritania*	16 0 N	16 28 W
100	Seoul, *S. Korea*	37 30 N	127 0 E
86	Serov, *Russian Fed.*	59 42 N	60 32 E
86	Serpukhov, *Russian Fed.*	54 53 N	37 25 E
84	Sétif, *Algeria*	36 10 N	5 26 E
84	Settat, *Morocco*	33 4 N	7 37 W
87	Sevastopol', *Ukraine*	44 36 N	33 31 E
79	Severn, *r., U.K.*	51 50 N	2 21 W
89	Severnaya Zemlya, *is., Russian Fed.*	80 0 N	96 0 E
84	Seville, *Spain*	37 24 N	5 59 W
91	Seychelles, *Indian Oc.*	5 0 S	55 0 E
84	Sfax, *Tunisia*	34 45 N	10 43 E
98	Shache, *China*	38 27 N	77 16 E
97	Shahjahanpur, *India*	27 53 N	79 55 E
87	Shakhty, *Russian Fed.*	47 43 N	40 16 E
99	Shanghai, *China*	31 13 N	121 25 E
99	Shangrao, *China*	28 28 N	117 54 E
79	Shannon, *r., Rep. of Ire.*	52 39 N	8 43 W
99	Shantou, *China*	23 23 N	116 39 E
99	Shaoguan, *China*	24 54 N	113 33 E
99	Shaoxing, *China*	30 2 N	120 35 E
99	Shaoyang, *China*	27 43 N	111 24 E
58	Sharon, *U.S.A.*	41 14 N	80 31 W
62	Shasta, Mt., *U.S.A.*	41 20 N	122 20 W
58	Shawinigan, *Canada*	46 33 N	72 45 W
60	Sheboygan, *U.S.A.*	43 46 N	87 36 W
79	Sheffield, *U.K.*	53 23 N	1 28 W
59	Sheffield, *U.S.A.*	34 46 N	87 40 W
62	Shelby, *U.S.A.*	48 30 N	111 51 W
59	Shelbyville, *U.S.A.*	35 29 N	86 30 W
58	Shenandoah, *r., U.S.A.*	38 56 N	78 12 W
99	Shenyang, *China*	41 50 N	123 26 E
58	Sherbrooke, *Canada*	45 24 N	71 54 W
62	Sheridan, *U.S.A.*	44 48 N	106 58 W
61	Sherman, *U.S.A.*	33 38 N	96 36 W
80	'sHertogenbosch, *Neth.*	51 42 N	5 19 E
99	Shijiazhuang, *China*	38 4 N	114 28 E
100	Shikoku, *i., Japan*	33 30 N	133 0 E
97	Shillong, *India*	25 34 N	91 53 E
95	Shiraz, *Iran*	29 36 N	52 33 E
100	Shizuoka, *Japan*	35 2 N	138 28 E
85	Shkodër, *Albania*	42 3 N	19 30 E
96	Sholapur, *India*	17 43 N	75 56 E
62	Shoshone Mts., *U.S.A.*	39 25 N	117 15 W
61	Shreveport, *U.S.A*	32 30 N	93 45 W
99	Shuangyashan, *China*	46 37 N	131 22 E
13	Siberia, *f., Asia*	62 0 N	104 0 E
83	Sibiu, *Romania*	45 47 N	24 9 E
101	Sibuyan I., *Phil.*	12 20 N	122 40 E
84	Sicily, *i., Italy*	37 30 N	14 0 E
80	Siegen, *Germany*	50 52 N	8 2 E
106	Sierra Leone, *Africa*	8 30 N	12 0 W
99	Sikhote-Alin Range, *mts., Russian Fed.*	45 20 N	136 50 E
97	Siliguri, *India*	26 42 N	88 30 E
87	Simferopol', *Ukraine*	44 57 N	34 5 E
110	Simpson Desert, *Australia*	25 0 S	136 50 E
94	Sinai, *pen., Egypt*	29 0 N	34 0 E
102	Singapore, *Asia*	1 20 N	103 45 E

PAGE	PLACENAME	LATITUDE	LONGITUDE
67	Sint Maarten, *i., Neth. Antilles*	18 5 N	63 5 W
60	Sioux City, *U.S.A.*	42 30 N	96 23 W
60	Sioux Falls, *town, U.S.A.*	43 32 N	96 44 W
99	Siping, *China*	43 15 N	124 25 E
84	Siracusa, *Italy*	37 5 N	15 17 E
94	Sivas, *Turkey*	39 44 N	37 1 E
52	Skagway, *U.S.A.*	59 23 N	135 20 W
81	Skellefteå, *Sweden*	64 45 N	21 0 E
81	Skien, *Norway*	59 14 N	9 37 E
84	Skikda, *Algeria*	36 53 N	6 54 E
85	Skopje, *Macedonia*	41 58 N	21 27 E
79	Sligo, *Rep. of Ire.*	54 17 N	8 28 W
83	Slovakia, *Europe*	49 0 N	19 0 E
82	Slovenia, *Europe*	46 0 N	15 0 E
86	Smolensk, *Russian Fed.*	54 49 N	32 4 E
62	Snake, *r., U.S.A.*	46 12 N	119 2 W
62	Snake River Plain, *f., U.S.A.*	43 0 N	113 0 W
79	Snowdon, *mtn., U.K.*	53 5 N	4 5 W
61	Snyder, *U.S.A.*	32 44 N	100 5 W
71	Sobral, *Brazil*	3 45 S	40 20 W
113	Society Is., *Pacific Oc.*	17 0 S	150 0 W
107	Socotra, *i., Yemen*	12 30 N	54 0 E
81	Söderhamn, *Sweden*	61 19 N	17 10 E
85	Sofia, *Bulgaria*	42 41 N	23 19 E
94	Sohag, *Egypt*	26 33 N	31 42 E
106	Sokoto, *Nigeria*	13 2 N	5 15 E
80	Solingen, *Germany*	51 10 N	7 5 E
112	Solomon Is., *Pacific Oc.*	8 0 S	160 0 E
107	Somalia, *Africa*	5 30 N	47 0 E
61	Sonora, *U.S.A.*	30 34 N	100 39 W
74	Sorocaba, *Brazil*	23 30 S	47 32 W
101	Sorsogon, *Phil.*	12 59 N	123 58 E
83	Sosnowiec, *Poland*	50 18 N	19 8 E
84	Sousse, *Tunisia*	35 48 N	10 38 E
108	South Africa, *Africa*	30 0 S	27 0 E
12	South America,		
110	South Australia, *d., Australia*	29 0 S	135 0 E
58	South Bend, *U.S.A.*	41 40 N	86 15 W
59	South Carolina, *d., U.S.A.*	34 0 N	81 0 W
102	South China Sea, *Asia*	12 30 N	115 0 E
60	South Dakota, *d., U.S.A.*	45 0 N	100 0 W
75	South Georgia, *i., Atlantic Oc.*	54 50 S	36 0 W
111	South I., *New Zealand*	43 0 S	171 0 E
100	South Korea, *Asia*	36 50 N	128 0 E
60	South Platte, *r., U.S.A.*	41 7 N	100 42 W
79	Southampton, *U.K.*	50 54 N	1 23 W
53	Southampton I., *Canada*	64 30 N	84 0 W
111	Southern Alps, *mts., New Zealand*	43 20 S	170 45 E
110	Southern Cross, *Australia*	31 14 S	119 16 E
79	Southern Uplands, *hills, U.K.*	55 30 N	3 30 W
89	Sovetskaya Gavan, *Russian Fed.*	48 57 N	140 16 E
84	Spain, *Europe*	40 0 N	4 0 W
59	Spartanburg, *U.S.A.*	34 56 N	81 57 W
110	Spencer G., *Australia*	34 30 S	136 10 E
114	Spitsbergen, *is., Arctic Oc.*	78 0 N	17 0 E
85	Split, *Croatia*	43 32 N	16 27 E
62	Spokane, *U.S.A.*	47 40 N	117 23 W
60	Springfield, *Ill., U.S.A.*	39 49 N	89 39 W
58	Springfield, *Mass., U.S.A.*	42 7 N	72 36 W
61	Springfield, *Mo., U.S.A.*	37 14 N	93 17 W
58	Springfield, *Ohio, U.S.A.*	39 55 N	83 48 W
62	Springfield, *Oreg., U.S.A.*	44 3 N	123 1 W
89	Sredne Kolymskaya, *Russian Fed.*	67 27 N	153 35 E
97	Sri Lanka, *Asia*	7 30 N	80 50 E
96	Srinagar, *Jammu & Kashmir*	34 8 N	74 50 E
73	Stanley, *Falkland Is.*	51 42 S	57 51 W
89	Stanovoy Range, *mts., Russian Fed.*	56 0 N	125 40 E
85	Stara Zagora, *Bulgaria*	42 26 N	25 37 E
58	State College, *U.S.A.*	40 48 N	77 52 W
59	Statesville, *U.S.A.*	35 46 N	80 54 W
81	Stavanger, *Norway*	58 58 N	5 45 E
87	Stavropol', *Russian Fed.*	45 3 N	41 59 E
86	Sterlitamak, *Russian Fed.*	53 40 N	55 59 E
58	Steubenville, *U.S.A.*	40 22 N	80 37 W
61	Stillwater, *U.S.A.*	36 7 N	97 4 W
81	Stockholm, *Sweden*	59 20 N	18 5 E
62	Stockton, *U.S.A.*	37 57 N	121 17 W
79	Stoke-on-Trent, *U.K.*	53 1 N	2 10 W
82	Strasbourg, *France*	48 35 N	7 45 E
82	Stuttgart, *Germany*	48 47 N	9 12 E
83	Subotica, *Yugo.*	46 4 N	19 41 E
72	Sucre, *Bolivia*	19 2 S	65 17 W
107	Sudan, *Africa*	14 0 N	30 0 E
58	Sudbury, *Canada*	46 30 N	81 1 W
94	Suez, *Egypt*	29 59 N	32 33 E
94	Suez Canal, *Egypt*	30 40 N	32 20 E
96	Sukkur, *Pakistan*	27 42 N	68 54 E
103	Sulawesi, *d., Indonesia*	2 0 S	120 30 E
101	Sulu Archipelago, *Phil.*	6 50 N	120 50 E
101	Sulu Sea, *Phil.*	8 30 N	120 25 E
102	Sumatra, *i., Indonesia*	2 0 S	102 0 E
102	Sumbawa, *i., Indonesia*	8 45 S	117 50 E
87	Sumy, *Ukraine*	50 55 N	34 49 E

V

PAGE	PLACENAME	LATITUDE	LONGITUDE
81	Vaasa, *Finland*	63 6N	21 36 E
96	Vadodara, *India*	22 19N	73 14 E
82	Vaduz, *Liech.*	47 8N	9 32 E
57	Valdez, *U.S.A.*	61 7N	146 17W
73	Valdivia, *Chile*	39 46S	73 15W
59	Valdosta, *U.S.A.*	30 51N	83 51W
82	Valence, *France*	44 56N	4 54 E
84	Valencia, *Spain*	39 29N	0 24W
70	Valencia, *Venezuela*	10 14N	67 59W
80	Valenciennes, *France*	50 22N	3 32 E
84	Valladolid, *Spain*	41 39N	4 45W
70	Valledupar, *Colombia*	10 31N	73 16W
84	Valletta, *Malta*	35 53N	14 31 E
73	Valparaíso, *Chile*	33 2S	71 38W
94	Van, L., *Turkey*	38 35N	42 52 E
62	Vancouver, *Canada*	49 13N	123 6W
62	Vancouver, *U.S.A.*	45 39N	122 40W
62	Vancouver I., *Canada*	50 0N	126 0W
81	Vänern, *l., Sweden*	59 0N	13 15 E
112	Vanua Levu, *i., Fiji*	16 33S	179 15 E
112	Vanuatu, *Pacific Oc.*	16 0S	167 0 E
97	Varanasi, *India*	25 20N	83 0 E
81	Varangerfjorden, *est., Norway*	70 0N	29 30 E
83	Varna, *Bulgaria*	43 13N	27 57 E
81	Västerås, *Sweden*	59 36N	16 32 E
81	Vatnajökull, *mts., Iceland*	64 20N	17 0W
81	Vättern, *l., Sweden*	58 30N	14 30 E
81	Växjö, *Sweden*	56 52N	14 50 E
70	Venezuela, *S. America*	7 0N	65 20W
82	Venice, *Italy*	45 26N	12 20 E
80	Venlo, *Neth.*	51 22N	6 10 E
64	Veracruz, *Mexico*	19 11N	96 10W
108	Vereeniging, *South Africa*	26 41S	27 56 E
89	Verkhoyansk, *Russian Fed.*	67 25N	133 25 E
89	Verkhoyansk Range, *mts., Russian Fed.*	66 0N	130 0 E
58	Vermont, *d., U.S.A.*	44 0N	72 30W
82	Verona, *Italy*	45 27N	10 59 E
84	Versailles, *France*	48 48N	2 8 E
84	Vesuvius, *mtn., Italy*	40 48N	14 25 E
81	Viborg, *Denmark*	56 28N	9 25 E
61	Vicksburg, *U.S.A.*	32 14N	90 56W
110	Victoria, *d., Australia*	37 0S	145 0 E
62	Victoria, *Canada*	48 26N	123 20W
73	Victoria, *Chile*	38 13S	72 20W
108	Victoria Falls, *f., Zimbabwe/Zambia*	17 58S	25 45 E
52	Victoria I., *Canada*	71 0N	110 0W
108	Victoria, L., *Africa*	1 0S	33 0 E
82	Vienna, *Austria*	48 13N	16 22 E
102	Vientiane, *Laos*	18 1N	102 48 E
102	Vietnam, *Asia*	15 0N	108 0 E
101	Vigan, *Phil.*	17 35N	120 23 E
84	Vigo, *Spain*	42 15N	8 44W
97	Vijayawada, *India*	16 34N	80 40 E
64	Villahermosa, *Mexico*	18 0N	92 53W
83	Vilnius, *Lithuania*	54 40N	25 19 E
89	Vilyuysk, *Russian Fed.*	63 46N	121 35 E
73	Viña del Mar, *Chile*	33 2S	71 34W
59	Vineland, *U.S.A.*	39 29N	75 2W
83	Vinnitsa, *Ukraine*	49 11N	28 30 E
101	Virac, *Phil.*	13 35N	124 12 E
67	Virgin Gorda, *i., B.V.Is.*	18 30N	64 26W
67	Virgin Is. (British), *C. America*	18 30N	64 30W
67	Virgin Is. (U.S.A.), *C. America*	18 30N	65 0W
59	Virginia, *d., U.S.A.*	37 30N	78 45W
59	Virginia Beach, *town, U.S.A.*	36 51N	75 59W
63	Visalia, *U.S.A.*	36 20N	119 18W
101	Visayan Sea, *Phil.*	11 40N	123 40 E
52	Viscount Melville Sd., *Canada*	74 30N	104 0W
97	Vishakhapatnam, *India*	17 42N	83 24 E
83	Vistula, *r., Poland*	54 23N	18 52 E
86	Vitebsk, *Belorussia*	55 10N	30 14 E
112	Viti Levu, *i., Fiji*	18 0S	178 0 E
89	Vitim, *r., Russian Fed.*	59 30N	112 36 E
74	Vitória, *Brazil*	20 19S	40 21W
84	Vitoria, *Spain*	42 51N	2 40W
71	Vitória da Conquista, *Brazil*	14 53S	40 52W
87	Vladikavkaz, *Russian Fed.*	43 2N	44 43 E
86	Vladimir, *Russian Fed.*	56 8N	40 25 E
99	Vladivostok, *Russian Fed.*	43 9N	131 53 E
85	Vlorë, *Albania*	40 28N	19 27 E
87	Volga, *r., Russian Fed.*	45 45N	47 50 E
87	Volgograd, *Russian Fed.*	48 45N	44 30 E
86	Vologda, *Russian Fed.*	59 10N	39 55 E
106	Volta, L., *Ghana*	7 0N	0 0 0
74	Volta Redonda, *Brazil*	22 31S	44 5W
87	Volzhskiy, *Russian Fed.*	48 48N	44 45 E
86	Vorkuta, *Russian Fed.*	67 27N	64 0 E
87	Voronezh, *Russian Fed.*	51 40N	39 13 E

W

PAGE	PLACENAME	LATITUDE	LONGITUDE
80	Waal, *r., Neth.*	51 45N	4 40 E
60	Wabash, *r., U.S.A.*	37 46N	88 2W
61	Waco, *U.S.A.*	31 55N	97 8W
107	Wad Medani, *Sudan*	14 24N	33 30 E
80	Wadden Sea, *Neth.*	53 15N	5 5 E
52	Waddington, Mt., *Canada*	51 30N	125 0W
100	Wakayama, *Japan*	34 12N	135 10 E
82	Wałbrzych, *Poland*	50 48N	16 19 E
79	Wales, *d., U.K.*	53 0N	3 30W
112	Wallis, Îles, *is., Pacific Oc.*	13 16S	176 15W
108	Walvis Bay, *town, South Africa*	22 50S	14 31 E
111	Wanganui, *New Zealand*	39 56S	175 0 E
83	Warsaw, *Poland*	52 15N	21 0 E
82	Warta, *r., Poland*	52 45N	15 9 E
59	Washington, *U.S.A.*	38 55N	77 0W
62	Washington, *d., U.S.A.*	47 43N	120 0W
58	Waterbury, *U.S.A.*	41 33N	73 2W
79	Waterford, *Rep. of Ire.*	52 16N	7 8W
58	Waterloo, *Canada*	43 28N	80 31W
58	Watertown, *U.S.A.*	43 59N	75 55W
60	Waukesha, *U.S.A.*	43 1N	88 14W
60	Wausau, *U.S.A.*	44 58N	89 40W
60	Wauwatosa, *U.S.A.*	43 4N	88 2W
114	Weddell Sea, *Antarctica*	73 0S	42 0W
99	Weifang, *China*	36 44N	119 10 E
111	Wellington, *New Zealand*	41 17S	174 47 E
99	Wenzhou, *China*	28 2N	120 40 E
82	Weser, *r., Germany*	53 15N	8 30 E
80	West Frisian Is., *Neth.*	53 20N	5 0 E
75	West Indies, *is., C. America*	21 0N	74 0W
59	West Palm Beach, *town, U.S.A.*	26 42N	80 5W
80	West Schelde, *est., Neth.*	51 25N	3 40 E
88	West Siberian Plain, *f., Russian Fed.*	60 0N	75 0 E
58	West Virginia, *d., U.S.A.*	39 0N	80 30W
110	Western Australia, *d., Australia*	25 0S	123 0 E
96	Western Ghats, *mts., India*	15 30N	74 30 E
106	Western Sahara, *Africa*	25 0N	13 30W
112	Western Samoa, *Pacific Oc.*	13 55S	172 0W
111	Westport, *New Zealand*	41 46S	171 38 E
111	Whangarei, *New Zealand*	35 43S	174 20 E
58	Wheeling, *U.S.A.*	40 5N	80 42W
61	White, *r., U.S.A.*	33 53N	91 10W
107	White Nile, *r., Sudan*	15 45N	32 25 E
86	White Sea, *Russian Fed.*	65 30N	38 0 E
52	Whitehorse, *Canada*	60 41N	135 8W
63	Whitney, Mt., *U.S.A.*	36 35N	118 18W
110	Whyalla, *Australia*	33 4S	137 34 E
61	Wichita, *U.S.A.*	37 41N	97 20W
61	Wichita Falls, *town, U.S.A.*	33 54N	98 30W
79	Wicklow Mts., *Rep. of Ire.*	53 6N	6 20W
82	Wiesbaden, *Germany*	50 5N	8 15 E
79	Wight, Isle of, *U.K.*	50 40N	1 17W
103	Wilhelm, Mt., *P.N.G.*	6 0S	144 55 E
80	Wilhelmshaven, *Germany*	53 32N	8 7 E
58	Wilkes-Barre, *U.S.A.*	41 14N	75 53W
66	Willemstad, *Neth. Antilles*	12 12N	68 56W
58	Williamsport, *U.S.A.*	41 16N	77 3W
59	Wilmington, *Del., U.S.A.*	39 46N	75 31W
59	Wilmington, *N.C., U.S.A.*	34 14N	77 55W
59	Wilson, *U.S.A.*	35 43N	77 56W
62	Wind River Range, *mts., U.S.A.*	43 5N	109 25W
108	Windhoek, *Namibia*	22 34S	17 6 E
58	Windsor, *Canada*	42 18N	83 0W
65	Windward Is., *C. America*	13 0N	60 0W
65	Windward Passage, *str., Carib. Sea*	20 0N	74 0W
60	Winnipeg, *Canada*	49 53N	97 10W
53	Winnipeg, L., *Canada*	52 45N	98 0W
60	Winona, *U.S.A.*	44 3N	91 39W
59	Winston-Salem, *U.S.A.*	36 5N	80 18W
82	Winterthur, *Switz.*	47 30N	8 45 E
110	Winton, *Australia*	22 22S	143 0 E
60	Wisconsin, *d., U.S.A.*	44 30N	90 0W
80	Witten, *Germany*	51 26N	7 19 E
83	Włocławek, *Poland*	52 39N	19 1 E
82	Wolfsburg, *Germany*	52 27N	10 49 E
110	Wollongong, *Australia*	34 25S	150 52 E
79	Wolverhampton, *U.K.*	52 35N	2 6W
100	Wonsan, *N. Korea*	39 7N	127 26 E
60	Woods, L. of the, *Canada/U.S.A.*	49 15N	94 45W
108	Worcester, *South Africa*	33 39S	19 26 E
79	Worcester, *U.K.*	52 12N	2 12W
58	Worcester, *U.S.A.*	42 14N	71 48W
89	Wrangel I., *Russian Fed.*	71 0N	180 0 0
83	Wrocław, *Poland*	51 5N	17 0 E
99	Wuhan, *China*	30 35N	114 19 E
99	Wuhu, *China*	31 23N	118 25 E
80	Wuppertal, *Germany*	51 15N	7 10 E
82	Würzburg, *Germany*	49 48N	9 57 E
98	Wutongqiao, *China*	29 21N	103 48 E
99	Wuxi, *China*	31 35N	120 19 E
99	Wuzhou, *China*	23 30N	111 21 E
110	Wyndham, *Australia*	15 29S	128 5 E
62	Wyoming, *d., U.S.A.*	43 10N	107 36W

X

PAGE	PLACENAME	LATITUDE	LONGITUDE
99	Xi'an, *China*	34 16N	108 54 E
99	Xiangfan, *China*	32 20N	112 5 E
99	Xiangtan, *China*	27 55N	112 47 E
71	Xingu, *r., Brazil*	1 40S	52 15W
98	Xining, *China*	36 35N	101 55 E
99	Xuzhou, *China*	34 17N	117 18 E

Y

PAGE	PLACENAME	LATITUDE	LONGITUDE
89	Yablonovy Range, *mts., Russian Fed.*	53 20N	115 0 E
62	Yakima, *U.S.A.*	46 36N	120 31W
89	Yakutsk, *Russian Fed.*	62 10N	129 20 E
100	Yamagata, *Japan*	38 16N	140 19 E
88	Yamal Pen., *Russian Fed.*	70 20N	70 0 E
97	Yamuna, *r., India*	25 20N	81 49 E
97	Yangon, *Myanmar*	16 45N	96 20 E
99	Yantai, *China*	37 30N	121 22 E
106	Yaoundé, *Cameroon*	3 51N	11 31 E
86	Yaroslavl, *Russian Fed.*	57 34N	39 52 E
100	Yatsushiro, *Japan*	32 32N	130 35 E
95	Yazd, *Iran*	31 54N	54 22 E
61	Yazoo, *r., U.S.A.*	32 22N	91 0W
86	Yekaterinburg, *Russian Fed.*	56 52N	60 35 E
99	Yellow Sea, *Asia*	35 0N	123 0 E
52	Yellowknife, *Canada*	62 30N	114 29W
62	Yellowstone, *r., U.S.A.*	47 55N	103 45W
107	Yemen, *Asia*	15 55N	48 30 E
89	Yenisei, *r., Russian Fed.*	69 0N	86 0 E
95	Yerevan, *Armenia*	40 10N	44 31 E
99	Yichang, *China*	30 43N	111 22 E
98	Yining, *China*	43 57N	81 23 E
102	Yogyakarta, *Indonesia*	7 48S	110 24 E
100	Yokohama, *Japan*	35 28N	139 28 E
59	Yonkers, *U.S.A.*	40 56N	73 52W
79	York, *U.K.*	53 58N	1 7W
59	York, *U.S.A.*	39 58N	76 44W
110	York, C., *Australia*	10 58S	142 40 E
58	Youngstown, *U.S.A.*	41 5N	80 40W
62	Yuba City, *U.S.A.*	39 8N	121 27W
65	Yucatan Channel, *Carib. Sea*	21 30N	86 0W
85	Yugoslavia, *Europe*	44 0N	20 0 E
57	Yukon, *r., U.S.A.*	62 35N	164 20W
52	Yukon Territory, *d., Canada*	65 0N	135 0W
63	Yuma, *U.S.A.*	32 43N	114 37W
99	Yuzhno Sakhalinsk, *Russian Fed.*	46 58N	142 45 E

Z

PAGE	PLACENAME	LATITUDE	LONGITUDE
80	Zaandam, *Neth.*	52 27N	4 49 E
83	Zabrze, *Poland*	50 18N	18 47 E
86	Zagorsk, *Russian Fed.*	56 20N	38 10 E
82	Zagreb, *Croatia*	45 49N	15 58 E
95	Zagros Mts., *Iran*	32 0N	51 0 E
108	Zaïre, *Africa*	2 0S	22 0 E
108	Zaïre, *r., Zaïre*	6 0S	12 30 E
108	Zambezi, *r., Mozambique/Zambia*	18 15S	35 55 E
108	Zambia, *Africa*	14 0S	28 0 E
101	Zamboanga, *Phil.*	6 55N	122 5 E
58	Zanesville, *U.S.A.*	39 56N	82 1W
108	Zanzibar, *Tanzania*	6 10S	39 12 E
87	Zaporozhye, *Ukraine*	47 50N	35 10 E
84	Zaragoza, *Spain*	41 39N	0 54W
106	Zaria, *Nigeria*	11 1N	7 44 E
94	Zarqa, *Jordan*	32 4N	36 5 E
81	Zealand, *i., Denmark*	55 30N	12 0 E
80	Zeebrugge, *Belgium*	51 20N	3 13 E
99	Zhangjiakou, *China*	41 0N	114 50 E
99	Zhangzhou, *China*	24 57N	118 36 E
99	Zhanjiang, *China*	21 5N	110 12 E
99	Zhejiang, *d., China*	29 15N	120 0 E
99	Zhengzhou, *China*	34 35N	113 38 E
83	Zhitomir, *Ukraine*	50 18N	28 40 E
99	Zibo, *China*	36 50N	118 0 E
82	Zielona Góra, *Poland*	51 57N	15 30 E
108	Zimbabwe, *Africa*	18 0S	30 0 E
86	Zlatoust, *Russian Fed.*	55 10N	59 38 E
94	Zonguldak, *Turkey*	41 26N	31 47 E
83	Zrenjanin, *Yugo.*	45 22N	20 23 E
98	Zunyi, *China*	27 41N	106 50 E
82	Zürich, *Switz.*	47 23N	8 33 E
82	Zwickau, *Germany*	50 43N	12 30 E

Map Projections

Map projections are the means by which the earth's curved surface can be transferred to or projected upon a flat surface, like the pages of this atlas. They are systematic drawings of lines representing parallels or meridians on a flat surface. They show either the whole earth or some portion of it. No single map projection can represent the earth's spherical surface without some distortion or areas, shapes, directions, or distances.

Although in practice nearly all projections are derived mathematically, most are more easily visualized if you think of a light shining through the grid of parallels and meridians on a globe. The shadows these lines would cast on a flat piece of paper would form a projection. The piece of paper could also be rolled into a cylinder or a cone. Thus, there are several kinds of projections. Theses are azimuthal, cylindrical, and conical (*See* diagrams below).

Azimuthal

Cylindrical

Conical

An Azimuthal projection is constructed by the projection of part of the globe onto a flat surface which touches the globe at only one point. The zenithal gnomonic projection (A) touches the globe at a pole. This projection is good for showing polar air routes, because the shortest distance between any two points is a straight line. Air-route distances from one point (e.g. Capetown) are best shown by the Oblique Zenithal Equidistant projection (B). Azimuthal projections are best for larger scale maps of small areas so that distortion around the edges is not too great.

Cylindrical projections are constructed by projecting a portion of the globe onto a cylinder which touches the globe only along one line, e.g. the equator. This line is the only one true to scale, with distortion of size and shape increasing towards the top and bottom of the cylinder. The Mercator projection (A) is one kind of cylindrical projection. It avoids distortion of shape by making an increase in scale along the parallels. Although there is still size distortion, the Mercator's best use is for navigation since directions can be plotted as straight lines. The Mollweide projection (B) is a cylindrical projection on which the meridians are no longer parallel. This is an equal-area projection, which is useful for mapping distributions. In this case, it is "interrupted" or cut apart in the oceans. Cylindrical projections are best for mapping the whole world.

Conical projections use the projection of the globe onto a cone which caps the globe and touches it along a parallel. The scale is correct along this line and along the meridians. In the simple conic projection (A), the scale is correct along the heavy parallel and the meridians. Bonne's projection (B) is another conical projection. It is an equal-area projection, but there is shape distortion around its edges. Conical projections cannot cover the entire globe. They are best suited for mid-latitude or temperate regions with large longitudinal extent, e.g. Asia.

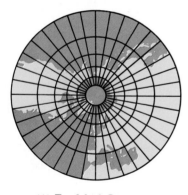

(A) Zenithal Gnomonic

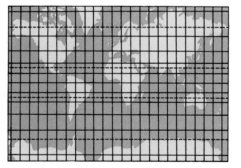

(A) Mercator

(A) Simple Conic

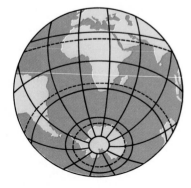

(B) Oblique Zenithal Equidistant

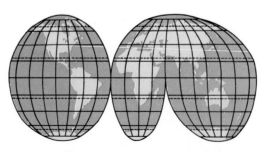

(B) Interrupted Mollweide

(B) Bonne

In this atlas, many projections are used. They have been carefully chosen for their specific advantages. The names of the projections appear below the bar scales on the maps. Almost all of the world and continental maps are equal-area projections. Most of the large-scale maps are conical projections, which have correct shapes and true directions.